Best Practice

Praise for Best Practice

"This is a fabulous book! Judy makes us want to apply her methods, often right after reading a sentence. The bonus is that the tools she gives us for practicing music can really apply to myriad areas of our lives. This is the kind of book I imagine every musician will enjoy."

– Liz Carroll

"Filled to the brim with practical insights, solid advice and wisdom that will benefit all traditional musicians, regardless of instrument, style, genre or skill level. There are vast wells of information in these pages that you can dip a toe, swim or dive deeply into. This is a rich and finely wrought work and I highly recommend it."

– Happy Traum

"A very lively, entertaining and friendly book which I'm sure will be a boon to players everywhere. Contains a wealth of exceptionally useful advice for musicians of any level."

– Kevin Burke

"A wealth of ideas and tools for making progress as a musician, all presented – in keeping with the book's own advice – in small, clear, achievable steps."

– Jeffrey Pepper Rodgers
founding editor, *Acoustic Guitar* magazine,
author, *The Complete Singer-Songwriter*

"A veritable bible of a practice guide. Players of all levels and all styles will benefit from reading this very well thought out, very thorough and accessible approach."

– Natalie Haas

"Kudos to Judy for sharing this highly organized, empowering approach to the practice of practice. It's a celebration of and for the adult learner. What a gift to players of all levels!"

– Shannon Heaton

"As a resource for any musician who wants to improve on their own, this book has it covered. Judy has compiled a treasure trove of ideas in a concise and easy to access format. She has an insight on the way humans think and learn that makes this book a joy to work with."

– David Leonhardt
renowned jazz pianist

"Having this guidebook is a godsend. I highly recommend it for all musicians, regardless of instrument, level or genre."

– Mary Flower
award-winning guitarist

Judy Minot

Best Practice

Inspiration and Ideas for Traditional Musicians

TradBridge Press • Asbury, NJ

Copyright ©2021 by Judy Minot. All rights reserved. This book, including illustrations, may not be reproduced, in whole or in part, in any form or by any electronic or mechanical means, including information storage and retrieval systems (beyond that copying permitted by Sections 107 and 108 of the U.S. Copyright Law, and except by reviewers for the public press), without written permission from the publisher.

ISBN 978-0-578-87044-1

Publisher's Cataloging-in-Publication data

Names: Minot, Judy, author.
Title: Best practice : inspiration and ideas for traditional musicians / Judy Minot.
Description: Includes index. | Asbury, NJ: TradBridge Press, 2021.
Identifiers: ISBN: 978-0-578-87044-1
Subjects: LCSH Musical instruments--Instruction and study. | Folk music. | World music--Instruction and study. | Performance practice (Music) | BISAC MUSIC / Instruction & Study / General
Classification: LCC MT170 .M56 2021 | DDC 784.193--dc23

Library of Congress Control Number - 2021904654

Cover painting: "In the Lightness of Being" ©2019 by Amanda Reilly Sayer. Used with the kind permission of the artist.
Author photo by Martin Lynn.

Published by TradBridge Press, Asbury, NJ.
More information and practice resources available at www.judyminot.com/bestpractice

For my mother, Patricia Minot,
who has always called me a musician
no matter what I did for a living.

Contents

Acknowledgements

Introduction 1

1	"Practicing" Is a Practice	5
2	Baggage	6
3	Minimum Effort for Maximum Effect	8
4	Being Present	9
5	Working with the Practice Pyramid	10
6	I Will Sound Good	12
7	Mind-Body Coordination	13
8	Being a Beginner	14
9	Having a Plan	15
10	Is It Training or Talent?	17
11	Going Slower is Faster	17
12	Beginner's Mind	18
13	Metronome	19
14	Physical Self-Care	20
15	Please Explain That More Slowly	21
16	You Can Play by Ear	23
17	A Space of Your Own	24
18	Taking Notes	25
19	When Not to Have Ambition	25
20	Play Better with Phrasing	26
21	The 20-Minute Interval	28
22	Attention	29
23	Motion is Lotion	30
24	Overwhelmed	31
25	The Benefits of Being an Adult	33

26	Practice, Play with Others, Get a Teacher	34
27	"At Speed"	35
28	Interrupt the Loop	35
29	A Mirror	36
30	The Gap (Between Taste and Ability)	37
31	Just Keep Showing Up	38
32	Tailor-Made Technical Exercises	38
33	Subtle Thoughts	40
34	Keeping the Beat in Your Body	41
35	Posture	42
36	When You Can't Practice	43
37	Tune Structure	44
38	Be Your Own (Great) Teacher	45
39	Fear of Theory	46
40	Playing Without Mistakes	46
41	Simplifying a Tune	47
42	The Myth of 10,000 Hours	49
43	Left Hand – Right Hand	50
44	Shift Gears	51
45	Attentive Listening	51
46	Finding a Teacher	52
47	Keep "One Point"	54
48	Listening for Patterns	55
49	Musical Priorities	56
50	Sing	58
51	A Musical Community	58
52	Conquering "Tunesia"	59
53	Enlargen	61
54	Tracking Small Wins	63
55	Yeah, But…	64

56	Your Body Clock	65
57	Recovering	66
58	Which Notes Do I Need?	67
59	Rotation of the Shoulders	68
60	Get Up	70
61	Stop Trying to Be Perfect	70
62	Thinking Ahead	71
63	An Extra Limb	73
64	Avoidance	73
65	Give Me That Rhythm	74
66	M Is for Mindfulness Practice	75
67	A Beautiful Sound	76
68	Don't Try Harder. Try Softer.	78
69	Sword Has Sword Nature	78
70	Don't Play with Pain	79
71	Performance Anxiety	81
72	Are You Having Fun Yet?	81
73	Opening Up Space	82
74	Discernment vs. Criticism	83
75	Are You Breathing?	85
76	Sing and Play	86
77	Normative Beliefs	86
78	Playing and Knowing	87
79	Interleaving	88
80	Very Slow Practice	90
81	One Thing at a Time	91
82	Four Stretches	92
83	Playing as Play	93
84	Relaxing Your Face	94
85	All Notes Are Not Created Equal	95

86	Musical "Words"	96
87	Engage Your Senses	98
88	Play What You Know	99
89	Your Three Things	100
90	Visualization	100
91	Before You Start	102
92	Acting "As If"	103
93	When the Bell Rings, Get Up!	104
94	Head and Neck Position	105
95	How to Jam	106
96	Ring Finger, Little Finger	108
97	Mental Flexibility	109
98	Positioning Exercise	110
99	Watch and Listen	111
100	Sleeping with a Key	112
101	When to Move On	113
102	Learning the Secret Language	114
103	Make vs. Allow	115
104	Upper Body Stretch	116
105	Creating Lift	117
106	Wild Takes	119
107	A Direct Connection	120
108	Learn a New Skill in 45 days	122
109	Spaced Repetition	123
110	Headwind	124
111	You've Got Five Minutes	124
112	Human Potential – A Story	125
113	Dynamics	126
114	The Tone Starter	127
115	Time Off	128

116	Smile	129
117	What Key Is It In?	130
118	Stop While You Feel Good	131
119	What's Next?	132
120	What's on the Technology Menu?	133
121	Playing Fast and Slow	133
122	What You Have	135
123	Mute	135
124	Making a List	137
125	Six Human Needs	138
126	Rhythmic Precision	139
127	Embodying the Tune	140
128	Wu (Weight Underside)	141
129	Everyone Is My Teacher	143
130	The Dotted Quarter Swap	144
131	Playing with Distractions	146
132	Accepting Limitations	148
133	Practice "Upside Down"	149
134	Free Play	150
135	Heuristics	151
136	Habit vs. Willpower	152
137	Fly Blind	153
138	Set Yourself Up for Success	154
139	Timed Modules	155
140	Your Inner Critic	156
141	Tensegrity	156
142	Phrasing and Expression	158
143	Sooner, Not Faster	159
144	How Good *Am* I?	160
145	The Two-Tempo Rut	161

146	Playing with Swing	162
147	Mukudoku	163
148	Playing with the Masters	164
149	Learn on the Fly	165
150	Comfort Zone	168
151	How Does It Really Go?	168
152	Ikkyo, Nikkyo, Sankyo	170
153	Checkerboard	172
154	Personal, Pervasive, Permanent	174
155	Wasted Motion	175
156	A New Environment	175
157	People Will Like My Playing	176
158	Scales and Arpeggios	177
159	Do Say Do	179
160	Ending the Tune	180
161	Jumps	180
162	Rich Musical Soil	182
163	Look Up!	182
164	Child's Pose	183
165	Simplify Your Approach	184
166	Pleasure, Praise, Fame, Gain	184
167	Make It Stick with a Memory Trick	185
168	Plays Well with Others	186
169	Continuous Growth	187
170	The Last Thing You Hear	189
171	Neurogenesis	191
172	Wake Up Your Warm-Ups	192
173	The Gift of Listening	193
174	Relaxed Hands	193
175	Harness the Power of Metaphor	195

176	Both Hands Together	196
177	Between the Shoulder Blades	197
178	The Next Note after the Hard One	198
179	Develop Counterarguments	199
180	Relaxing while Playing Fast	200
181	Transitions	201
182	Embracing Uncertainty	202
183	Consonants	203
184	Give Yourself a Gold Star	204
185	Six Direction Spine Stretch	205
186	Writing It Down	208
187	Shine	210
188	Piano	211
189	Aimaisa	212
190	I Can't Hear Myself	212
191	It's All Your Voice	213
192	Making a Recording	214
193	Fast Practice	215
194	The Presentation Rule	218
195	Overlearning	219
196	Goal Setting	219
197	Simple Idea! Why So Difficult?	221

Appendix A – The Practice Pyramid 223

Appendix B – Jamming Best Practices 226

Appendix C – Harmony Basics 228

Appendix D – Four Basic Principles 232

Appendix E – Breathing Exercise 234

Notes 236

Index 239

About the Author 250

Acknowledgements

I am incredibly grateful to many people who have helped make this book a reality. Countless friends in the musical community have been supportive of the idea from its inception. Susan Donoghue, Nancy Neff and Linda Zdepski were attentive listeners, offering sanity, hilarity and encouragement. Thanks also to Jan Hempel, who taught me to keep showing up for practice, and to Amanda Reilly Sayer who offered the serene painting on the cover.

Among my many teachers, some have been memorable and life-changing. David Leonhardt is a mentor and friend whose ideas about music, practice and self-knowledge suffuse these pages. Lisa Ornstein taught me to work with my brain instead of against it. In the practice of aikido I have been deeply influenced by the teaching of Dan McDougall, Veronica Burrows, David Nachman and Shuji Maruyama Sensei. Thank you for your patience, attention and generosity.

I particularly want to thank Jim Besser. In these days of self-publishing, I was fortunate to benefit from the skills of a talented editor. Without his guidance this would have been a poorer offering. Thanks also to Susan Cohen who generously came out of "indexing retirement" to work on the book, and to Maryellen Costello and Mary Roth who provided meticulous manuscript editing and very valued perspective.

My family has been my bedrock. Ben Minot knows how to remind me of the ways to be a better person. Martin Lynn has been cheerleader, webmaster and a great backboard for ideas. Finally, my deepest thanks go to my husband, partner and best friend, Chun Wai Liew, who provided calmness, common sense and delicious sustenance throughout a creative process that encompassed a global pandemic.

Introduction

Best Practice is written for non-professional, adult musicians, of any experience level, who play traditional music.

The term *traditional music* can refer to regional musical styles from any part of the world. A defining characteristic of these styles is that they have historically been learned and transmitted person-to-person, by ear, rather than through written music. The focus is often on playing for dancers or on playing together as social event in itself, rather than playing for paid audiences. Traditional musicians of many styles have started to refer to their music as "trad," and that's the term I use most often in this book.

In the 21st century, technology and the ease of travel combine to make it possible to learn this music, even if we didn't grow up in an area where it originated. Yet, even though the music itself is more accessible, adult trad players still face obstacles in becoming better musicians.

We Need a Teaching Style that Suits Adults

> If we studied an instrument as children or teens, the teaching was likely oriented toward goals like performing, band competitions, or even a career in music, playing common or "orchestral" instruments like clarinet, saxophone, piano or violin.
>
> Absent the goal of competing or performing, adults may feel great relief, but it can leave us feeling aimless, wondering why we're going to all this trouble. Why spend hours practicing when I could relax and watch a movie after work instead? It's not as if I depend on it to make a living, after all.

We're Often Self-Taught

The vast majority of trad musicians are learning without formal instruction. We may attend workshops and use online resources to learn, but without the structure, guidance and feedback provided by a teacher we struggle to maintain our commitment and enthusiasm for practicing.

Many of Us Don't Know How to Practice

Many adult musicians aren't really sure of the most effective way to spend their practice time. Almost everyone I've spoken to admits they have no idea if the things they spend time on will help them achieve their musical goals *effectively* or *efficiently*. This is often true even if they have a teacher.

We all know that repetition is involved, and time, and consistency. But *how much* time should we spend? *What* should we work on during that time? Should we focus on notes, ornaments, speed, intonation? How much music theory do we really need to know? What should our goals be for each day, each week or longer?

As adult musicians we may not expect to become famous and take the world by storm. At the same time we have a right to want to improve and to take ourselves seriously as musicians. This book was written to address that desire.

How the Book Is Structured

Musical mastery is achieved through incremental progress. We may not notice a change after one day's practice. Improvement happens over weeks, months and years.

This book is written for you to read in a similar fashion to the way you practice: in small, regular measures.

Each chapter offers a single concept or idea. Many chapters describe practice techniques. Others address the "mind game" of creativity and practice. Some are about ensuring your body provides the most effective support for your playing.

It may surprise you to find these subjects jumbled together rather than presented in a more ordered or structured way. There's a reason for this approach: To learn deeply and permanently, we need to absorb new material in small quantities. We need time to try out new ideas, practice with them in mind, and even forget about them and come back to them later.

If I had organized the content subject by subject, it would certainly have been easier for me! But I feared readers would read the entire book in a few sessions, thinking "OK, I got that!" They might walk away with three or four new ideas to try. My hope is that when you finish this book you'll already be in the habit of using far more than three of the ideas contained in it.

There are 197 self-contained chapters. You may want to read a chapter before you sit down to practice, or one every day or week, or whenever you want. You could read them in order, skim until you find one that appeals, or use the *sortes sanctorum* method: Flip through the pages, stick in your finger in a random spot and see what you come up with.

Even though the subject matter is spread out, there is some progression throughout the book. Some of the initial chapters apply to beginners along the road to mastery and self-knowledge. Some later chapters build on concepts from earlier on.

I wrote over a period of many months. During that time I was playing and practicing myself. Many subjects surfaced for me again and again. I often had to be reminded of things I thought I already knew. For that reason there are themes that recur throughout the book.

Each chapter ends with an "intention." This short statement sums up the ideas in the chapter. In the practice of yoga, teachers often provide a concept, aspiration or statement at the beginning of class that helps students focus as they practice. This idea translates well to music practice.

Becoming a better musician and becoming a better person have much in common. Both involve listening to others, being honest yet kind to yourself, and integrating humor and humility into your daily activity.

My experience as a musician, a martial arts instructor, a yoga teacher, and even as a broadcast video editor are represented here. I've incorporated learning from neuroscience, psychology, meditation, and subjective "research." Sometimes I may go a little far afield, but I hope I always relate the topic back to its relevance to our practice.

Writing about music, as the wags say, is like dancing about architecture. If I use words or ideas that seem out of context or don't quite make sense it's only because I was trying (and failing) to express the inexpressible.

I hope you will keep this book near where you play. Abuse it. Make notes and drawings. Highlight it. Dog-ear and mark up favorite pages. Do whatever you need to help you remember things and find them again.

Happy practicing!

1   "Practicing" Is a Practice

We all want to play better. We've all, at some time, experienced practicing as drudgery. Even though we love the music, love the instrument(s) we play, love playing, and may even love practicing itself, there are many times when sitting down to do it feels like swimming through glue.

It may be hard to find the time, or hard to focus our attention. It may feel frustrating or unrewarding that we seem to make little progress. It may seem like there's so much to do that it's overwhelming. It may just feel like we'll never achieve our goals, or that we have no idea what steps to take to approach them.

Many players, even though they'd love to become better, put their instruments away until they can summon up good feelings again – in a day, a month, or a year. For some musicians, the word "practicing" is so psychologically loaded that they use a different one.

None of these negative associations are necessary. You **can** look forward to practicing, and you can incorporate techniques that help you improve faster and make playing music itself an enjoyable activity. You can look forward to practicing and even bring joy to the time spent practicing.

The first step is to ***let go of the idea of practicing as a means to an end.*** Practicing is not something you need to "get through" to get to the good part. Instead, begin thinking of practicing *as a practice,* an activity you engage in for its own sake.

The "practice of practicing" can be valuable time when we learn more about our instrument, our musical "voice," and even ourselves as human beings. When we look at it this way, we can approach practice with focus, deliberation and even respect.

Put It into Practice

Here's how to begin making *practicing* a *practice*.

Use just a small portion of your practice time to engage in some musical exploration. Set your metronome at a slower tempo than you usually play. When you find a trouble spot, pause. Play the spot again. Identify the problem as clearly and deliberately as you can.

You may have thoughts about how long it may take if you always go at this rate, or how many other mistakes remain after you address this one. Especially if you find you're focused on the outcome, see if you can stay with whatever you're working on. Be patient, curious, even playful.

Today I'll try to think about practicing in a new way. Instead of a means to an end, I'll begin to think of it as a valuable time in which I learn more about my instrument, my voice, and myself as a human being.

2 Baggage

Like many of my musician friends, I had classical music training as a child. When I started playing trad, it took me a while to put a finger on what made this music so appealing and so different from the musical culture I'd been trained in.

Trad Music Is Inclusive

Playing trad music is part of a community experience. People get together in homes, bars and coffee houses to learn and play together. Even the most well-known musicians are accessible. The enjoyment of the group is far more important than playing perfectly.

Trad Music Is Made for Dancing

Playing with a danceable beat is essential, even if no one is dancing. In contrast to "composed" music, traditional tunes are typically played over and over until the musicians (or dancers) feel like stopping.

Trad Music Is Social

In a jam session or musical get together, there's often as much conversation as playing. Politics, religion and other divisive issues are (almost always!) left at the door.

Trad Music Allows for Individual Expression

Some musicians assume that classical music is "superior" to traditional styles due to its complexity. Yet the playing of a trad tune is far more open to the performer's interpretation, and therefore requires a flexible, responsive relationship to the music. Rhythm (i.e. chord) players are far more free to choose their own harmony for backup.

Trad Music Is a Living Tradition

The music changes. Even living composers don't claim a "definitive" version of their tune. Players share and swap information about tunes: stories about the composer, the region where they're from, regional variations, who popularized them... Playing and sharing the music becomes part of transmitting a historic and cultural tradition.

Trad Music Is an Aural Tradition

Sheet music is available, and often shared widely, but it's used as a reference. If you want to know how the tune really sounds, you won't find that in the sheet music. You have to listen to someone play it. Because trad players generally learn by ear, they tend to be great listeners as well.

When I thought through these differences, I realized I was carrying a lot of "baggage" from my classical training: assumptions about what it means to be a good musician, and even about why I play.

Today I'll consider my assumptions about what it means to be a "good" musician, and compare them to what is important in playing trad. Maybe there's some baggage I can leave behind.

3   Minimum Effort for Maximum Effect

Great players make it look easy. Yet we know from our own experience that achieving that level of mastery is not easy at all. Most of us are aware of the time and focus it takes to learn to play an instrument well. What most of us *don't* realize is that *the ability to relax while playing* – that ability to "make it look easy" – *is an important skill of its own*, one that's worth practicing in its own right.

For over 25 years I practiced and taught the martial art of Kokikai Aikido. My teachers would often tell us to use "*minimum effort for maximum effect.*" This is an extremely useful concept that translates well to playing and practicing music.

In aikido, *minimum effort for maximum effect* refers to the idea that when we're soft and relaxed, we can also be more flexible, open, aware, *and* powerful. Something that was barely possible to do can instead become almost effortless.

Here is a question for you:
How often do you pay attention to whether you're relaxed as you play?

For most of us the answer is, "Not very often." Once in a while you may think to yourself, "Wow, my shoulders really *are* tight." You might notice you were tired or achy after playing for a while. But that is quickly forgotten and normal habits are resumed.

What if, the next time you practiced, in addition to learning fingerpicking and bowing patterns, learning tunes or perfecting an ornament, you were to give that same level of attention to *making your playing more effortless*? The answer is, you would open the door to an amazing, even *unimaginable* level of capability and creativity.

What do you want from your playing? Better tone? Fewer mistakes? More speed? Freedom from stage fright? To memorize more easily or have more fun? All of these and more will happen, as you *practice playing with minimum effort*. That's your incentive. Be as clear as you can about it.

Put It into Practice

> First, simply *make a commitment* to incorporate the idea of "minimum effort" into your practice and playing. It's not difficult, but it takes some persistence and patience. (Those are two words you'll hear a lot in this book!) There are ideas and techniques in the chapters that follow to help you keep this concept "front of mind."
>
> Start practicing by just focusing on one element. It might be the way you hold your instrument, your facial expression when you hit a hard passage, or a tension spot in one shoulder.
>
> Set aside 3-5 minutes at the beginning of your practice session. Mindfully and slowly go through the movements that you want to happen. Try to be aware of how your body feels. Really *sense the feeling of being relaxed and effortless* as deeply as you can. Imagine a microscope zooming in on individual muscles and muscle fibers.
>
> Then move on to your regular practice. Check in on yourself periodically: Did you revert to playing with effort? If so, can you call up that effortless feeling, even for a few moments?

Teaching yourself to use less effort when playing can be frustrating, even slippery. To learn to let go of habitual tension, we have to practice slowly and deliberately, especially at first.

It may not seem like much is happening, but rest assured that every time you do one of these "check-ins" you'll reinforce, in your mind, the importance of relaxing as you play.

Today I'll begin to practice playing with minimum effort.

4   Being Present

There are days when, as I practice, I want to jump up and do something else. It's frustrating, since often when I'm *not* practicing, *I wish I had more time to practice.*

We all have the habit of doing one thing while thinking of something else. I might be eating the most delicious meal, one I've anticipated for weeks, and instead of enjoying it, I'm worrying about something I'm going to do tomorrow.

My time (and my life) are finite. I may be unusual, but I take very seriously the idea that I don't have time to waste. I need to get the most out of the hours I spend practicing. That's why, for me, **developing a mental habit of being fully engaged in what I'm doing, or being "present," is as important as practicing the instrument itself.**

People sometimes talk about being "present" or, "in the moment" the way you might say, "I want to spend more time reading": as if it were an objective you could achieve if you only had more time. "Maybe next month, after I retire, I'll get the chance to be more in the moment."

Being present and engaged in your lived experience doesn't take time. *It gives you back time*: the time you already have, that you spend imagining you're somewhere else.

Put It into Practice

> Whatever you're doing right now, pause for a few seconds and notice that. Say to yourself, "I am here, doing this, feeling this."

Taking this mindful pause feels good. Whenever I take a pause to be present, it feels like I'm living my life, instead of riding an express train to somewhere else.

It can be hard to be "in the moment" when the moment doesn't feel so good. But playing music? That is pure joy. I try to remind myself of that every time I sit down to play.

Today I will try to be present while I play. I'll look up and remember: "I'm here, doing this, hearing this, seeing this, feeling this!"

5   Working with the Practice Pyramid

The Practice Pyramid[1] is a powerful tool for self-assessment as we practice. It is described in detail in Appendix A.

Once you've familiarized yourself with the elements of the Practice Pyramid, you'll have the ability to incorporate *five key elements* into your practice, and to zero in on them, one at a time.

The base of the Practice Pyramid consists of *staying relaxed* and *playing in time*. Whenever you're practicing a tune or a part of a tune, you should play *in time* (or "in rhythm"), i.e. without hesitations or hiccups. A metronome is an excellent tool to keep you "honest."[*]

In addition, as you practice make sure you're relaxed. Check in with yourself: Is your breathing uninhibited? Are your shoulders and arms hunched? Is your stomach clenched? Is your face tense?

If you're playing with tension or unable to play in time, then *let go of one of the other three elements*. Either play *more slowly*, play *a shorter section* or loop of the tune, or *give up playing perfectly*.

I noticed two things as I began using this tool. First, it's difficult to be honest with myself. For example, I don't like to admit that I hesitate over mistakes ("The metronome is speeding up!"), or that I'm not relaxed as I play.

Second, it's can be surprisingly tough to let go of one element in my playing. I don't want to go slower! I don't want to play less of the tune! I don't want to play with mistakes!

A third realization, at least for me, was that I spent far more time on one aspect of playing (getting the notes correct) than others (relaxing, or playing the whole tune). When I started letting go of "perfect" and relaxed into playing entire tunes, I began playing faster with far less effort. I quickly got better at playing entire tunes without pausing.

If you find that one option in the Practice Pyramid doesn't come naturally or easily to you, it may be worth working on that one even more.

---

[*]Certain types of tunes, including airs, songs and accompaniment to Morris dances, are not played to a fixed rhythm. Every musician, however, should be *capable* of playing in time for those tunes when it is appropriate.

Today I will use the Practice Pyramid as a tool during my practice. I'll adjust one of the three optional elements until I can play in time, and without tension.

6   I Will Sound Good

My piano teacher suggested I start each practice session with an intention. Since I'd first met him in a yoga class, I wasn't that surprised that he made use of this idea. What did surprise me was the intentions he recommended: "I will sound good," and, "Everyone will like my playing." I already was using intentions as I played, but I would tell myself things like, "I will keep my hands relaxed, or, "I will focus on what scale I'm using to improvise." *My focus was on technique, his was on having positive thoughts about playing.*

You already know that you play better when you feel good about yourself. You may have experienced the opposite: that devastating crash of capability that comes from fear, insecurity and the onrush of negative thoughts.

The tendency to bring up negative thoughts is just something the mind does.

Addressing this tendency to self-criticism is an important – even vital – element of our practice. Retraining ourselves to be positive, to believe in ourselves, to have useful observations about our playing instead of defeating ones, takes time and persistence. Yet it has as much effect on our playing as the technical aspects of making the sounds.[*]

Put It into Practice

> Decide what you'd like to think about your own playing. Be forewarned: The thought, "I will sound good," may not feel believable at first. Give it your full attention anyway. Repeat it to yourself several times.

---

[*] *Positive Mind* is one of the four basic principles of Kokikai Aikido. There's more about them in Appendix D.

Put it on a sticky note, and stick it where you can see it while you practice. Every time you see it, make an explicit reminder to yourself.

You may want to repeat your positive intention at other times during the day, too. Do what you need to make *positive mind* into *an intentional practice.*

Here's a bonus: letting go of negative thoughts about ourselves, and having more positive ones, can benefit far more than our music practice. It can have far-reaching effects in our daily lives as well.

Today I will sound good.

7 Mind-Body Coordination

As a musician I use many ideas I learned in martial arts training. Many people are surprised at this. They wonder what self-defense has to do with music. The answer boils down to mind-body coordination.

We tend to divide the activities of playing into the *physical* and the *mental.* The physical aspects include how to hold the instrument, technique, strength and flexibility, and the repetition of certain movements until they become automatic. A few of the mental aspects are listening itself, learning where the notes are, and memorizing tunes.

The idea of *coordinating the mind and the body* is not something most of us think about. Our standard practice in daily life is to engage one or the other: *either* mind *or* body. While exercising we daydream or watch TV. While engaging in mental activities like reading or studying, we sit inactive.

In contrast, in the practice of many martial arts, mind-body coordination is fundamental to the teaching. When the mind and body are coordinated, it's not just possible, but easy to do things that might seem incredible.

You can **bring the attention of your mind to your body** (focusing on posture, or on relaxing while you play) or you can **start with a mental**

concept (finding your center of balance, or imagining a deeply-held confidence in your ability) and ***see how it affects your body.****

You'll get instant feedback if you're even moderately successful. You may find that your sound changes, or you have more ease in playing. If you make a note of the changes it will help you remember to keep working on coordinating your mind and body.

Today I'll begin to work on coordinating my mind and body. I'll either bring the attention of my mind to my body, or start with a mental concept and see how my body reacts. Then I'll listen: Do I sound better? Do I play with more ease?

8   Being a Beginner

As adults we're used to having knowledge and expertise about something – perhaps about many things. Playing trad music can often put us in the position of feeling like beginners again. This can feel uncomfortable, even discouraging.

It's not only beginning musicians who may feel clueless and awkward. Anyone who has made the shift as an adult from classical to trad, learned a new instrument when they're already accomplished at another, or walked into their first jam or workshop after playing for many years alone at home, is likely to feel discomfort at being "such a beginner." It's worth taking a moment to acknowledge that it takes courage to overcome this discomfort.

When we're kids it's no big deal to be a beginner. In karate, band or gymnastics class, we're with a bunch of other clueless kids. The teachers are all adults, and their authority and experience is assumed and accepted.

Now that we're adults ourselves, being a beginner is more complicated. The gap between our abilities and those of our teachers and mentors seems wider, (especially if some are younger than we are). We can be

---

* I use the Four Basic Principles of Kokikai Aikido as a mnemonic to help me coordinate my mind and body. For more about the Four Principles, see Appendix D.

hyper-aware of our own failings and insecurities, and flat-out disbelieving of our own talent and ability.

Subtly, or not so subtly, our thoughts turn to reasons why we should stop trying:

> "I feel ridiculous."
>
> "It's absurd to want to do this at my age."
>
> "I'm going to sound horrible and feel childish."
>
> "I'm accomplished at so many things. I'll just keep doing those things."
>
> "It will be *x* years before I'm any good, and then I'll be too old."
>
> "Those people have talent. I don't have talent."

When my mother was 33, she wanted to go back to college to get her undergraduate degree. She had four kids. The youngest was two. She told *her* mother she was afraid by the time she finished she'd be "so old" that there wouldn't be any point. My grandmother responded, "You may be 37 or even 40 when you're done. But if you don't start, you'll be 40 anyway, without a college degree." My mom's degree led to a 30-year career as an arts manager.

I know people from ages 30 through 75 who've started playing trad music for the first time. Some played music as kids; others had never played before. Some chose simple instruments like tin whistle or harmonica, others took up violin, piano or flute. Other friends have challenged themselves to learn music by ear, to perform in public, or to compose tunes.

It's difficult to be a beginner again. But you can do it.

Today I will acknowledge the courage it takes to be an adult musician. I'll remember that being a beginner is especially difficult now that I'm an adult.

9   Having a Plan

One of the best things my teacher does is to give me very clear instructions about how to organize my practice time. There's nothing more daunting than sitting down to practice and thinking, "How do I start? Is this the right thing to work on?"

With a little forethought and preparation, you can provide yourself with these same clear instructions. When you do, your practice time will be more efficient and enjoyable, because you'll know what you did and why.

Put It into Practice

Take a few minutes to think through some questions. Write down the answers. Think about those answers as they relate to your practice goals for just the next few weeks.

- What's your focus? Is it mastering a certain technique? Memorization? A music theory thing? Learning a particular tune or set of tunes? Refreshing familiar repertoire?
- On a given day, how long do you want to work on each element (technique, tune, idea)?
- What tunes do you want to work on? List them.
- How many days do you expect to work on a tune or a technique before moving on?
- What are your goals for each element, each day?

The exact answers – even the questions you ask – aren't as important as having articulated your goals. You can use the answers as your general plan to organize your practice time for the next week or month.

The key is to *write it down*, and *put it somewhere you can see it when you sit down to play.*

How you divide the time when you practice can vary. You don't have to stick to your plans. Big rocks may get dropped in the pond of your serene practice routine: a last-minute gig, a jam session with fun stuff to work on, life, whatever. It doesn't matter. You can always get back to the plan, or rewrite it. *It's having a plan in the first place that makes the difference.*

Today I'll create a plan for practice. It can be just an outline that will help me sit down and get started.

10   Is It Training or Talent?

You may believe you can only be a good musician if you have talent to begin with. That's pretty discouraging. It's not true either.

When a magician does a magic trick, we intuitively know he or she spent many hours working on every detail: practicing in front of a mirror, continuing the smooth patter and making distracting body movements. The trick is no less impressive because of all the hard work that goes into it. Yet I've never heard anyone say, "He was just born with a talent for doing magic tricks."

There *are* people with certain musical talents. But no one, not even the most talented musician, can play a complex, delicate, moving performance without *consistent, attentive practice.* As for talented people who don't apply themselves to their art: Can they be great? I don't know. I do know many musicians who consider themselves to be "moderately" talented, who are passionate about the music they choose to play and work consistently on improving. *Those people always achieve results.* Many of them are downright incredible.

Today I'll try to let go of the question of whether I'm talented, and sit down to practice.

11   Going Slower is Faster

We *all* focus too much on **how fast we play**, and too little on **how we sound**. And we *all* avoid practicing slowly, even though we're told, over and over, that it works.

There are times to build up speed. But we're often better off practicing *slowly and attentively much of the time.*

Slow practice is effective. It allows us to find the notes reliably and comfortably. It lets us build important habits like listening, playing in time, being calm while playing, relaxing, and thinking ahead.

The paradox of slow practice is that once you can do these things slowly, speed comes almost by itself.

In teaching the martial art of aikido, when I can get students to slow down the execution of a technique, they *always* make immediate, noticeable progress. To be effective, aikido requires you to be relaxed, calm and centered. When a self-defense technique is slowed down, as with a slowed-down tune, it may not seem so fun, or even realistic. But when students do slow down, they may realize that their shoulders tense when they raise their arms, or that they flinch at a certain point, or some small change in body position that affects the outcome. If you never practice except at full speed, it's almost impossible to recognize any of these sensations, and certainly not possible to correct them.

Many aspects of learning happen more quickly when we move slowly.

Today I will practice more slowly. I'll use the slower speed to help me notice the details of my playing and make any corrections as needed.

12   Beginner's Mind

We've all noticed that children learn quickly. This seems particularly true when children learn music. One reason may be that children approach learning with an open mind. They're ready to receive new ideas, with few, if any, preconceived notions. Without previous experience or previous teaching, they absorb what they're told and try it wholeheartedly.

A well-known story in the Zen/martial arts tradition involves a student who comes to a famous master to request teaching. They sit down together and the master sets out tea. As the student talks about his previous experience, his diligence, his years of study, and all the reasons he would be a worthy pupil, the master pours tea into the student's cup.

He pours and pours until the tea overflows the cup, dripping onto the table and then the floor. Finally, the acolyte can't restrain himself. "It's full! There's no room for any more!" he cries.

"This is you," the master replies, gesturing to the cup. "How can I teach you unless you first empty your cup?"

Paradoxically, the idea that we are knowledgeable can be a major obstacle to learning and growth. When a new idea is presented, we throw up roadblocks: objecting, arguing, listing the reasons that it won't work. If a suggestion or correction is made, we "shoot the messenger," faulting their experience, training or method. The more accomplished we become, the more difficult it is to keep this mindset.

Unlike the martial arts, whether we play well is not a life-or-death issue, but there are parallels. In the best of all possible worlds, we play balanced on a knife-edge. On the one side is competence, self-assuredness, comfort. On the other is complete openness and receptivity. To be able to play this way, we have to *practice it every time we sit down to play*. We have to practice having beginner's mind.

Beginner's mind is an attitude that can allow us to learn faster and play more sensitively.

Today I'll consider what it means to have "beginner's mind." I'll try to notice when I may be resisting a new idea or instruction, no matter who is offering it, and switch from thinking about "what I know" to "what I can learn."

13   Metronome

When I was eight, my piano teacher told me to practice with a metronome. She probably assumed that after she told me to, I did it. I never did.

When I was 48 and started taking jazz piano lessons, my teacher told me always to practice with a metronome. When I tried, I was shocked: I was an accomplished pianist, I played Chopin and Brahms, but I couldn't keep the beat.

Since then, I've spoken to many highly accomplished musicians who have told me they *always practice with a metronome.*[*]

Why Play with a Metronome

You'll realize when you tend to slow down (which we all do when we're unsure or having trouble) or speed up (which we do when

---

[*] or some other external device that keeps the beat, such as a backing track or playing along with a recording.

using weaker fingers, for example). This will help you quickly identify trouble spots that you might not have noticed

As you get better at hearing minute changes in your own tempo, you'll also get better at listening to an external source and making changes so you can stay right on the beat. This will help you when playing with others.

An electronic metronome is cheap. There are free apps. You can even open a web browser and search "metronome."

You may think a metronome isn't necessary. Maybe you usually play along with recordings or a backing track, or you tap your foot (usually).

Try it.

Tip: If you can connect headphones to your metronome, you may find it a lot easier to hear over the sound of your instrument.

Today I'll begin making the metronome a valuable practice tool.

14   Physical Self-Care

One way we describe "good health" is to say we are in *harmony*. Music and health have a symbiotic relationship: Music can affect our mental wellbeing, which has an impact on physical health. At the same time, good mental and physical health both help us make better music. It makes sense to take care of the body that lets us enjoy, and play, the music we love.

The entire body is involved in playing. We're aware of things like fingers, hands, arms, lips that make contact with the instrument, but we also need the rest of the body – muscles in our legs, hips, abdomen and spine – to support us when we sit or stand. The body provides regular air and blood flow. We need our brains to play, too, and our mental processes benefit from good physical health.

Physical self-care is a practice, with all the same issues as music practice. It's not something that we become experts at in a day or a week. We need to make time for it, be consistent, set reasonable goals, assess progress, avoid overcommitting, and, above all, find ways to make it enjoyable.

Many ideas in this book could apply to an exercise routine as easily as they do to music practice.

Get exercise in the way that feels right for you. Move around and breathe fresh air if you can. Whether it's hiking, swimming, walking the dog, chopping wood, dancing, or something else, make it your own.

Taking care of yourself is important. The rewards can include more than just better mood, more energy, stamina and better sleep patterns. A healthier body can help you be a better musician.

Today I will take stock of how I'm caring for my body. What have I been doing? Is it enough? Is it worth doing more to help me be a better musician?

15   Please Explain That More Slowly

We have all encountered a section of music that trips us up again and again. Most of us address a problem area like this by repeating it, over and over, until we experience some improvement. This works much of the time, but some challenges are more persistent. We may come back the next day and the problem has arisen again, in the same place, almost exactly the same way.

There is a better way to approach this type of persistent trouble spot. It begins with the assumption that *what our brains are seeking is more clarity.* We may *think* we're being clear, but somewhere there is ambiguity about what's supposed to happen, and our brains are either filling in the gap with mistakes, or just plain freezing up.

I remember trying to explain a smartphone app to a friend who was not tech-savvy. I had no idea that I was going much too fast for him to follow. When he tried to repeat what I did, I realized I'd made the assumption that he understood much more than he actually did.

Your brain is like my friend learning how to use that app. It just wants you to slow down, and break each element into smaller steps.

When we pick apart the section of music that's causing us trouble, down to its tiniest component parts, our brains respond very well. Often the problem can be easily solved.

Put It into Practice

Here are a few ways to break down a trouble spot:[*]

- Do you know *what the notes are* that you're trying to play? Can you picture where they are on your instrument?

- Can you "play" the section *with each hand separately*? On stringed instruments can you finger the notes without bowing or plucking? Can you bow or pluck the strings without fingering?

- Can you *name every note*, in time, as you play it? What about before you play it?

- *What's happening in your body* as you play? What part of your shoulder/arm/hand are you using? Does the sound change when you make even small changes in your hand, finger or arm position?

- *Look at your fingers and hands* as you play. Does it help to remember the way it looks?

- *What part of the instrument are you looking at*? What happens if you change that? Or don't look at all?

- Are there any *differences in what you do* when you play very slowly vs. at a more typical speed for you?

Treat your brain like a good friend. If you explain what you're trying to do, slowly and clearly, it will understand and remember.

Today I'll respond to my brain's need for clarity. When I'm having trouble with something, I'll break the section down and examine every element to help me understand and remember.

---

[*] Why not keep a list of these, and add any more you discover for yourself along the way?

16   You Can Play by Ear

Many people who've learned to play from sheet music have told me they can't play by ear. Often their reasons *sound* logical: "It's particularly difficult on my instrument," or, "I've tried it many times, I'm just not talented like some people."

Repeating the music you hear on your instrument is intuitively a simpler task for your brain than seeing something on paper and reproducing it as sound. Think about learning to talk vs. learning to read words. Which one can babies do?

Playing by ear is just a skill. It can be learned like any other skill. Often when people fail at learning by ear, it's because they started with something too difficult. You'll have more success if you start with something simple and build gradually.

Put It into Practice

Sing the Tune

Can you sing the tune? It doesn't matter if you have a "good" voice or if you can hit all the notes. Do you *know what each note should be*, or are you "fudging" some of it because you don't know?

Play What You Hear

Try to sing something, and then play it on your instrument. If you have any trouble, simplify: Slow down. Sing fewer notes – even just two. What you sing doesn't have to be a real tune. Just practice singing a few notes and then playing them

Learn the Rhythm

Try beating the rhythm of the melody with your fingers. If there's a section you're not sure about, slow down – use a metronome if you can. Or try listening to a recording, and slow it down until you can hear it clearly.*

---

*If you don't already use a "slowdowner" app, I highly recommended that you do. There may be a bit of a learning curve to get started, but once you do, you'll find that the ability to make loops, save your settings, even change keys, will increase your practice efficiency in many ways.

No matter how well you learn by ear, some tunes are harder than others. You can make use of these three ways to help you learn faster.

Today I'll revisit learning by ear. I'll see if I can start simply and build gradually.

17   A Space of Your Own

You spend a lot of time in the place where you practice. Even if it's just a little corner, why not make that space your own? Small things can make practicing more comfortable and enjoyable.

Organize your practice space so you have what you need close to hand. For me that includes a clock with a timer, a metronome, a pen that writes nice and dark, sticky notes, a notebook, a music stand and a mirror. I also have some personal preferences: a three-hole punch, highlighters (to mark the hard parts), correction fluid, my tablet computer and headphones, and reading glasses.

Make your space inviting, somewhere you want to spend time. In my old house, my piano was in a family room with tiny windows. The piano was an upright, so I played facing the wall. The aging Tensor lamp used to fall on my head whenever I adjusted it. One day I decided to hang some artwork over the piano – a painting by a friend. I got a new light and replaced my wobbly table with a sturdy one that I could use to write on. I even traded my hard, wooden bench for a fancy padded "artist bench." Suddenly the idea of practicing was much more appealing.

Gradually I have developed a practice space that's 100% about me, for me, and tailored to my needs. Just thinking about it makes me look forward to spending time there.

Today I will look at my practice space with a new eye. Are the things I need close by? Is it inviting and comfortable? Is it mine?

18 Taking Notes

My husband is a college professor. One of his common complaints is that students don't take notes. They think they'll remember everything. As musicians we aren't much better. Day after day we make headway, and assume that tomorrow we'll be able to pick up right where we left off. The next day we sit down and we're a blank slate with no idea what we did yesterday – especially if it wasn't actually *yesterday*.

A few notes can save a lot of time, and keep us pointing toward a goal consistently enough to achieve it.

My own notes are brief. I might list a particular technical exercise, a tune name and what I was focused on, and maybe notes on my progress. It might look like this:

> June 12 –
> E string intonation. Tunes in F !!!
> Le rêve du Quêteux - string crossing B sect

I also make notes on particular tunes, often directly on sheet music or electronic PDFs. I may highlight tough passages so that when I come back to practicing the tune I can work on those sections first. I may write notes on the "fine tuning" of the tune: "Don't speed up during B section," or "Check transitions!"

This is what *I* do, and of course you may do something else. I may do something else next year. You could use an app, or electronic documents, or paper and pen. No matter what you choose, some form of note-taking is a powerful aid for practice.

If you know it's for your own benefit, taking notes doesn't have to be a burden.

Today I'll find a way to take notes on the things I want to remember.

19 When Not to Have Ambition

In teaching yoga, I try to help students understand that there's no "perfect" expression of a yoga pose. Everyone has a different body, and different levels of flexibility and strength – and even these change over time. A perfect yoga pose is really one in which you're focused on how it feels, breathing deeply and evenly, and trying to release any tension that isn't necessary to hold the pose.

When I began practicing yoga, I didn't have any expectation that I'd be "good" at it. I liked how it felt to try to breathe and relax. I wasn't concerned with what my poses looked like to others, as long as I walked away feeling I had gotten something from the class: some flexibility, some strength and some balance.

One day it occurred to me that I had difficulty finding that equanimity when I practiced music. I wondered if it was because I have so much ambition to be a better musician. In yoga I didn't really have any goal at all. I just came to class, did the work and left.

Goals are great. They help keep us motivated and pointed in the right direction. Thinking about the long-term future, however, isn't very useful *while we're practicing.* In fact, it can be disheartening.

Let your practice time be free of any ambition to "be" someone. Instead focus on the way it feels and sounds right now.

Today as I practice, I'll try to let go of goals, ambitions and comparisons. I'll try to focus on the way it feels and sounds right now.

20   Play Better with Phrasing

One of the simplest ways to make your playing sound instantly better is to bring out the phrasing in a tune. It's not always easy to hear phrasing, however, especially if you're not used to it.

When we sing or talk, we use phrasing naturally. Consider the best public speakers you've heard. Whether they were giving a speech, reading poetry, or presenting a talk, they use their voices to give meaning, emotion and life to their words.

These same patterns and rhythms exist in music. Musicians can do what good speakers do: We can create and emphasize musical phrases through changes in rhythm, dynamics, and emphasis. When we do, we'll give the music meaning, emotion and life.

If you're not used to listening for phrases, it just means you need to pay a little more attention to them. It's likely that once you start uncovering them, you'll realize you heard phrasing all along without realizing it.

Singers, flute and whistle players, and accordion and concertina players need to pay particular attention where they make space to breathe or to change bellows direction. Musically, it makes an enormous difference when you ensure that these spaces happen at the ends of phrases, rather than in the middle of them, or randomly.

Put It into Practice

> A great way to find the phrasing in a tune is to sing it.* *Think of the places where you naturally want to breathe as the spaces between phrases.* Where do you naturally take a breath? What if you played around with where that happens?
>
> Do you need to open up space to breathe that doesn't exist in the tune? How would/could that work?
>
> Can you make two short phrases out of a longer one? What if you did the opposite: made a longer phrase without breathing?
>
> Do you like the sound better if you breathe in one place, versus another?
>
> A common "road sign" pointing to the end of a musical phrase is *a longer note.* It functions like a period at the end of a sentence. If you were reading out loud, you'd pause to let the listener absorb the meaning of the sentence. Can you do the same with the longer notes, without changing the rhythm?

Once you have more practice listening for phrases, they'll begin to come out more naturally in your playing. Just like reading out loud, or reading poetry, there's no one right way to phrase a tune. The music may lend itself to phrasing a certain way, but you're free to do it differently.

---

* Use nonsense syllables, and don't worry about the quality of your singing.

Today I'll look more carefully at phrasing. I may try singing to help make the phrasing more clear. I'll start listening for phrasing and see if I can bring it out more in my playing.

21   The 20-Minute Interval

It's a good idea to divide longer sessions of practice into roughly 20-minute segments.

There are several benefits to dividing practice time up this way.

First, by building variety into practice, we're **building more complex cognitive connections**. A large body of research shows that varying the type of mental and physical activity we do helps with both memory and learning.

Second, **it's easier to stay focused for short periods of time**. Few of us can maintain mental focus for longer than 20 minutes. Taking a short break, stretching, moving around and then shifting gears can help us stay more attentive.

Third, after each brief period, **it feels like you've made definitive progress**. At the end of the practice session, you'll have made progress in three, or four areas. That's a good feeling.

Finally, breaking it up **makes it easier to schedule practice time**. I *try* to schedule an hour to practice, but some days I don't have an hour. I have 20 minutes now and *maybe* 40 minutes later, if everything goes as planned. By using 20-minute blocks, I can be more flexible with my practicing and feel like I'm making progress, even if I didn't practice for as long as I'd hoped.

Put It into Practice:

Here's an example of how you might block an hour into 20(ish)-minute time periods.* What you work on is completely up to you.

---

* There's no rule that says you have to practice for an hour. Choose a length of time that's right for you, that you can do consistently and that leaves you feeling energized, not exhausted.

- An exercise (e.g. intonation practice, 2-note violin chords) – 5-10 min.
- Learn a new tune 10-15 min.

  [5-minute break]
- Review material from yesterday [20 min.]

  [5-minute break]
- Memory practice: Try to start six tunes I "know" [5 min.]
- Work on new tune some more *or* continue detailing yesterday's material [15 min.]

In progressing from segment to segment, I try to vary the type of mental and physical effort I'm using. If I'm doing a technique exercise that's physically demanding, I'll switch to something that's more relaxing, like working on my posture with a tune I know, or sight reading that may be sloppy but in time.

Today I'll organize my practice time in 20-minute segments.

22   Attention

You can think of attention as food that nourishes your goals. As you develop the ability to maintain your attention, your practice time will become more and more productive.

When you become aware of the power of attention and start learning to focus, hone, and develop that tool, *you will perceive the difference* in your practicing and playing.

As you develop this power, you can even use it to support other purposes in your life. Whatever you goal may be, it will be fed by the power of your attention.

Today I will begin learn to use of the power of my attention.

23   Motion is Lotion

If you're already dividing your practice time into 20- (or so) minute sessions,* why not do a few stretches during your breaks? Intense focus, habit and physical fatigue can cause us to stiffen and slouch over the course of a long practice session.

Deliberate movement helps our joints stay flexible and transports oxygen and nutrients to our muscles and joints. A few gentle stretches can give us the physical "reset" we need to continue practicing with focus.

As you do the movements, pay attention to your overall posture and breathing. Try to keep your spine and the back of your neck long and your breathing regular, deep and even. Do each movement five times (or five times on each side, where applicable).†

Arms and Legs

- Make gentle arm circles at the shoulder, then do the same at the wrist in both directions. Switch arms.

- Bring movement into the legs with gentle leg swings: Swing one leg back and forth like a bell clapper, gently and easily. Switch legs.

- Lift one leg to the front and shake your foot as if you were gently shaking off water. Switch legs.

Head and Neck

- Bend your head forward *gently*, and bring it straight up again. As you bring your head to the erect position, lengthen the back of your neck. Imagine creating space between the vertebrae.

- Turn your head toward your left shoulder, only as far as you can without strain. Then go to the right. Move slowly and easily.

---

* See 21 – The 20-Minute Interval

† Video of these movements is available at www.judyminot.com/bestpractice/

- Tilt your head gently toward your left shoulder, letting the muscles on the right side of the neck lengthen. Then tilt toward the right. To intensify this stretch, you can extend the arm on the side that's lengthening.

Hands

- Hold your left arm out in front of you, letting the arm and hand relax. Make a gentle fist with the thumb outside the fingers. Hold this curled shape as you bend the wrist. Stop just at the point where the fingers start to uncurl. Hold this position for five seconds.
- Now uncurl the fingers and bend your wrist backward, as if you were gesturing "Stop!" Hold for five seconds.
- Repeat with your right arm.

Cautions:

Always exercise common sense with your own health. Move to a point of comfort, not pain. If you have a back or neck injury or another health concern, or if you experience pain during one of these stretches, stop and seek professional advice. If you have balance issues, hold onto something and move slowly.

Today when I take a break, I'll bring some movement into my joints.

24 Overwhelmed

> "I didn't know where to start, what to practice first, how many things to practice, what would do any good, what would change my playing. So no matter what I practiced felt like a drop in the bucket. Therefore it didn't feel like it was helping."
> – Kenny Werner[*]

This work toward mastery, the practice of music, is *difficult*. Even the word *mastery* itself sounds daunting. Our progress usually seems slow,

---

[*] https://youstu.be/G9M90QCwKGs

stepwise, sometimes even nonexistent. There are so many things to work on. They all seem impossible. So much music is available to listen to. There are so many others to compare ourselves to.

All these feelings and thoughts can add up to paralyze us.

Human beings have evolved to prefer secure, immediate rewards over uncertain future gains. It's quite natural that our brains put up roadblocks to doing something that's so demanding and unproven. Yet you know you want to become a better musician. *There are things you can do to help yourself to feel less overwhelmed.*

Put It into Practice

> ***Accept that there is never an end to what you can learn.***
> This is a fact that every musician faces. Even the greatest musicians just can't be great at everything. We can see that as an overwhelming hurdle, or we can become OK with it. In fact, we can decide to be really excited about it. The reason it's exciting is that in no matter what direction we focus our efforts *there's always an infinity of creative possibilities open to us.* Once we do that, we can focus on what we want to learn today.
>
> ***Start out each week with a small, measurable goal.***
> Make this a regular habit. Be very specific about finding a short-term goal with an achievable result that you can perceive/hear/distinguish. Write it down: Learning a chord progression. Playing low D reliably. Remembering how "Far Away" starts. When you find yourself sliding into despair over your lack of overall progress, remind yourself, "I only need to work on *this* right now."[*]
>
> ***Organize your practice time.***
> Being organized really helps you sit down and get to work. I find if I take too much time wondering where to start I don't work on anything meaningful and I don't work consistently on any one idea.
>
> Instead, every week or two I think through what I'll work on and write it down. I might include a list of tunes, exercises, habits and/or techniques. If you exercise regularly you probably don't come up

---

[*] See 54 – Tracking Small Wins

with a new exercise plan every day. Make "getting down to practice" as easy as sitting down and following the plan.*

Remind yourself of the progress you've made. Pull out a tune you know well and haven't played in a while. This may help you remember why you love playing, and help motivate you to practice.

Today I can acknowledge the feeling of being overwhelmed and take some steps that will help make it easier to practice.

25 The Benefits of Being an Adult

Sometimes when I play with other musicians there are skilled players in the group who are quite young. This can lead to discouraging thoughts about aging and its effects on playing.

When this happens I try to remind myself that "mature musicians" like me have advantages that kids don't have. An important one is a ***better understanding of our own affinities***. We know what we're good at, what motivates us and what appeals to us.

Some musicians enjoy research: learning about the history of a tune or style. Others like to see how people dance to it. Some like to build things: instruments, cases, custom practice chairs. I have friends who prefer to compose, others who enjoy arranging. You may want to learn many instruments or dig deeply into one.

Our ***professional and life experience*** – another thing young people don't have – can help inform how we learn and practice. For me that includes martial arts, yoga, meditation, a career in entertainment and marketing, classical music training, and raising a child. Together, these affect how I organize my time, how I interpret what I'm learning, and how I interact with my teachers, play with others and set goals.

Another benefit of being an adult musician is that we're ***self-motivated***. It's my choice to play, not my parents' pushing (not that my parents had to push terribly hard). It's my money spent on instruments and teachers, and my time spent practicing, procrastinating, traveling and jamming. I

---

* See 9 – Having a Plan, 21 – The 20-Minute Interval, 111 – You've Got Five Minutes.

also know that if it turns out something's not for me (like playing the low D whistle), even after investing time and money into the effort I can stop with no recriminations.

Finally, although we may make a few bucks here and there, most of us have **no plans to make a career of music**. We're free to fully enjoy every aspect of the musical life, including practice time, experimenting, playing alone, playing with others, lessons, instrument-making, recording, taking workshops, and, if it should happen, performing.

Today I'll reflect on the benefits of being an adult musician striving for mastery.

26   Practice, Play with Others, Get a Teacher

When I first started playing trad music, a fiddling friend told me, "There are three things you need to do to get better: Practice, play with others and get a teacher."

You already know you need to *practice*.

Playing with others may seem daunting, but it will do more than help improve your playing. Joining a musical community can help motivate and inspire you, not to mention the fact that it's fun.[*]

Finding the right teacher can be a challenge for trad musicians, and many of us do without a regular teacher. Still, while workshops are helpful, there's a great benefit to working with someone who can give you individualized instruction.[†]

My friend was on the right track. Practice is necessary, but playing with others and having a teacher really boost your progress as a musician.

Today I'll keep in mind: Practice, play with others and get a teacher.

---

[*] More about a musical community at 51 – A Musical Community

[†] More about finding a teacher at 46 – Finding A Teacher

27   "At Speed"

The idea that we have to play things "at speed" is not very useful. It can even be harmful and destroy the joy of playing. A tune that might be played beautifully – melodically, evocatively, rhythmically – can become a source of dissatisfaction if we're too focused on speed.

Professional musicians are great models but there are many things we can emulate besides the speed at which they play.

If your primary goal is to play "at speed," then every time you play you're likely be focused on how fast you're playing (or not playing). This is not a productive mental state for learning, absorbing or listening.

For most tunes, "optimal speed" is arbitrary. Unless you're playing for a dance or with a band, **the optimal speed for a tune is the one where you sound best**. Aim for quality, musicality and enjoyment. Let speed come last, and then only if it sounds better that way.

You have a limited time to practice. Why not spend that time playing beautifully, rather than trying to crank up the metronome and feeling bad that you're not "there" yet?

Today I'll let go of the need to play "at speed." I'll focus my attention on playing for musicality and enjoyment.

28   Interrupt the Loop

It's easy to fall into a mindless loop as we practice. Many of us have spent years learning music by rote. It may seem like the best way, or even the only way to learn. In reality, too much repetition can actually waste precious practice time, especially if it is done mindlessly.

When we repeat any task more than a few times we stop paying attention to what we're doing. The brain, like a computer looking for maximum efficiency, recognizes a rote process, assigns it to the background, and starts to engage in other tasks. Our minds drift, and the thoughts we have often have nothing to do with our musical goals.

Mindless repetition creates an issue with memory as well: When we are mentally "checked out" we don't make good, strong memory connections. We remember best when we are awake, aware and fully engaged in what is going on at the present moment.

The easiest way to become more present is to **_interrupt your repetitive practice loop._**

Put It into Practice

When you realize you're grinding away mindlessly, try this:

- Play the passage you're working on *once*. Stop.
- Ask yourself: "How did it feel? What do my hands look like when I do it this way? What did it sound like? What is going through my mind?" Make your observations as detailed as you can.
- Now try again. What has changed? What is the same? Is anything better?

This practice technique is an excellent way to "jog" your mind back to fuller awareness of what you're doing. It will help you make more efficient use of your practice time.

On the other hand, it takes focus to practice this way. It can also feel less musically rewarding to keep stopping and starting. There's no need to practice this way all the time. But if you really want something to sink in, give it a try.

Today, if I realize I'm caught in mindless repetition, I'll try interrupting the loop.

29   A Mirror

Practicing with a mirror can tell me a lot of things:

- Is my posture correct?
- Is my bow straight?

- Are my arms relaxed?
- Is my face calm?

Looking at the mirror reminds me to get out of my own head, to sit up, to relax and listen. It reminds me that I like to play for and with others.

If you can, find a mirror and set it up in your practice space. If you can't, just practice in front of a mirror for today. You'll find it to be a good teacher.

Today I'll try practicing in front of a mirror.

30 The Gap (Between Taste and Ability)

There's an interview with Ira Glass, host and producer of NPR's *This American Life*, that's often quoted by creative people. Glass points out that when we first begin to do anything creative, the first couple of years can be frustrating. The reason is that at the beginning we're just *not that great at it*.

> "But your taste," he says, "the thing that got you into the game, your taste is still killer. And your taste is good enough that you can tell that what you're making…is kind of a disappointment to you."[2]

It's tempting to quit at this point. It's hard to imagine a future time when your ability will measure up to your taste. What you have to know, Glass says, is that *this feeling is normal.* Everyone goes through it.

Even if you're not a beginner, chances are you've experienced this feeling when trying something musically new. It's helpful to be reminded that this is an absolutely normal part of the process of developing any creative skill. Your ability to tell good from "not there yet" is what will help you improve. If you can stay motivated and carry on, you will get past this stage.

It helps to remind yourself that many people are so daunted by the *idea* of playing an instrument or of becoming a musician, they never even try. You are already much farther along than that.

Today I'll remember that when beginning anything new, it's normal to be terrible at it...at first. I'll need to give my ability the chance to catch up with my taste.

31 Just Keep Showing Up

One evening before aikido class I was changing in the locker room with my friend Jan. A girl of about seven had just finished her swimming lesson. As we put on our black belts and tied them, her eyes lit up.

"You're *black belts*?" she asked.

"Yes, we are," said Jan, smiling.

No matter how jaded you are, impressing a 7-year-old feels pretty good. As the girl and her mom left, Jan looked at me and said quietly, "...and it's not as hard as you might think. All you really need to do is keep showing up."

Working toward mastery in any discipline can be hard work. Even though it's sometimes wonderful, at other times practicing can feel repetitive and frustrating and the progress can be slow. One of the hardest things to do is just to show up: to sit down in the chair and get started. Sometimes that feels like all we can do. But at those times, that's also all we need to do.

Oh, and my friend Jan? She's now a fourth-degree black belt and just finished writing her first book.

Today I'll show up to practice.

32 Tailor-Made Technical Exercises

There are books and books of technical exercises for musicians. I find it to be more satisfying to create my own. It's fun to make them up. I base them on music I'm working on, which makes them feel more relevant than exercises from a book. That relevance makes it easier for me to stay interested when I practice them. And if I do get bored with an exercise, I can make up a new one.

Put It into Practice

Here's how to create your own tailor-made technical exercises

- First, ***identify a passage you have trouble with***.

- Then ***look for the source of your difficulty.*** Whether it's a weak finger, an intonation issue or a pattern you're not used to, be specific.

- Next, isolate that area, and ***create a limited set of repeatable notes*** that *focuses on the issue you've identified.*

- Your exercise might consist of playing the section in different rhythms, on different strings or in different keys, swapping out notes, or something else. There are unlimited options depending on what you decide the issue is and what interests you.

Tips on Practicing Efficiently

Go slowly, especially at first. The speed you choose should be slow enough that you can ***pay attention to detail***.

Start with ***awareness of the physical***. Feel the way your fingers and hands are moving; the position of your arms. Scan your body for tension, and check your posture and breathing.

Then bring your attention to ***rhythm and timing***. A metronome is invaluable for technical exercises. Are you playing in time? Do you tend to slow down or speed up? Is the rhythm of the music being brought out in your playing?

Always ***play exercises as musically as you can***. If you can't think of what you're playing as "real music," try changing something about the exercise to make it more interesting to play.

Finally, ***listen to the activity of your mind***. What kinds of thoughts float around in your head? Are they mostly positive or negative? Are you impatient? Bored? Distracted? See if you can replace frustration with fascination, criticism with curiosity.

Bringing this much focus to technical exercises takes effort. The good news is that when you *can* maintain your concentration in this way, you'll spend far less time on a given exercise before hearing things change.

Today I'll create my own technical exercise.

33   Subtle Thoughts

> "Your beliefs become your thoughts,
> Your thoughts become your words,
> Your words become your actions,
> Your actions become your habits,
> Your habits become your values,
> Your values become your destiny."
>
> – Gandhi

I once heard the Buddhist teacher, Gil Fronsdal, talk about the power of subtle thoughts. He described how, in his early days doing meditation practice he became interested in the idea of falling in love.

Most of us think of falling in love as something that happens outside our control. We say things like, "It was kismet," and, "It was meant to be."

Fronsdal wanted to investigate that belief. His meditation practice involved noticing thoughts as soon as he became conscious of them. As it happened, there was a woman at a meditation retreat he found interesting. He was able to distinguish a point when his thoughts about her shifted. He actually "heard" himself think: "Hmm, she has [such and such] qualities. *I could be in love with her.*"

He realized that it was only *after* that thought occurred that he began the process of "falling in love."[3]

Normally we aren't aware of subtle thoughts. Just like when we "fall in love," we obey the emotions they generate without realizing where they came from. This can have a profound effect on our musicianship. I may have subtle thoughts like these:

> "I am a bad person because I don't practice consistently."
> "I will never get very good at this, so why bother?"
> "Everyone thinks I'm the worst player in the group."

If I'm not aware of them as thoughts, I'm likely to act on the emotions they generate: feeling bad, deciding not to practice, staying home from the jam session.

Learning to recognize the subtle thoughts, and to identify them as *just* thoughts, not reality, takes practice. But as we begin to do it, we can develop a greater capacity to reach our goals.

Today I'll give consideration to subtle thoughts and how they affect my practice.

34   Keeping the Beat in Your Body

Classical musicians are trained not to tap their feet or even move their bodies to keep time. This is not true for trad musicians! Foot tapping is so ingrained that traditional musicians often have difficulty *not tapping*, for example when making a recording.

Trad musicians don't tap their feet just because they feel like it. Many, perhaps even most, foot-tapping musicians train themselves to tap consistently. In one group fiddle class our teacher would stop the class if we were not all tapping our feet *strongly*! In a workshop on Swedish polskas, we spent the first 20 minutes learning to tap to that unusual 1...3 beat.

Benefits to foot tapping include:

- Helping you keep the rhythm
- Signaling the rhythm to anyone else who's playing
- Making your playing more rhythmic and danceable

Can you tap your foot reliably on the beat? Try making it something you practice.[*] At first it may feel like rubbing your belly and patting your head, but it won't be long before you're very consistent. See how it changes your playing.

---

[*] If you play an instrument like accordion or bagpipes that occupies your lap, try just tapping your toe.

Today I'll start practicing tapping my foot.

35 Posture

You may have negative associations with the idea of improving your posture. Somewhere around 1960s I think good posture became associated with rule-driven conformity, along with wearing a suit and tie (or pearls and heels), hence, in my opinion, its poor reputation.

Good posture affects far more than how others react to us. The way we hold our bodies affects our playing. Good posture helps us stay relaxed, reducing the likelihood of injury and making playing itself more enjoyable. For many of us, a change in posture can lead to an immediate improvement in sound.

Playing with good posture is a habit. Like so much of our practice, changing a habit takes persistent attention, humility and even a bit of humor.

Put It into Practice

> Before you start to play, take a moment to assess your posture. Start by putting both feet on the floor. Lengthen your back: Lift your chest to take some of the C-curve from your upper spine. Position your head above your shoulders instead of craning it forward. Sit in this position for a few moments. Take a couple of deep breaths. Each time you exhale, allow yourself to relax. Try to experience the feeling of being upright, balanced, open, relaxed, and ready.
>
> Try to make this your starting point, physically, at the beginning of every session of playing. As you get lost in practicing and playing, you'll slip back into old postural habits. That's to be expected. If you can periodically remind yourself to bring back this feeling, even once or twice as you practice, you're on the right track.
>
> It can help to use a mental cue as a reminder. An image, say, of a tall tree or a photograph of someone you admire, or even a few words on a notepad, can bring back the whole feeling. Make sure your image encourages a feeling of balance, openness, relaxation, and readiness.

Most of us are quite unused to giving attention to our posture. It may be uncomfortable or even painful at first. You may feel stiff. If that's true for you, don't dismiss the whole idea and go back to your usual slouched, cramped playing. For now, just work on getting a sense of what it feels like to sit in a relaxed, upright, comfortable way. If it does feel better, you'll have more incentive to come back to it.

Good posture is a lifelong practice. Approach posture as something that you will continue to work on. Good posture will reward you by making it more enjoyable to play, and helping you sound better in the bargain.

Today I'll work on playing with better posture.

36 When You Can't Practice

There are days when we just can't get to our instruments. I am sure that professional musicians have days when they don't feel well, have to travel or drop everything to deal with a plumbing emergency. It must be stressful. Luckily my livelihood doesn't depend on maintaining my "chops" by playing every day. And yet many musicians feel guilt when they can't practice every day.

If this sounds like you, you may want to regard time when you can't practice as an opportunity to recharge and remember why you like to play. (Do this after you've dealt with the plumbing emergency, obviously.)

If you actually have time but can't play (say, because of an injury or noise restrictions), using the time for musical "research" can be time well spent. Go through a shelf of tune books: Maybe you'll uncover some new gems. Listen to recordings of lessons and workshops, or dig through your notes and handouts. This may be the time to test that music notation software or puzzle through a bit of music theory.

Regular practice is essential to improve at our instruments. Practicing every day is not a realistic expectation for most non-professionals. Yet time spent away from the instrument can be a benefit, allowing us to step back, recharge, and come back with fresh energy and enthusiasm.

Today, if I'm unable to get to my instrument, I'll consider it time for recharging. If I can, I'll find an activity that helps me stay in touch with my musicality.

37 Tune Structure

Understanding the structure of a tune will help you learn it more quickly, play it more accurately, and remember it more easily. Many of us absorb this information more or less intuitively, yet it's worth taking a moment to be explicit about a tune's structure.

The majority of trad tunes have an A part that repeats, and a B part that repeats. (We usually say that they're structured "AABB.") The two sections may be the same length, or one may be longer or shorter.

Not all tunes are structured AABB, by any means. A tune may be played AABA, or AAB. There may be a C, D, or E section, and sometimes a section is played three or four times. A tune may even be played one way in one tradition and a different way in another.

When you can mentally fit the notes and phrases in a structural framework, it will help your ear make sense of the music, making it easier to remember the notes themselves.

Whether you prefer to learn by ear or with sheet music: Listen to a tune once through, glance through the music, or ask someone in the group what the structure of the tune is before you start playing. This might seem obvious, yet sometimes musicians (myself included) jump into playing a tune, and find out halfway through that the structure isn't what they assumed.

That information can then become part of your mental "dossier" on the tune, along with the overall rhythm (jig, reel, etc.), the key, and anything else you choose to remember.

The Kid on the Mountain – slip jig in G – 5 parts

Today I'll make sure I understand the structure of the tunes I play.

38   Be Your Own (Great) Teacher

Shuji Maruyama Sensei, the founder of my aikido style, often tells students, "Be your own instructor." This sounds counterintuitive. It is a *martial* art, and in that tradition we're taught to respect our teachers and do what we're told. One would expect that the instructor would be 100% in charge of the instructing.

Of course, no one is simply a vessel into which the teacher pours expertise and wisdom. Whether intentionally or not, we observe, compare, make decisions, and personalize instruction for our own use.

Musicians spend many more hours practicing alone than martial artists do. This means that, in reality, we are *already* our own teachers much of the time. So how can we do a better job at it? **How can we be more "teacherly"?**

We need to observe and identify the characteristics of the best teachers, and then use them *to become better teachers…of ourselves.*

Put It into Practice

Here are three characteristics of a great teachers that you can incorporate into your practicing:

> One of the most important traits of the best teachers is **kindness**. Most of us quickly become judgmental, frustrated and impatient with ourselves when we can't do something. What kind of a teacher would have such an attitude toward a student? I would prefer a teacher to be warmhearted and forgiving of my mistakes. I want a teacher to remind me of the positive aspects of what I've done as well as the things I can improve.
>
> Another characteristic is something I'll call **skillfulness.** A great teacher can watch a student, and while they may think of 15 things that are wrong, *they will only make one suggestion*, or perhaps two.
>
> When a great teacher gives advice, they make sure to **suggest something the student can actually accomplish at their level.** That way the student can perceive their own progress.

You deserve a great teacher. You can learn to be one.

Today I'll practice being a great teacher…of myself.

39 Fear of Theory

Music theory developed as a *way to explain what musicians already were doing.* Music came first. Someone played or sang something and said, "That sounds good!" Then people (usually different people) developed music theory to figure out why everyone seemed to like it.

It's definitely not *necessary* to know theory in order to play trad music. On the other hand, there's no need to be afraid of it. If it could help, (and it can), why not learn about it?

If you have a strong aversion to music theory, it's worth asking yourself if that's because you've had a bad experience. An enthusiastic friend or teacher may have swamped you with too much, too fast. Or perhaps what you learned didn't seem relevant.

If you think that might be the case, consider trying to take in music theory in very small doses. Trad music offers a great opportunity for doing this, because most traditional styles follow fairly basic rules of harmony. If modern jazz is the differential calculus of music theory, then trad music is addition and subtraction.

Start with a simple goal, like understanding the key and scale used in one tune. Once you've worked a few ideas into your playing, it's up to you if you want to learn more.

You don't have to be afraid of music theory.

Today I'll address my reluctance to learn music theory. Maybe I could stand to learn just a little.

40 Playing Without Mistakes

How much attention should we give to mistakes? What mistakes should we let go by? What is a "mistake," anyway? Is it possible to play "without mistakes"? These are great questions.

As musicians, of course we can't just play any old thing. There's an expectation of keeping the time and playing something like the melody at the very least. Yet more than once I've played "badly" and still obviously affected my listeners. This was a reminder to me that *an important goal of playing is to communicate.*

What might change if we *stopped trying to play without mistakes*? Not that we ignore them, but remove the unrealistic and counterproductive goal of eliminating them entirely. What if we even stopped calling them *mistakes*? Maybe we could label them as *things we want to change* in our playing, and work to understand them?

What if you thought of mistakes as gifts that help you identify what to work on? If you did that, then when you heard an issue in your playing, instead of thinking, "Aw, snap!" you might think, "Great! I can work on that!" Would that make your practice time more enjoyable?

These are just ideas. You are free to think about your mistakes in any way you choose. It's worth considering whether you're thinking about them in the way that's most helpful to you.

Today I will think about mistakes. Would thinking about them in a different way be more helpful to me?

41   Simplifying a Tune

If a tune is too challenging, why not simplify it? No trad composer is going to roll over in their grave when we play a few notes differently.

Look to simplify if there's a section of a tune that's giving you trouble. If a reasonable amount of practice isn't helping, see if you can avoid the problem by changing the notes. There may be a physical issue: a reach, stretch or jump you can't make. Maybe it's just flat out something that isn't appropriate at your level of ability.

Put It into Practice

> An easy way to start simplifying is by leaving out notes. In a 4/4 or 2/4 tune (march, reel, hornpipe, etc.), try leaving out every other

note. In a jig-type tune where the notes are in groups of three, start with leaving out the middle note.

You can do this to just a section that's causing a problem, or to the whole tune – for example if you want to play along with others and you can't play as fast. Once you've cut out notes, you can always add some of them back if you feel like it.

The result doesn't have to be perfect. You can play a pretty "bare bones" version of a tune, especially if you're playing it with others. A good tune, even reduced to half the notes, is still a good tune. The goal is to be able to play along and have fun.

Anticipate spending a bit of time on trial and error. Can you play three fast notes in a row as long as you get a little pause on a longer note afterward? It depends on you, and your instrument.

Then plan to practice the new, simplified tune (or section) until you're used to playing and hearing it in the new way. It may be helpful to write it out or record it, so you can remember what you did.

Here are examples of the first line from two tunes, a jig and a reel. Both are commonly played for American contra dances. The top line shows a fairly standard version. The next has some of the notes removed, the third line even more, and the fourth line is a hybrid. Even if you're not a sheet music aficionado you should get the general idea: trim, trim a bit more, and then add back in until you get something you like *and* can play.

Old Gray Cat

Traditional

The Moon And Seven Stars

Traditional

[Musical notation: four staves labeled "typical", "var.1", "var.2", "var.3" in 6/8 time, key of G major]

Simplifying a section, or a whole tune, can make it work better on your instrument and make it more playable for you. It can help you relax, play more fluidly and sound better.

Simplifying a tune is great training for your ear. It can help you develop confidence in your musical judgment. Listen to which notes sound essential and which don't, which notes seem to give the tune its personality and which ones could be varied or left out altogether.

Simplifying is just as respectable a way to vary a tune as making it more complex. Once you've worked out a simplified version, it's an option that's available for you any time.

Today I'll work on simplifying a tune.

42   The Myth of 10,000 Hours

When my friend was a child, her mother insisted she practice violin for an hour a day. She would go dutifully into the basement, open a book, and read it while playing scales and arpeggios. When her mother opened the basement door she heard practicing, and so closed it, smiling. Her daughter was hard at work.

When I was a teenager I practiced piano for three hours a day. I watched the clock, daydreamed, and when that time was over I felt released.

It's strange that, even though many of us have such negative associations with long practice hours we continue to believe in the importance of quantity over quality when it comes to practice time. Journalist Malcolm Gladwell did musicians no favors by extolling the benefits of long practice hours. He even branded it as the "10,000-Hour Rule." According to Gladwell, the key to success *in any field*, including music, is practicing a minimum of 10,000 hours. Some quick math puts this at 20 hours a week for 10 years.

Anders Ericsson, whose research was the basis of Gladwell's idea, is adamant that Gladwell's 10,000-Hour Rule is wrongheaded.[4] Ericsson insists that *we should always practice in a focused and mindful way*, identifying weaknesses and intentionally pushing ourselves outside our comfort zone. He uses the term "deliberate practice" to describe effective practicing.

This is good news for adults who and are looking to achieve some level of mastery and enjoyment in our playing. We can make plenty of progress using the time we have, whether it's 10 minutes or an hour a day, as long as we spend that time well.

Today I will let go of the debilitating idea that I must practice long and tedious hours to achieve musical progress and mastery. I will use "deliberate practice" to make the best use of the time available to me.

43   Left Hand – Right Hand

Most of us spend 100% percent of our practice time playing our instrument with both hands. An excellent practice technique, one that works for many instruments, is to separate the hands and play them one at a time. It can be quite revealing.[*]

Select just a part of a tune – say, a few measures where you're having a difficulty – and try playing with one hand at a time. For instruments with a fingerboard or fretboard, finger the notes or chords without plucking, strumming or bowing. Do this a few times. You may have to go more slowly than you might have expected. It's surprising how much our

---

[*] For some instruments (wind instruments, concertina), this process may be daunting, impossible or perhaps just very interesting!

mental model of playing depends on using both hands. Then switch hands: Bow on open strings, or pluck or strum without fingering.

Practicing using one hand at a time often uncovers issues we never would have noticed. Sometimes, when we do notice, those issues seem so obvious that we wonder how we could have missed them.

Today I'll try practicing with one hand at a time.

44 Shift Gears

It may seem paradoxical, but frequently "shifting gears" – changing your routine – can actually be an aid to practicing.

Novelty is a powerful trigger for the storing of information in memory. We all have memories that stand out because of they were unusual: seeing a cow standing in the middle of the highway, steamy-delicious fish 'n' chips eaten on a frigid pier, the first night in a new country.

My piano teacher frequently forces me to upend my routine. I may be working on a left-hand technique, a set of exercises or a style of music. Just as I get comfortable and think I'm "getting it," he shifts to something else. My aikido instructors do the same thing: never teaching the same techniques for two classes in a row. It took me years to realize the power of this teaching method.

Change wakes us up. Working on a new tune, changing the order of what you practice, or trying something completely different can enliven your entire practice session. It can make everything we practice – including the reviewed tunes and even technique exercises – feel more interesting and worthwhile.

Today I'll try shifting gears.

45 Attentive Listening

It's safe to say that the average musician listens to music more closely than a non-musician. At times, we may just let the melodies wash over us, but we also have the ability to hear details that the non-musician doesn't discern.

It's worth trying to see how far we can take this idea of *informed* or *attentive listening*. How intensely can you listen? What can you find out? Why not try it?

Put It into Practice

> Set yourself up in a decent listening environment with few distractions. (My preference is in the car.) Cue up a favorite tune.
>
> To get started, pick a simple arrangement: a solo instrument, or a melody player with a one backup instrument.
>
> As you listen, try to pick out as many details about the performance as possible. You might listen for *tone, attack or dynamics*. How did the musician(s) *start and end* the tune? Are there *harmonies*? *When are they introduced*? What is the *arrangement*? When does each musician enter, what parts do they play and when? Is there an *intro*? An *outro*?
>
> Like an archeologist, brush off and examine every fragment and look at the way it contributes to the whole.

Don't let this become a homework assignment. It's something to do for yourself, and in your own way. Follow your own interests - if you want to figure out the violin bowing, or want to explore the chording, go for it.

Attentive listening is a skill. The more you do, it the better you become. In the process of listening, I've often recognized things I want to avoid in my playing. If this happens to you, it's nice to know that you're developing your own preferences and that you're aiming high!

Today I'll listen attentively to a piece of music that I enjoy.

46   Finding a Teacher

Finding the right teacher can be daunting. When you were in junior high school, all you needed to do was sign up for clarinet lessons. Now that you live in rural Pennsylvania and want to play uilleann pipes, your options may seem more limited. Fortunately, with ingenuity, technology, and a bit of legwork, you can usually find a teacher who is right for you. Here are a few avenues to try.

Connect with the Local Music Community

Do you take part in a jam session or any other musical gathering? (No? Why not?) Ask those musicians. Ask at music stores. Go to local concerts. Introduce yourself to the musicians you like and ask if they know good teachers. Use social media, look for online user groups for your instrument, reach out to random high school classmates, send out a group text message. It never hurts to spread the word that you're a musician looking for a teacher.

Attend Workshops and Music Camps

There are music camps and workshops offered all over the U.S. and the world. They may be focused the general (learning and playing folk music), the particular (nyckelharpa, Acadian music), or anything in between. Camps offer opportunities to "try out" teachers and teaching styles, and can give you the chance to learn what works best for you. With a bit of travel (sometimes not much at all) and a dose of bravery, you'll connect with a community of musicians like you, get plenty of encouragement, and find a potential source of teachers.

Use the Internet, and Ask

Many excellent professional musicians supplement their touring and recording income by giving lessons online. You might assume an artist is too busy to give lessons. They may be, but they may not. Video calling has opened an expanded pool of students to traditional music teachers, and more and more of them are willing to make use of the technology.

More Thoughts

Don't assume that only well-known musicians are effective teachers. A "name" musician may not be the right teacher for you. Seek out a teacher who *listens well,* who can *express ideas that are helpful to you,* and who gives you not just tunes but *insight on how to practice more effectively* and *how to sound better*.

A student-teacher relationship is not a lifelong commitment. Let a teacher know if you only want to take a few lessons, or if you want to take them at a different frequency than they suggest. Feel free to stop if it's not right for you. Any experienced teacher has seen plenty of students come and go, and has been in the student's chair themselves. They will understand.

Today I'll think again about getting a teacher. Maybe I'll find the right one for me.

47 Keep "One Point"

When I returned to playing piano as an adult, my teacher had himself just finished a course in the Alexander Technique.[*] In one of my first lessons, he told me to focus on an area a few inches below my navel, in the center of my body. He said this would help me stay relaxed and balanced. The idea was identical to one we use in aikido, which we call *keeping one point*.

It seems nonsensical, but simply **focusing the mind on this part of the body** can have a perceptible effect on our ability to do martial arts, music, or, really, almost anything. There's nothing particularly special about this area of the body. So why might it work?

There's a lot going on when we play an instrument. In addition to the physicality of playing, the mind is busy recalling, thinking ahead, being aware of our body, listening (to ourselves and others), comparing, and more. Having a focus, one that's in our own bodies, that's actually near the physical center of balance, seems to help unify all that activity.

Ultimately it doesn't really matter why it works, if it does work. And the only way to find out is to try.

---

[*] The Alexander Technique is a method of addressing the way we habitually move and hold our bodies. People in many professions, from actors to musicians and dancers, use it to increase freedom, speed and accuracy of movement and reduce tension.

Today I'll take a few minutes to find my one point. *I'll investigate whether focusing on one point helps me to feel more calm or centered as I play.*

48 Listening for Patterns

Many of the tunes played in traditional music are easy to learn, remember and pass along. One reason is that most trad tunes have repetitive musical and rhythmic patterns.

Learning to pick out these repetitive patterns can help you learn tunes more quickly. Particularly if you want to improve your ability to learn by ear, listening for patterns is essential. Most people who learn easily by ear do this instinctively. Luckily, if you're not one of those people, it's not difficult to learn how to do.

Put It into Practice

>Here's the written notation for the Irish polka, "The Britches Full of Stitches." You don't need to be able to read sheet music to pick out the repeating note patterns.

The Britches Full of Stitches

Traditional (Ireland)

A few of the patterns are marked below:

The Britches Full of Stitches

Traditional (Ireland)

In the A section there is a pattern of four notes that's circled. It's repeated three times. In the B section there's a similar pattern that's marked with underlines. Both the A and B sections of the tune end with the same phrase. In fact, there are two more repeating patterns I didn't highlight because the sheet music got too messy.

This boils down to the idea that *to play this tune you don't need to learn 32 bars of music.* Only eight measures are unique. The rest are repeats, echoes or whatever you want to call them.

It's great ear training to practice *listening* for patterns. Any time you want to learn a new tune, listen to it a few times and deliberately pick out repeating note patterns. Do your best to make clear in your mind exactly where they happen. This "prep work" will give you a head start as you learn the tune.

Today I'll listen to a tune that I want to learn by ear. Instead of trying to play it right away, I'll listen for repeating patterns.

49   Musical Priorities

Here's an exercise to help you explore aspects of "playing correctly" so you can decide which contributes most to the sound you want. It's adapted from *Metaphors for the Musician*, by Randy Halberstadt.[5]

Establish a Benchmark

Pick a tune – or a section of a tune, if you prefer – that you can play comfortably.

Play it once, the best you can, whatever that means to you.

When you're done, notice the choices you made – even if you made them without thinking. Did you play at a fast speed and sacrifice your ability to incorporate every nuance? Or vice versa? Did you try to play in time, or to throw in every possible extra note? Were you working to avoid wrong notes?

Perform Your Experiment

You're going to isolate variables about the way you choose to play, in the tradition of scientific inquiry. Then you'll judge the results.

You'll be testing to find out *which of these four aspects is most important to making you sound good:*

- Playing in time/on the beat
- Playing the "right" notes
- Playing fast
- Playing musically

Record your experiment. You may think you know what the results will be, but listening will make the details clear and unforgettable.

For each setup, you'll focus on one variable. Otherwise try your best to play the tune the way you normally do.

Playing in time/on the beat: Make sure that no matter what you do, you don't speed up, slow down or even hesitate over a difficult or wrong note. Use a metronome and wear headphones if possible.

Playing the "right" notes: Concentrate on getting every note right.

Playing fast: Set a fast tempo and try to stick to it.

Playing musically: Try to use dynamics, phrasing and every other idea you have to make the tune sing.

When you're done, play back the recordings. Which do you prefer to listen to? Make detailed (but kind!) observations. If this were your good friend playing, what would you suggest they work on first? Next? There's no right answer. Hearing the difference in your own playing will help you clarify what's important *to you.*

Today I'll try an experiment to help clarify my musical priorities.

50   Sing

I asked jazz pianist David Leonhardt how I could make my improvisation more melodic. He said, "Practice singing what you're going to play."

Dave is just one of many teachers I've worked with who encouraged singing. When we sing, we naturally bring out rhythmic patterns, introduce dynamics, and shape phrases that are separated by our breathing.

Many musicians I've spoken to are uncomfortable singing. It's a sad state of affairs that so many of us believe we "don't have a good voice" or "aren't good singers." According to composer John Krumm, "In cultures that hold the belief that everyone can sing, *everyone can sing,*" (emphasis added). John writes, "Your voice is beautiful because it sounds like you and not someone else."[6] He believes that singing is a right, and he calls the fact that people are afraid to use their voices a tragedy. I agree.

Whether or not you call yourself a "singer," or ever intend to sing in public, your voice is a tool. It's one you already possess, that will help you become a better musician. You have a right to sing with your own beautiful voice.

Today I'll sing.

51   A Musical Community

One of the greatest benefits of playing trad music is the way it can provide connection to a community. Modern culture has a way of separating us from each other in self-sufficient dwellings that contain all the entertainment and recreational options we require.

Playing traditional music will change that, if you let it. There are jam sessions, workshops, performances, pickup bands and festivals – literally hundreds of opportunities to participate in, and build, a musical community.

It's hard to exaggerate the importance this community can have in your life. Here's just one example:

With the onset of the COVID-19 pandemic, people were unable to take part in normal social routines. Many people felt very isolated. Trad musicians immediately looked for creative ways to keep the connections going using every tool they could find. They used web conferencing, video streaming and jamming apps. They made recordings and videos together; set up tune swaps, online workshops, camps, concerts and watch parties. They even held "virtual" dances. Although none of this could replace playing and jamming in-person, these events were a vital lifeline during an extremely difficult time.

If you haven't already done so, find a way to join your musical community. Find a jam session nearby, or a music camp or workshop you can attend. It doesn't matter if it's not a perfect match for you. Think of it as a starting point. The people you'll meet can help you find more opportunities to play and learn.

As a shy person myself, I know that reluctance – even fear – to join such a group can be a big hurdle, even for an experienced player. My advice: Take a deep breath and give it a try. Your courage will pay off 1000%.

Participating in a community is a measure of musical "success" that's often overlooked and undervalued. Trad music offers us that community, if we will take the opportunity.

Today I'll work to enlarge my musical community.

52   Conquering "Tunesia"

You've practiced the tune diligently. You sit down in the jam session. Someone says to you, "Hey, why don't *you* start a tune!" And you *cannot dredge a single note of the tune from your memory.*

The first thing to remember is: There's no need to get frustrated. This happens to everyone.

The second is: *You have to practice remembering a tune, just like you have to practice playing the tune.*

Here are some tips for building better tune memory.

Put It into Practice

Build Multiple Neural Connections

We remember things best when we build *multiple neural connections* to the memories. It's like building a strong rope out of many thin threads.

Every part of your experience with the tune can be used to build stronger connections. Who did you learn it from? Where were you at the time? What instrument was it played on? Are there other memorable occasions when you've heard it? Is there anything about your experience of playing or hearing the tune that adds to its "personality" for you?

Another way to build strong neural connections is to use multiple senses. Our brains seem to be wired to do a better job at remembering things we see and touch. Try *writing things down* about the tune: the key signature, the rhythm (i.e. jig/step dance/bourrée), the first few note names. *Use your eyes*: Look at your fingers on the instrument, or at the sheet music, or at some notes you've written. *Use your sense of touch*: Draw your attention to the feeling of your fingers on the strings, keys or buttons.

Use Recall Aids

All trad musicians use recall aids to help them "find" a tune and pull it out of their memory banks. There are a lot of things can we know about a tune that can help us in recall.

Listen for a memorable part of the melody, and use it as a "hook." (Yup: the *hook* helps you *fish* the tune out of the memory *ocean*.) Does it sound like another tune? Like a soft drink jingle? The hook can be anywhere in the tune. Once you find it, practice using it to find your way back to beginning.

Use the *things you wrote down*: the key, what note it starts on, the first few notes, as recall aids. Try to connect those in your mind with the name of the tune.

Make up your own mnemonic. Many musicians call "Egan's Polka" "The FABA" because the first four notes are F-A-B-A.

When you *are* able to remember the tune, keep track of what helped and what didn't help. The technique that worked for you on one tune may also work on another.

Use Spaced Repetition

Spaced repetition[*] is a well-established way to build tune recall. Keep a list of tunes that you want to be able to remember at will. Spend time every practice session going through a few of them. You only need to play enough to say, "Yes, I can remember it." If so, move that tune to the bottom of the list, but if the answer is, "No," then try again tomorrow.

Today I'll be more methodical about remembering tunes. It takes practice, just like learning to play the tune.

53 Enlargen

When you're practicing a tune and run into a trouble spot, are you able to play *just that part of the tune* without going back to the beginning?[†]

If not, you have plenty of company. But it *is* a limitation. It can make it frustrating – even impossible – to work just on a section you're having difficulty with. By the time you go back to the beginning, you're likely to have forgotten what you were working on.

Here's a process for learning to work on a challenging area, and then work it back into the rest of the tune without getting lost. Accordionist Jeremiah McLane coined the term *enlargening* to describe this process.

Put It into Practice

- Set the metronome to a relaxed speed. Make it slow enough that it's not a struggle to play the tune.

---

[*] See 109 – Spaced Repetition

[†] This assumes you're playing from memory, rather than from sheet music.

- Play the tune up to your trouble spot. Stop. Now, *before you forget*, play just the notes of the trouble spot again. If you can't do that, can you sing them?

- If you can't do either of those things, go back to a place you *can* start from (it may be the beginning, that's OK). Slow the metronome down a bit. This time as you play *remind yourself to pay special attention when that section is coming.* Again, stop just after you play it and try to play or sing just that section again.

- If you can't play but you can sing it, next time see if you can play it. If you *can't* sing it, make sure you're clear on what the notes *actually are.* Listen carefully to your audio source or go back to sheet music.

- Once you can repeat just the trouble spot, *turn off the metronome.* Play the section a few times, using all the techniques you usually use to iron out wrinkles.[*]

- *Turn the metronome back on again.* See if you can back up a little in the tune and play from there. Again, if you can't find the notes, back up until you can. This time, focus on the notes *just before* the trouble spot, and see if you can include them in your practice loop.

- Keep going in this way until you can play the tune from the beginning, get to the spot you're working on, and play through it. Does it feel different now?

As you *enlargen* the area you're working on, you may uncover more, or different issues. It's up to you to decide what to work on now, ignore, or save for later.

This can seem like a frustratingly slow process at first, but it has many benefits. You'll be deepening and strengthening your knowledge of this particular tune. At the same time you'll build your ability to listen and repeat melodic content. That will help with everything you play.

Today I'll look at whether I can play just the part of a tune I want to work on. Then I'll work on enlargening *my area of practice, bit by bit.*

---

[*] For ideas on working out wrinkles, see 32 – Tailor-Made Technical Exercises

54 Tracking Small Wins

It can be difficult to perceive the incremental gains we make in one day's practice. *We need to find ways to shed light on our progress.* Practice is more pleasurable when we can tell it's helping us improve. Without a doubt, one of the biggest obstacles we face is that *if we don't have fairly constant reminders that we're improving, we won't be motivated to practice.*

The basic idea is simple: *We need to identify and clearly articulate short-term goals that are both measurable and achievable.*

Put It into Practice

Set out goals for yourself that can be achieved in a day or a week.

A goal for the day might be:

- Being able to play the notes of the tune, or even just the "A" part, without looking at the music
- Playing the tune in rhythm, even at a very slow speed
- Taking the speed up by 10% - for the whole tune or just part of it
- For a tune I already know, adding just one skill I'm currently working on (e.g. adding a bowed triplet, playing an alternate chord progression, or playing the tune three times without stopping)

A goal for the week might be:

- Playing through a set of chord changes in three keys without stopping or hesitating
- Playing the tune without music at a certain speed
- Sitting down, picking up the instrument, relaxing, and playing the tune the first time, at a slowish speed, without major problems
- Playing a difficult note, or set of notes, with good tone

Keep Track

Your note-taking habit will pay off here.* Every day (or so) scribble a few words. Here are some of mine:

Point au Pic – 75%!!!
A section – bowing pattern practice.

The act of writing itself helps remind us that we're making slow but steady progress. If we need the proof, we can look back at our notes.

It took me a long time to learn to do this. I usually overestimated what I could do in the time I had, and so was continually disappointed with myself. It took dialing my goals way back, and keeping track, to be able to see that change was happening.

Today I'll begin setting measurable and achievable daily and weekly goals. Then I'll track my progress.

55   Yeah, But...

All of us resist new ideas. This resistance can be a real roadblock to progress and growth.

It's normal to want to hang onto any comfort level we may have achieved, especially as many of us live with a fairly constant barrage of self-criticism. When our ideas are challenged in a way that might upset that comfort, we have all kinds of justifications and rationales for why we're not going to do it.

"I'm doing fine with this method."
"He's a good teacher but some of his ideas are over the top."
"I've tried that once before and it didn't work."
"It could work, but it will take a really long time that way."

Eighth dan aikido instructor Veronica Burrows calls these *yeah, buts*.

---

* See 18 – Taking Notes

I'm as susceptible as anyone to "Yeah, butting." I tend to think my first teachers were the best. I stick to old habits and avoid trying new things. And I will spin a *very* convincing internal monolog to justify my resistance and persuade myself that it's absolutely *not* about *my* unwillingness to try something new.

Thoughts like this are evidence of inflexibility in our thinking. *Inflexibility does not help the creative artist in any way, ever.*

When I hear myself thinking, "Yeah, but...," I try to admit, "*I'm resisting a new idea,*" plain and simple. What I am doing is ruling out the possibility that this new idea might actually work better than what I'm doing.

If you want to grow, to learn, to become more capable, fluent, musical, more able to learn quickly, to improvise, then your *yeah, buts* are holding you back.

Learn to recognize *yeah, buts* and *not* act on them. Try something you're not used to doing. Listen to a new idea with an open mind. Think, "*Yeah, OK!* I'll try it. What could it hurt?"

Today I'll listen for my internal monolog of resistance. I'll try to let go of "Yeah, but..." and say, "Yeah, OK! I'll try it. What could it hurt?"

56   Your Body Clock

Our bodies are attuned to a circadian rhythm. All our physiological processes, and therefore our mental processes, involve an ebb and flow based (for most people) around a 24-hour day.

Certain responses in the body are quite easy to measure, such as alertness (highest at mid-morning), coordination and reaction time (fastest in the afternoon) and cardiovascular efficiency and muscle strength (best around 5pm).[7]

We can combine this understanding of circadian rhythm with our subjective experience to help us practice more efficiently. For example, morning is a good time for me to tackle a new tune or song or project because I'm more focused and energetic. But it's also a time when I have to be careful not to get sidetracked: I often decide that's the time I *must* organize my workspace, or transcribe that 6-page piano rag – and if I do, my most effective practice time will vanish.

In the evening I may not have the ability to focus as well, but I *can* be very relaxed and creative. That's a great time to just play for the sake of playing – to let my playing infuse *me* with energy. I've found it's also a great time to work on improvisation or musicality.

Afternoons can be a dull time for me, creatively, as I'm often distracted with things half-done or planned. That can make the afternoon a good time to do work that doesn't take a lot of mental commitment. (This is a better time to transcribe that piano rag.)

Your body clock, and the way it affects your energy and creativity, is unique to you. Get to know your daily rhythms and decide for yourself how to apply that knowledge to your practice.

Today I'll get to know my body clock and apply that knowledge to my practice.

57 Recovering

We all have a hard time relaxing and finding our focus after something difficult has happened. We can be playing as well as we've ever played, pouring out great music, and something happens that knocks us out of the "zone."

It doesn't matter if it's a difficult passage, an itch, or something external. Our bodies retain the tension: The fingers stay cramped, we stiffen our jaws, we lose flexibility and mobility. Our minds also remain stuck in that past event, contributing thoughts that are subtle ("Phew, I did OK. I can't believe I slowed down, *again*! Did anyone notice?) or dramatic ("What is that buzz? Maybe something's broken! How could I afford to repair it?").

This is an annoyance when we're practicing. It can be devastating if we're performing.

In aikido we use a practice technique with wooden swords to help us learn to recover quickly. Musicians don't have to do use swords, but *we can practice recovering quickly*, whenever we recognize we've been knocked out of our "happy place."

Put It into Practice

- To recover quickly, you need to stay focused but also relaxed. Drawing the attention of your mind on your center of balance or *one point** gives you a kind of mental ballast, helping you right yourself more quickly.

- Rather than focusing on *making yourself sound good*, try focusing on your body. Breathe deeply and evenly. Relax your shoulders and any other areas that are habitually tight. Check your posture. Let your instrument settle comfortably in your hands.

- Open your ears. Rather than trying to play a certain way, listen. See if you can keep from "trying" – trying to sound a certain way or trying to play certain notes. Allow your body to respond to the sound and follow that sound back to the great music.

- Smile.

When you're practicing, as opposed to playing "out" or performing, you can stop playing, get these steps clearly into your mind and body, and start playing again. Eventually you'll be able to try to do it without stopping.

Today I'll practice recovering.

58   Which Notes Do I Need?

Before you start playing a tune, try this:

Run through the tune, or a part of the tune, and figure out what notes are needed to play it.

---

* *One point* is described under the Four Basic Principles in Appendix D.

You obviously don't need every note available on your instrument to play a given tune. So it's worth asking: For this tune, which ones *do* you need? The answer might be interesting.

- It might use all the notes in a D major scale (or all the notes in a different scale, like G or C).
- It could use the notes in a D scale, but not sound like it's in D. If so, can you figure out what note might be the "root note" or tonal center of the scale?
- A tune might use just *some* of the notes in the scale – maybe only five or six of them.
- It might use all the notes in a scale plus one more. (For some reason we call that an accidental, as if it were an accident, when it's obviously not.)

You might ask some other questions, like:

- Are all the notes within a narrow range, or are they spread out from very high to very low?
- Are certain notes played more than others? Which ones?

If you do this to a few tunes, just now and then, you may begin to notice patterns, which will, in turn, help you remember and play the tunes. It can also be a confidence-builder to know that, no matter what, you only need a finite number of notes to play this tune.

Today I'll look at exactly how which notes are needed to play a tune I'm working on.

59 Rotation of the Shoulders

Most of us habitually sit and stand with our shoulders rounded and rolled forward. One of the best ways to start changing this habit is to *learn to externally rotate the shoulders.*

When you externally rotate the shoulders, the weight-bearing of a held instrument (flute, violin) is transferred from the shoulder girdle – lots of small, overstressed muscles – to the latissimus dorsi or "lats" – big, broad muscles that are spread over the back.

When we settle the shoulder blades down over the back of the ribcage, our arms do less work, and movement comes from more powerful areas of the body like the back of the torso and the pelvis. We sit up taller and breathe more naturally. These results don't take years to achieve – they happen immediately.

Put It into Practice

Practice this movement first without your instrument using one of the following two methods.

Standing Method

Stand with your legs wide, and open your arms to the side with your palms down. Now simply rotate your palms upward. Rather than just turning your wrist, let that action extend all the way up your arm to your shoulders. The movement you feel in your shoulders and shoulder blades is external rotation. Try to feel the front muscles of your shoulders lengthen, the front of the rib cage opening, and the shoulder blades settling down over the back of the rib cage.

"Child's Pose" Method

From a kneeling position, bend forward at the waist with your arms outstretched, palms on the floor. Draw the outer arms down and towards each other so that the inner creases of the elbows face toward the ceiling.

The movement in your shoulders as you do this is external rotation.

Sit up, and try to replicate this external shoulder rotation movement while you are sitting.

Once you get the hang of what it feels like to externally rotate your shoulders, try doing it while holding your instrument. Finally, externally rotate your shoulders before you start playing, and see how long you can keep that feeling.[*]

---

[*] Video of these movements is available at www.judyminot.com/bestpractice/

If you like the way this feels, certain exercises and stretches can help you maintain more open and relaxed shoulders. Look for stretches that are intended to open up tight areas in the front of the chest, and exercises that strengthen the upper back muscles.

Today I will learn how to externally rotate my shoulders.

60 Get Up

One way to make better use of practice time is, counterintuitively, to get up out of the chair. Why? We're most effective when we are deliberate and attentive. There's a limit to how long anyone can stay attentive before becoming distracted and playing mindlessly.

There's no need to berate yourself for not being able to focus longer than you can. What *is* important is to practice a kind of "meta-awareness." When your focus is wavering, get up, move around, stretch your hands, look at something different.

I use a timer to make sure my break doesn't extend too long, but that's not necessary for everyone. If you want to come back to your instrument, you will.

Practicing in these shorter, more focused bursts can help us approach the instrument, the tune, the problem, with a fresh perspective.

Today I will get up, move around, and re-approach my instrument, the tune, the problem, with a fresh perspective.

61 Stop Trying to Be Perfect

I have a friend who is a professional orchestra musician. Occasionally I would talk to her about the appeal of traditional music. I knew she associated trad with simple melodies, played in unison and repeated many times. She often mentioned that she enjoyed the complexity and harmonic interest of classical music, hinting that these were missing from the trad music I had given her to listen to.

One evening my friend attended a large holiday gathering at my house. There were musicians of all levels, playing a variety of instruments. There was music from multiple traditions, plus carols of the season, even a bit of Queen and Tom Lehrer. Everyone joined in, singing or playing.

My friend called me the next day, very enthusiastic. "That's the element that is missing with my classical friends," she said, "It's not fun! They're too focused on sounding perfect! They won't play in public. Some of them won't even play with friends if they don't think it will sound exactly the way they want it to sound."

Many of us do struggle with the idea that we must sound perfect before we let anyone listen. Fine singers won't sing, great players won't play, because someone might hear something they didn't like.

Stop striving to be perfect. Have some fun.

Today I'll stop trying to be perfect, and have more fun.

62   Thinking Ahead

One way to become faster and more fluid in our playing is to be deliberate about thinking ahead. In a perfect world, we could play a tune, fully engrossed in the music, without thinking "about" anything at all. This is not possible for tunes we're in the process of learning or refining. *Deliberately thinking ahead* can get us to that point faster.

Often, as we play, our attention is on *what just happened*:

> "That was supposed to be a C#...I think."
> "Oops, the little finger again."
> "Missed the string crossing."

We can get so caught up in these thoughts we may lose track of where we are in the tune.

If we're able to *think ahead*, we're much more likely to play with calmness:

> "Transition to B part: go down, not up."

"Unison coming, get little finger ready."

"Going to a low note, relax fingers even more."

If you're unable to think ahead, it may be because you're not in the habit. Or, you may be so cognitively and physically overwhelmed, you can barely keep up with what you *are* doing, much less what's about to happen.

To get into the habit, you need to practice. If you're overwhelmed, you need to simplify and, probably, slow down.

Put It into Practice

Develop your own exercise for thinking ahead, based on what you're working on. Using a metronome is important to keep you honest. As you play, *consciously, explicitly* think ahead, using whatever cues you need (chords, fingering, notes, positioning, concepts, etc.) to help you to get the sound you're looking for.

Remember that if it's a struggle, you can reduce your cognitive load: Slow down, shorten the loop, simplify your playing, until you have less difficulty. Then you can add elements back, one by one.[*]

Pay attention to *what works for you*. Are visual cues more effective than verbal ones? How far ahead should you think? What happened when you slowed down?

Write down what you did. Come back tomorrow and try it again.

This practice can work quite quickly to help you play tunes with more calmness and equanimity.

Today I'll practice thinking ahead.

---

[*] Use the elements of the Practice Pyramid, detailed in Appendix A, to break down this process.

63 An Extra Limb

I grew up playing classical music. I was taught to play exactly what was on the page. Unless I had memorized a piece, I was always reading as I played.

When I first started learning trad and playing by ear, I felt some fear. What if I forgot what came next? At the same time, I felt a sense of relief that I didn't have to constantly check the sheet music. In some ways, playing without having to read felt like playing with an extra limb.

Pickpockets and magicians make a living using the knowledge that *what we see dulls our ability to hear and even feel.* Musicians know this intuitively.

When we don't have to read, we listen better. When we listen better, we play better.

When our eyes aren't focused on the page, we can also pay more attention to how our bodies feel. This includes not just our fingers and hands, but our breathing and overall posture. It stands to reason that this will improve our playing as well.

Today I'll give my eyes a rest. I'll put the sheet music away.

64 Avoidance

When I've been away from my instrument for a few days or more, I sometimes find myself avoiding getting back to practicing or playing. I realized this didn't make sense, because I knew how much I missed playing.

When I haven't been practicing, one thing that quickly happens is I lose track of what I was working on: which tunes, what the problems were, where the excitement was, and what I hoped to do next. I feel I've lost my forward movement.

I realized that I avoided picking up my instrument because I associated it with the unpleasant feelings: having stopped making progress, and having to sort out what to work on.

It was quite a revelation to realize that *the very reasons I was avoiding practice were because I missed the effects of practicing*: knowing what to do every day, and feeling that I was making progress.

The answer was contained in the realization of how much I love playing. After that it was easy to set aside a few minutes for my instrument.

Today I'll remember that unsettled and frustrated feelings may come from a disruption in practice – and the answer is: Pick up the instrument you love to play.

65   Give Me That Rhythm

In trad music, every musician is a drummer. We're all responsible for maintaining and supporting the beat. It's not only because there may not be a "rhythm" instrument among a group of players. It's because, by clarifying the beat, we give shape to the music. When we play with others, expressing the rhythm clearly is even more vital, as it helps everyone play together.

We can look at rhythm in a "big picture" way, in terms of the overall rhythmic feel of the tune. Once we understand that feeling we can look at individual rhythmic patterns within the tune.

Overall Rhythmic "Feel"

When you play for an American contra dance, all the music is sorted into three categories: "reels" (stuff with four beats), "jigs" (stuff with two groups of three beats) and "couples dances" (mostly waltzes).

Listen to where the strong beats are. Are there four strong beats in a measure, making you feel like marching? Are there two? Or, as for a waltz, are there three?

Rhythmic Patterns Within the Music

What are the rhythmic patterns in the melody itself? If you sing nonsense words to the tune (or as they might say in Ireland, "lilt" it), or drummed the melody on your knee, what notes would you stress? Which ones might you glide over? *Highlighting the rhythm in the melody* plays a major role in shaping the texture of the tune, and in bringing out its essence and poetry.

You could think of the first idea as giving dancers a clear sense of *when to step*. The second might help them express other elements of the dance: a hip sway, a "balance," a jump or a graceful turn. These more subtle rhythmic patterns are what give tunes the qualities that make them danceable as hop jigs, hambos, slides, step dances, 5-beat waltzes, etc.

Improving your ability to bring out the rhythm isn't that hard. All the familiar practice techniques come in handy. Tapping your feet and playing with big physical movements can help, too. Simply giving the rhythm of the tune your consistent attention, though, will make a big difference all by itself.

Today I'll pay attention to the way I express rhythm.

66   M Is for Mindfulness Practice

Recently somebody asked me what mindfulness meditation has to do with playing music. Here is my answer.

Immersive Experience

> Meditation is essentially the practice of being present.* I practice staying connected to what is happening (even though the only thing "happening" is that I'm sitting). When the time comes to play music, I use this skill to stay more connected to the music as I'm playing.

Being Attentive to Thoughts

> Mindfulness meditation involves being attentive to our thoughts. It's like there's another, bigger "me" observing the little "me" think. Little Me says, "I am really terrible at this! I'll never get better!" and Big Me says, "That's just a thought. You don't have to engage with that." This helps me build the habit of staying aware of what is going on now, instead of getting lost in thoughts about what might happen, or what already happened.

---

* More about being present in 4 – Being Present

Listening

One way to practice mindfulness is to try to *listen*. Listening is different from thinking about what you're hearing, or what you're going to play. Just listening without expectations or judgements is a great practice for a musician.

Body Awareness

It's safe to say that most of us ignore our bodies unless we're in discomfort. When we *do* become aware of aches and pains, we get caught up in fear, anticipation, recollections, etc. A common mindfulness practice is to try to be aware of sensations in the body – not just negative ones – and to do so without getting "hooked in" to these associated thoughts.

This practice of better body awareness is an excellent tool for fine tuning our musical skills.

As I've become more skilled in these areas, my music practice has benefited:

- I'm able to notice when my posture could be better.
- I can quickly sense my own tension.
- I'm a better listener.
- I can pay attention to what I'm working on with more focus and for longer.

Mindfulness practice isn't a fit for everyone. If you do decide to try it, however, it can really help your music practice.

Today I'll consider engaging in a mindfulness practice.

67   A Beautiful Sound

Just a few simple notes, played beautifully, can go straight to our hearts. One important factor in creating that beautiful sound is what we call *tone*.

Most of us don't think enough about tone. When we do draw our attention to the quality of the sound, we can quickly bring more richness to our playing.

Try making it a goal to play with good tone *consistently*. You may have a tendency to treat tone as an afterthought: something you'll do after you've learned the tune, or after you get better at some other aspect of playing. It's important to integrate attention to tone into your playing whenever possible. From the very first note you play to the last, every time you play, practice listening for the quality of the sound, not just the notes and the speed.

Put It into Practice

> Hold your own tone workshop. This is a great time to record yourself, as it's far easier to hear your own sound on playback.
>
> - Play a few notes that don't require special effort. If you're playing a violin, just play one note on an open string. Play those notes as beautifully as you can.
>
> - Now that you've heard that sound, play the note(s) again, and let your ear guide you to making this beautiful tone happen more consistently.
>
> There *are* things you can do, or are doing, that will make the sound better, or worse. The amount of air or bow you use, the angle of your fingers, your posture and breathing, physical tension, even your thoughts. At the same time, you don't have time to run through a 25-point mental checklist before you play every note.
>
> There's nothing wrong with noticing these physical aspects, what hand position works or doesn't work, etc., but ultimately *your body will obey your ear*. **Work to develop your ability to hear the smallest details in your sound.**
>
> - When does your sound degrade? Is it at the beginning of a note? At the end?
>
> - Does your tone vary while the note is sounding? Can you change it?
>
> - When you get it right, do your best to *revel in that sound*. It's hard to overemphasize the importance of this idea. You want

your mind and body to *crave this sound*, the way you might crave dark chocolate, a poker win, or holding someone you love.

Once you've begun to distinguish the sound of better tone, it will work its way into your playing. You may not be able to recreate your best sound all the time. However, *listening* for good tone is the first step toward having a beautiful sound, all the time.

Today I will listen, and try to create a beautiful sound.

68 Don't Try Harder. Try Softer.

When we're focusing intently, the brain (poor brain!) has a tendency to want to "help" by doing things like tensing up the arms, holding the breath, hunching the shoulders. These responses may be useful for some things that are difficult, but not music.

We need to rewire the conditioning that makes us associate "trying" with physical tension.

Whenever your musical efforts are not bringing out the beauty you seek, instead of trying *harder*, try *softer*. Relax. Open up the chest. Extend the spine and let the shoulders relax. Let your center of balance sink into your hips. Breathe deeply and let your mind be at ease. Now listen. Do you hear a difference?

Today instead of trying harder, I'll try softer.

69 Sword Has Sword Nature

The founder of my Aikido style, Shuji Maruyama Sensei, used to remind us that "sword has sword nature." The phrase describes the way we should work *with* the quality of a weapon rather than *against* it. A sword has weight, a certain length, sharpness, and center of balance. Gravity directs it downward in a specific way.

Every instrument also has its own nature. Each has a different timbre or sound quality. In addition, every instrument is played in a distinctive way that affects the sound produced. For example, an accordion or fiddle player can sustain a note and keep making changes in the quality of the sound throughout that time. That's not possible on a piano or a mandolin: Once you've plucked or hit the string, you can't do much except cut it off sooner.

When we play with deep understanding of the nature of an instrument, our interpretation of a melody will adjust to make the most of that nature. On the fiddle I can add rhythmic notes on open strings. This is possible on an accordion, but it might sound forced or heavy. To play a tune that I originally heard on the fiddle and make it "fit" the accordion, I need to explore what the accordion does best.

Accordion has accordion nature.

Understanding this idea and putting it into practice may mean letting go of some aspects of a tune that I love. It may require a reworking of the tune. It may even mean that I don't play that tune on accordion, or don't make it a feature of my playing, much as I'd like to. All these are acceptable outcomes if the goal is to *work with the nature of the instrument.*

Today I will remember, "Sword has sword nature." I'll work with the nature of my instrument, not against it, to produce the music that fits me, my playing and my instrument.

70 Don't Play with Pain[*]

Pain while playing is not acceptable. It's a sign that something is wrong. There's no need to fear that pain will end your musical journey or that you'll need a surgical remedy. But we do need to pay attention and try to address the cause.

Playing an instrument puts repetitive stress and strain on joints, tendons and muscles. It's not surprising that this stress can sometimes cause pain. Yet there are musicians who spend many more hours

---

[*] This information is not a substitute for medical advice.

practicing the same instruments as we do, who do *not* have debilitating injuries. It stands to reason that there should be a way to play any instrument without pain.

When I started playing violin at age 54, I assumed that the limitations of an aging body would prevent me from getting far. After a year, I experienced debilitating shooting pains in my left hand. In year four, I developed neck and shoulder pain that made playing impossible for longer than 15 minutes at a time.

In both cases the problem was resolved by changing something about the way I played. I learned to relax my hands and fingers. I did regular stretches. I improved my posture while playing. I released tension in my shoulder and wrist. I changed the way I held my instrument.

In working out these issues, I spoke to various professionals: orthopedists, physical therapists, massage therapists and music teachers. Looking back, the ones who provided the most helpful insight and advice were knowledgeable about *body mechanics* – the way muscles, joints and tendons interact when we move. I received even more help from those who understood the *specialized issues of musicians*.

The sooner you become aware of pain and tension, the more quickly you can work to address it. **Habituating ourselves to pain makes it more likely that we will be seriously injured through repetitive stress.** Playing "through" pain, "sucking it up," or ignoring it are not helpful.

There is no one answer to the issue of pain while playing, any more than there is one instrument or one player who experiences pain. The answer, when it does come, will have as much to do with you – your own awareness and understanding – as from any outside help you seek.

Today I'll be aware of any pain I feel while practicing. I don't need to attach fear and dire predictions to my pain. Yet I will commit to a goal of playing without pain.

71 Performance Anxiety

Even if you're not a professional, there are still times when performance anxiety strikes. It doesn't matter how beautifully you can play: if you get flustered or anxious starting a tune at a jam, playing for your teacher, or playing onstage, all that practicing can go right out the window. The answer is to *take any opportunity you can* to "perform."

We have the same issue in teaching self-defense. An aikido student can be great at all kinds of techniques when they're practicing with people they know and are confident they won't be hurt. In a real-life attack, calmness and awareness – arguably their most valuable assets – can disappear in an instant.

To address this in aikido training, we gradually increase the level of challenge as students gain more experience. We introduce more elements of the unknown: unexpected attacks, bigger attackers, simultaneous attacks by several people. The highest-ranking students can be "tested" at any time without warning.

You can gradually acclimate yourself to "performing" using a similar approach. Start in the most low-key way you can: Play in a jam. Build from there. Start a tune or lead a song. Play for a friend. Festivals and music camps usually offer some kind of "camper's night." Get a friend, sit in the park and play some tunes. Try an open mic.

The point is: Don't back out of these chances. Nobody will get hurt, even if you mess up. You may not expect to "wow" anyone, but you'll be building your ability to remain calm in front of a crowd. And chances are you'll get plenty of support from your listeners.

Today I'll think about "performing." How can I gradually work my way from small to greater challenges until I feel more comfortable doing what I want to do?

72 Are You Having Fun Yet?

Music should be an addition to our lives, not a burden. Whenever I make a decision involving music, I try to remind myself that I choose to play because it gives me enjoyment.

I want to increase that enjoyment.

Should I take lessons? Should I get another instrument? Should I go to this jam session? Should I practice today? Should I bring my instrument on vacation? Should I join that band? The decision, for me, is based on the answers to these questions:

- Will it be *fun*?
- Will it be a *burden*?
- Am I doing it *because I want to*?
- Am I *not* doing something that might give me joy *because I'm afraid*?

Today I'll remember that music is an addition to my life. I'll think about the ways that I can increase the enjoyment and reduce the element of burden.

73   Opening Up Space

In my early professional years I worked in broadcast television as a video editor. One of the most time-consuming tasks was cutting interviews for documentaries.

Most people don't realize that taped interviews are heavily edited. This isn't done to change the meaning of what someone says, but to make their statements more coherent and concise. Television audiences have a short attention span, and people seldom speak in compact thoughts. Therefore, whenever someone is not visible on-screen, their voice track is carefully pruned.

As a newbie editor, my interviews often sounded unnatural. On paper, what I put together made sense, but the phrases sounded robotic – even hard to understand. I eventually learned that the key to making the track sound organic and intelligible was adding space. A little space for breath, a beat of silence, brings natural cadence to the speech, and can even be used to add emphasis.

Music, like speech, is communication. **One of the simplest ways to give a tune coherence is to allow the melody "space to breathe" by opening**

up space between the notes. I'm not referring to changing the rhythm or adding a pause, but *to ending the sound of the note early.*

Be attentive to where you can open up space in a tune. The easiest places are usually at the ends of phrases. It's a simple thing to add some silence instead of holding the note – especially a longer one – until the last instant.*

Try playing with this idea. Keep adding more and more space until you feel you've gone way overboard. You can always dial it back.

The result of this simple technique can be dramatic, and quickly give you many more options for playing a tune.

Today I'll try opening up space between the notes.

74   Discernment vs. Criticism

As we practice, we observe ourselves:
- I wasn't in tune.
- I was late.
- I messed up the ornament.
- I forgot the chord.
- I meant to use better phrasing.

To become a better musician it's important to be discerning. It's essential to know the difference between what we *want* to do and what we *are* doing. But we should not confuse *discernment* with *criticism*. Discernment is useful observation. Criticism is self-destructive judgment. Far too often, we spend our mental energies on the wrong side of the line between these two.

Self-criticism is self-destruction. Think of someone whose opinion matters to you. Imagine that person strongly criticizing you. Do you feel like

---

* People who are classically-trained sometimes protest, "But there's no written rest in the sheet music!" In trad music, rests are seldom written in. It's the musician's choice to decide where there should be space, and how much to add.

playing? Do you feel energized? Uplifted? Do you feel like practicing at all?

Discernment can be uplifting. When we practice discernment, we can learn and improve. We also increase our self-assurance, and our confidence in our own insight, understanding and skill in listening.

Put It into Practice

As you practice, pay attention to the thoughts that pop into your head. Listen for words like "never," "always," or "should." When you recognize these critical thoughts, explicitly replace them with more positive, constructive ones.

Instead of thinking:	*Try thinking:*
I *always* miss transitions.	That's interesting, I just missed the transition.
I *never* get this right.	I keep fumbling right here. Maybe that's a sign that I don't really *know* it.
So-and-so plays that much faster, what's wrong with me?	I actually can play that just like so-and-so, just a lot slower!
I'm so bad at this, I may as well give up.	I'm a weekend musician with a full-time job. I'm doing great.

Try coming up with alternatives to your mind's critical commentary. You can even make a game out of it. Slowly but surely, it will become a habit. You'll get better and better at listening to your playing in a way that's constructive, one that actually fuels learning and musicianship.

Today I'll try to be aware of the difference between discerning thoughts and destructive, critical commentary. When I notice critical thoughts I'll explicitly switch them for more useful, positive and constructive ones.

75   Are You Breathing?

> "I would start out my own solos...playing some pretty good stuff...but as I went along it would get worse and worse. What I realized is that as I played, I was just forgetting to breathe! The less oxygen I got, of course, the worse I played."
>
> — Béla Fleck[8]

Unless you're a wind player or a singer, chances are you don't think about breathing as you play. Many of us sit slouched, with a caved-in chest that makes it hard to breathe deeply. We take shallow breaths and may even hold our breath when we play tough passages.

When we breathe fully, it allows more oxygen to reach the cells in the body. Full, deep breathing relaxes the nervous system.

Put It into Practice

> *Incorporating breathing can transform any repetitive exercise.* Breathe in for a count during the exercise, and breathe out for the same count. Don't try to extend your breathing uncomfortably, just settle your attention on whether you're breathing in or breathing out.
>
> I often practice scales breathing in as I go up and out as I go down. You can coordinate breathing with musical phrases, long bow strokes or something that works for you.
>
> As you focus on your breathing, the musical part of the exercise may start to feel more comfortable and natural. Remember to stay relaxed and keep a posture that allows your chest to be open and expansive.

As you learn to draw attention to your breathing, it will become more comfortable to breathe naturally whenever you play.

Making a regular practice of breathing outside your music practice time also can be beneficial, even if it's only for a few minutes a day.*

Today I'll integrate breathing into my practice.

---

* I outline a method for breathing practice in Appendix E.

76 Sing and Play

For many musicians, one of the biggest obstacles to learning by ear is being able to *play what you hear*. If you've learned to play from music notation, you've learned to *play what you see*. You learned to associate a note on a page, or a letter name, with a physical action of your fingers, or perhaps a visual reference on your instrument.

When we hear a note and try to play it, we don't know that it's an "A" or a "C sharp." That may sound scary: so many opportunities to be wrong! Yet it makes intuitive sense that less effort is required by the brain: The sound goes from the ear to the instrument, without any visual, paper-based intermediary.

If you have difficulty learning tunes by ear, try singing a few simple notes and then playing what you sang.[*] If that's a struggle, then this is a skill worth practicing.

Put It into Practice

>Spend just a few minutes every day. Sing a few notes, then play them. Keep it at a level that you have some success. Make it fun and playful.

Even accomplished players and accomplished "ear learners" can get a great deal from creating a deliberate exercise of singing and playing. Improvising musicians often practice by singing their ideas first. Singing and then playing can increase your facility, phrasing and musicality, no matter what your playing skill.

Today I'll practice singing and playing.

77 Normative Beliefs

A normative belief is a belief in how things are, or how they ought to be. Normative beliefs are ideas that are so deeply ingrained that we don't question them. Some, like, "When you're waiting to pay, form a line," or,

---

[*] More about playing by ear in 16 – You Can Play by Ear

"Parents are responsible for taking care of their children," make it possible to live in an ordered society.

Some normative beliefs are not so helpful, especially if they impede our musical progress:

> "I'll never be able to play that fast."
>
> "I'm getting older, and so I won't be able to get much better."
>
> "I've never been much good at understanding harmony."

Make a list of five things you've *always believed without question* about your playing. These are (*some of*) your normative beliefs. Now that they're out in the open, you can examine and evaluate them.

You don't have to make a decision about whether they're right or wrong – certainly not today. You don't have to challenge them at all. Just let them hang out there. Say to yourself, "Hmm. I think *that*."

Over time, you may compare these beliefs to things in your experience. You may decide you agree, or not. But *if you don't ever articulate them, you won't have the opportunity to question them*. And perhaps you'll miss your opportunity to prove one or two of them wrong.

Today I'll try to articulate a few of my normative beliefs.

78   Playing and Knowing

Deliberate practice involves engaging the body and mind together as fully as possible. One way to engage body and mind together is to try to *know* every possible aspect of what we're playing.

To be more *knowing* about the music you're playing, you might ask yourself:

- Do I know where each finger is going to go *before I put my finger down*? Do I know what string each note is on?

- Could I play *just the strings without fretting them*? Or *put my fingers down without sounding any notes*?

- Can I say the *name of each note* before I put my finger down?

- Can I *sing the tune*? Can I sing it *using the note names*? How about singing the *chord names or numbers*?
- Could I write out the *chord chart or the note names* without using my instrument?

You don't have to be able to do *all* of these things. Choose one, or think of something else that it might help to *know*. Try this technique on a short tune section that's problematic for you. You're likely to find that you work your way through it more quickly.

Today I'll choose a section of a tune and work on knowing it.

79   Interleaving

Most of us use what's called a *blocked practice* method to practice. We focus on one thing and trying to learn it thoroughly before moving on. Another form of learning, often called *interleaving*, is more organic. It involves mixing different topics and skills together while learning.

Consider the difference in the way we're often taught subjects in like math and history in school: We focus on one topic, like multiplication tables, thoroughly before moving on to the next, like long division. Contrast that to the way we learn skills that we pick up over the course of our lives, like carpentry, baking or gardening, where we do a bit of this, and a bit of that.

By understanding why and how interleaving works, we can use it to our advantage, *intentionally* mixing up our learning to improve memory retention and speed our progress.

How Does Interleaving Work?

When we practice anything repetitively, the brain quickly identifies patterns and assigns that work to short-term memory. Like a computer's RAM, short-term memory can be accessed quickly, but it's also…short-term. If you focus on a different repetitive task, the tune you thought you had "memorized" may be replaced by how to quickly dice potatoes.

To make our learning truly "stick," we need to create problems that the brain can *only solve by pulling in information from other areas of memory*. This is the essence of interleaving: to associate different pieces of knowledge with the concept we're learning, in order to build stronger, more long-lasting neural connections.

Put It into Practice

We need to work in ways that emphasize the *context* of what we're doing and *keep us engaged and focused*. Here's an example from my own practice:

If I'm having difficulty with a passage, I resist the urge to keep repeating it. I may play it four or five times, and then stop and stretch. Then I'll try it in the context of the piece. I might switch back and forth: passage – whole tune – passage – whole tune. I'll slow it way down or speed it up. Play along with my favorite musician, then on my own. I'll play just the left hand, then just the right hand. I sing it. Look carefully at my hands. Close my eyes. Write down the notes. Say the note names out loud. I may do one technique one day and one the next.

Interleaving Is Not Task Switching

Be cautious of bouncing around *too much*. Stay with an idea long enough to get some benefit, to feel some satisfaction. For example, if you play a passage, then look for another online video of that tune, then play the passage, then look for versions of sheet music for the tune. You may be building different types of memory, but you're also switching to a different *type* of task. When we're deeply focused on something and then switch to something else, there's a cognitive cost associated with the switch.

Interleaving May Not Feel as Satisfying

Your typical method of blocked practice is probably going to feel more comfortable. It may seem like it works better. Your brain is likely to offer a convincing rationale as to why this won't work; that is, until you've experienced the advantages.

Experiments with subjects like math and history tests show that even when people think it doesn't work, interleaving is more effective, particularly with memorization and long-term recall.[9] If you don't believe it, by all means, try your own experiment!

We need to use every trick we can to learn more efficiently. This is one that's worth the effort to develop.

Today I'll practice interleaving.

80   Very Slow Practice

Sometimes it can be informative to practice slowly. *Very* slowly. Very slow practice involves playing as slowly as you can possibly stand to play.

Very slow practice takes effort. It forces us to address our lack of attention. One would assume playing at a very slow speed would give us time to do everything perfectly. Instead, the mind wanders at every space between the notes.

If we can be curious, attentive and "teacherly," very slow practice can be quite illuminating. You may want to consider a few ideas as you try it:

- Are you able to infuse your playing with the same musicality? Does the music take on a different character? What happens to the rhythms?

- At a slower speed, your body may lose its ability to play certain passages "automatically." Are you comfortable with that, or is there something you want to work on?

- Are there physical clues that can inform your practice? You may perceive tension, or an unnecessary movement, or even a stray thought that, at a faster speed, would go by unnoticed.

This practice can be uncomfortable. Use a metronome, because you'll have a tendency to want to creep back to a more typical speed. It's also not something you need to do every day. Very slow practice can be an effective tool to have in your practice toolbox.

Today I'll try very slow practice.

81 One Thing at a Time

Multiple studies have found that humans can't really multitask, even though we persist in thinking we can. Usually, when we think we're saving time by working on two things at once, we're actually unable to focus on either task and we lose focus and energy.

Often, while we may not be *intentionally* attempting to multitask, we do think about one thing while doing another. How many times have you been practicing, convinced you're working on where a fingering change or bellows switch will happen, and realize your attention has wandered to a wrong note, dynamics issue, or the cat that just walked into the room?

It's possible to build a greater capacity for attention and focus. We have a powerful incentive, because *focusing on one thing at a time is the most efficient way to accomplish more.*

Put It into Practice

> The first, and most difficult, step is to **notice** when your mind has wandered away from what you are doing now.
>
> Next, **make the shift**. Bring your focus back to your present task. Use a mental cue – just a couple of words, like "chord change pattern."
>
> Finally, **build positive associations** to help rewire your brain. Try to fully experience the enjoyment of that focus and attention. It may feel silly to do, but it helps remind yourself explicitly, "I'm doing this because I'm going to get better faster," or "It will be great when I can do this bellows change smoothly." You only need to hold this positive thought for a few seconds.

Building your ability to focus is incremental work. It may not seem like you're making progress. Our minds are like monkeys, looking for something new and interesting to latch on to. We can develop the ability to focus for longer periods, slowly but surely.

Today I'll work on developing my ability to focus on one thing at a time.

82   Four Stretches

Here are four stretches I learned from fiddler Lisa Ornstein. Try them at the beginning of your practice, or during a break.[*]

Unwinding

Imagine the way your left hand and arm would twist to put your fingers on the fingerboard of a violin. (You can probably visualize this even if you don't play violin.) Hold your arm in front of you and twist your hand and arm into that shape, keeping your shoulder relaxed. Now "unwind" your entire wrist, arm and shoulder until your hand is facing toward the left. Repeat this two more times.

Do the same on the other arm. Or, if you choose, you can "unwind" both arms at once.

Wrist Circles

Make fists with your thumbs tucked inside. Make gentle circles with your wrists. Do five in each direction.

Taking Off Rings

Hold out your left arm fairly straight in front of you. Let the hand and fingers drop. With the other hand, massage each finger in turn, starting with the pinkie. Start massaging each finger close to the hand. Rub and pull slowly as if you were taking off a ring. Give the finger tips a little extra massage. Massage all five fingers, then switch hands.

Neck Stretch

Tilt your head gently to the right and support it with your right hand. Feel the gentle stretch in the neck muscles. Take a deep inhalation and slowly exhale. Use your hand to help you return your head upright. Switch sides. If it feels good, try gently extending the opposite arm, holding it a foot or so away from your body.

---

[*] A video for these stretches is available at www.judyminot.com/bestpractice/

Cautions:

> Always exercise common sense with your own health. Do these stretches to the limit of comfort, not tolerance. Keep it simple and easy. Remember to breathe. If you experience pain during one of these stretches, don't continue.

Today when I take a break, I'll try these four stretches.

83 Playing as Play

> "Play is often talked about as if it were a relief from serious learning. But...play is serious learning."
>
> – Fred Rogers, a.k.a. Mister Rogers[10]

Our practice time is usually spent in methodical activities that are often planned out in advance. This makes sense: If we had to create a new plan every day, it would be harder to move forward. Sometimes, however, in focusing on following the plan, we can lose track of the joy we take in making music.

It's important to make room for play in our playing. On a regular basis, find some place for spontaneity, exploration, "whatever comes out." You might even call it "breaking the rules," or "not doing what you're supposed to be doing."

Pick up your instrument and just play whatever comes to your mind. A tune you love, something that sounds beautiful. Play a few notes, make something up, engage in a little silliness.

Spend a few minutes, or as long as you want, exploring the sounds of your instrument with no particular goal in mind. Open your ears to every sound, and follow the ones you like.

Engaging playfully with your instrument can be unexpectedly challenging if you're used to sticking to a plan. It's hard to let go of worrying about wrong notes, poor tone, or whether what you did was "correct." At the same time it can be energizing. As Mister Rogers pointed out, we learn a great deal when we are playful. Your ear will benefit and your body will absorb the lessons from what you do during your play time.

Today I will "play."

84   Relaxing Your Face

Most of us wince or tighten our mouths – a little or a lot – as we play. It may happen only when we're playing something tricky, or more often than that. Yet if you watch accomplished players, you can't tell from their faces that *anything* they are doing is difficult.

What you look like while playing might seem unimportant if you make the right sounds, but relaxing your face *can* actually help you play better. A facial twitch is a sign of tension, either in the mind, or somewhere else in the body. Since the body and mind are connected, if we relax the face, it subtly calms the mind. Playing with a more relaxed face can also help release tension in the hands, shoulders, and arms.

You might assume that as you become a better player, your face will naturally stop twitching. This is not the case. It's not difficult to learn, but if you don't pay attention to relaxing your face, it's unlikely to happen on its own.

Put It into Practice

> Start with a tune that's easy for you to play. Use a mirror for visual feedback. As you play, try to stay aware of what your face feels like. If you can let go of the tension in your face, does anything change in your body? Can you hear a difference? Is it easier to get the sounds you want?
>
> You may not be able to hear or feel an immediate change. Try assessing what's changed after a week.

Quite quickly you may find that your face is relaxed most of the time. At that point you can use your facial "tics" as tools: signs that you're having difficulty. You may not have made a mistake: The fear of a mistake, or something that causes extra effort or attention can be causing you to tense. When your face doesn't show tension any longer, you can be pretty sure you've worked out the issues.

Today I'll look at ways that relaxing my face can help me play better.

85   All Notes Are Not Created Equal

In some cultural traditions, music was often played without dedicated "rhythm" instruments like drums or guitars. The playing styles, and the tunes, evolved to incorporate the rhythm into the melody itself.

For this reason, certain notes, ornaments, or stylistic elements in trad tunes may serve a strong rhythmic function, more than a melodic one. Learning to distinguish these more rhythmic elements in your playing can help you make the tunes you play sound both more melodic *and* more rhythmic.

Put It into Practice

Since every style and every tune is unique, you may find this exercise easier or more challenging depending on the tune. If it is a challenge, don't toss the idea. Keep your ears open until the right tune comes along, and try applying it then.

> *Identify Rhythmic Elements*

- Sing, hum, or lilt the tune while moving your body. Whether you tap your foot, move your head, or drum on the steering wheel, which notes could you replace with a body movement?

- Have fun with this idea. What's the minimum you can reduce the tune to? Think of this as a kind of core melody.

- If a note is repeated often, especially alternating with others, (this is especially common in some fiddle styles) those notes are likely supporting the rhythm of the tune.

- Many players use ornaments as rhythmic elements – to emphasize the beat. Can you hear this in the playing of one of your favorite musicians?

Bring out the Melody

- Once you've identified the core melody, practice bringing that melody out. Try making everything else a little softer, or more detached, or less emphasized.

- Can you get the melody notes to sound like they flow, even if there are other rhythmic notes in between? Imagine you were playing two instruments at the same time: one that's playing the melody, and one that's drumming out the rhythm.

- This is a great time to record your efforts to give you a better perspective on how your sound changes.

Note for polyphonic instruments:
Pianists and stringed instrument players can sound two notes at the same time, making one louder or softer. Bellowed instrument players may not be able to make one note softer, but they can de-emphasize a note by making it shorter.

Today I'll look at how melody and rhythm are expressed within a tune, and see if I can emphasize that with my playing.

86   Musical "Words"

When I took up the one-row diatonic accordion, I was concerned it might be my "last straw" instrument: the *one too many* that would cause me to lose focus on everything else.

I persuaded myself it could be easy. "You just have to push the right buttons," I thought. "It can't be that hard: it only plays in one key!" Still, I knew that the diatonic accordion had its own challenges, in addition to the most obvious one: You have to push the right button *and* move the bellows in the right direction to get the right note. I hit on the idea of learning to play it like I learned to type.[*]

---

[*] Please bear with me for a few more paragraphs before you send an angry email about how music cannot be reduced to typing on a keyboard. *I agree with you*!

I'm from a generation that was offered touch typing class in high school. In class we spent a lot of time on repetition like this:

>cat cat cat cat
>fat fat fat fat
>sat sat sat sat
>cat fat sat cat fat sat

and, eventually:

>through through through
>would would would
>bring bring bring

The layout of a typewriter keyboard is far from intuitive. Yet after hours, and years, of touch typing, common words and letter patterns pour from my fingers without conscious thought.

I've read that as we get better at typing and reading, *our brains combine common patterns into one synaptic event*. My fingers automatically type words like "through" and "would." In fact, I'm so used to typing my own surname that I have to slow down to type words like "monitor."

What this means is that I can focus on my train of thought as I type. I give little or no attention to what finger goes where.

I applied this concept to learning the button accordion to help make the counterintuitive, push-pull aspect of the instrument less of a challenge. As I worked on a new tune, I looked for any scale or chord patterns that seemed common or familiar. When I picked these out, I repeated them, just as I did in typing class.

Since I was playing *music*, not learning to type, I also tried to make the melody sound beautiful and fluid. As I progressed, the patterns I worked on went from simple (cat cat sat sat) to more complex (through through would would).

Did it work? While I won't make bold claims about my button accordion playing, I will say my method was very helpful.

This idea has application to playing any instrument in any style. *Just as every language has common words and sounds, every musical tradition incorporates common musical patterns.*

Devote some attention to identifying those patterns that you hear often. Turn them into mini-exercises. Repeat them with attention and focus. The next time you encounter them, they'll be easier to play.

Today I'll start to identify common patterns, or "musical words," in the music or style I'm exploring.

87   Engage Your Senses

Most of us prioritize certain senses over others. We may think we're *listening*, when in fact we're *looking*. Or, we may pay attention to the feeling in some parts of our bodies (hands, fingers), and ignore the feeling in others (shoulders, back, hips).

When you're having trouble absorbing an idea or playing a passage, try an exercise to deliberately engage your senses. Musicians can't make as much use of our senses of taste or smell, but *we can heighten our awareness of what we see, hear and feel* to help us play better.

Put It into Practice

Play a passage slowly enough that it's close to the way you want it to sound. You may have to slow down the metronome and choose a small section – a couple of bars or notes, or two or three chords.

Sight

As you play, look at each of your hands in turn. Examine them in as much detail as you can. Look at angle of your fingers where they come in contact with the instrument. Look at your wrists, elbows, arms – anything that seems relevant. Try not to judge "good" or "bad." Just look, and be interested.

Feeling

> Close your eyes. What sensations do you feel in your fingers? Are they relaxed, tense? Experience the way your fingers feel as they contact with the instrument, with *as much specificity as you can*.

> Now scan your body. Sense the interrelationship of your fingers, wrists, elbows, shoulders, head, neck, back, even your hips and legs. Where do you feel tension or relaxation as you play? Sense the angle of your elbow to your shoulder. Where do your shoulder blades rest on the back of your rib cage?

Hearing

> Keeping your eyes closed, listen deeply. Without judgement, see if you can hear the finest differences in sound. Can you relate them to the way your body feels?

> Make adjustments to this exercise based on your instrument, your experience and your own inclination.

Make a habit of incorporating more of your sense "data" as you practice. It will help create stronger, more lasting learning.

Today I'll try an exercise to engage my senses of sight, feeling and hearing.

88   Play What You Know

We often focus on learning new tunes and new techniques. Why not set time aside to play something you already know? Devote your full attention to playing as *beautifully, musically, and evocatively* as you can.

Start the tune, and then stop. Whatever speed that was, start again just a little slower. Play *at that speed*, with every element of musicality you can. Use dynamics to give the tune an arc. Make the phrasing obvious. Open up space between the notes. Play in perfect time, and be rhythmic in your playing.

Keep it simple. Leave out things like ornaments, harmony notes, fancy strumming patterns or other technical additions, unless you can play them with complete ease.

Play through the whole tune. Let that experience settle into your body and your ear.

Now do it again, only more so. Try to accentuate everything you did the first time. If you were to evoke an emotional response in your listener, what emotions might they be?

Play this way as often as you can.

Today I'll play something I know, as well as I can.

89   Your Three Things

When I'm struggling with a passage of music, there are three things that always help me:

- Slow down
- Fix my posture
- Breathe deeply

What are your three things? You may be tempted to list more than three – but try to stick to just three. It's easy to remember and fairly quick to address just three things.*

Write them down. Put the list somewhere that you can see it. Whenever you struggle, refer to the list. Eventually, as soon as you feel things aren't going the way you want them to, you'll respond automatically by addressing your three things.

Today I will make note of my three things.

90   Visualization

Visualizing is a powerful learning tool for musicians. In some cases, visualizing can actually train the brain to make correct movements. It can

---

* If there are more than three, wait six weeks and switch one out.

also be used to change habitual mental reactions, such as performance anxiety.

Many people use visualization when they're unable to practice. It can also be used to help when you feel "stuck" – for example when you feel you just can't get past a certain problem in your playing.

Visualization involves creating very detailed mental images of the result we want. When you use visualization as a practice technique, several things are important:

- Take the activity seriously. Set time aside. Find a space that's comfortable and free of distractions.
- Make your imagined setting as rich and realistic as you can. Imagine not only the sound, but the way things look, feel, and even smell. Imagine the room you're in. Is anyone else in the room?
- As you imagine what your body feels like in this imagined space, include the feeling in your arms, neck and head. Imagine the way your body feels in space. Visualize your breathing, your posture and even the feeling in your stomach.

Put It into Practice

Here are some ways you can make use of visualization to achieve a musical goal. Pick one that makes sense for you.

- *Visualize to improve a technical aspect of your playing.* Create a detailed mental image of the way your finger comes down on the fingerboard, the hand position for a certain chord, or the way your embouchure or bow hand feel.
- *Use visualization to improve a difficult passage.* Visualize yourself playing beautifully and with ease.
- *Visualize to improve your understanding of harmony.* Imagine yourself playing scales, clearly understanding the name of each note, where it is and how it feels.
- *Use visualization to imagine playing more musically.* Picture yourself playing a tune you are working on. As you hear the sound, imagine the feeling of your entire body, the

instrument in your hands, and the effect of the sound on you and the space around you.

- *Create an alternate world in which you don't experience performance anxiety.* Imagine yourself about to perform or start a tune in a jam session. What is your breathing and posture like? What thoughts are going through your head? Open your eyes and close them deliberately. This time, visualize the experience the way you want it to be.

- *Open up to the artist in you.* Imagine yourself bursting with creativity, with music pouring out of you like an ocean. Choose a metaphor that appeals to you: the beach, sunshine, a supernova, or anything that makes you feel comfortable, capable, creative. This type of visualization can be rejuvenating, especially when you're feeling discouraged.

Visualization can help you unleash the incredible power of your imagination, so that it can better facilitate your playing.[11]

Today I will use visualization as a way to achieve a musical goal.

91 Before You Start

When we sit down to play a tune, we often begin without much forethought. This is not an issue when we're at home, alone. The resulting habit can have repercussions when we're playing with or for others.

You might bluff through a few parts you'd forgotten the notes for. By the second or third time through you may start to feel a bit more comfortable, yet at that point your self-esteem is already on the downslide. The next time someone says, "Why don't you start a tune?" you may shy away. That's not the result you want.

It's time to stop blundering blindly into tunes.

Put It into Practice

Before you start playing, *even when you're playing for yourself,* go through a quick mental checklist. It should be short, but focused. Here's mine:

What key is it in? What is the meter? What are the starting notes?
"Jig in G, starts on B, starts like 'Jingle Bells'"

What's the tricky part?
Do you know the transition/pickup notes between sections? What's the hardest part for you?

Hear/imagine the tune, and your best sound
Do a quick mental recap of the tune. Get the feel of it. Map it with your fingers. Play a few notes quietly if you can. Find a way to settle into the sound of your instrument – maybe by playing a few notes or a scale.

Begin from a position of physical and mental repose.
Set both feet on the floor. Relax your shoulders. Breathe. People *want* to listen to you play.

Today I'll begin a new habit when starting tunes.

92   Acting "As If"

Social psychologists say that *behavior change often precedes changes in attitudes and feelings.* In other words, if you want to change the way you feel about something, it's possible that behaving *as if* that is the way you feel can lead to a change in the way you *actually do* feel.

We can use this idea in our practice to achieve some of the results we want.

- If you don't feel like practicing, try *acting as if* you did want to practice.
- *Act as if* you're not afraid to play at a jam session.
- *Act as if* you believe in your own ability.

Here's another take on *acting as if*: When you're practicing something difficult, isolate the part that's giving you the most trouble. Before you play that section – that chord, that double stop, those five notes – take a moment. Internally persuade yourself that you are absolutely certain you can play it well.

What happened? If you were able to play better, even only one time, you've found out that *acting as if* you can do something *can change your result*.

Today I'll try "acting as if."

93   When the Bell Rings, Get Up!

I remember reading an article about a student of Zen living at a Japanese monastery. He was always late for four a.m. services. His teacher told him to set an alarm. He told the teacher that he did set an alarm, but when it went off he'd open his eyes, look at the ceiling for a few seconds, and the next thing he knew, he was waking up again, much later. The teacher's response was simply, "When the bell rings, get up!"*

When we know we have a commitment, especially one involving practice for a long-term goal, the mind almost always puts up road blocks. Why not lie in bed for a few more minutes, do the dishes, or clean out your email inbox?

There is a simple remedy: Decide in advance when you will practice, and when the time comes, get up and practice.

Today when it's time to practice, I will get up and practice.

---

* Zen teachers often try to provoke students to have a more direct experience of reality, unmediated by thought and cognition. The teacher in this case may have been indicating that the bell should prompt the student to get up without thinking.

94   Head and Neck Position

Keeping a neutral head and neck position can help us stay more relaxed and settled when we play.

Put It into Practice

Take a moment to think about how you habitually hold your head.

> Do you typically lift your chin when you play? Do you thrust your head forward? Do you look down? Turn your head to the left or right?
>
> You may not be used to having an awareness of your head and neck position. Sneak a look at yourself in the mirror as you play. Do a little "check in" the next time you're playing in a group of people.

Get a sense of what a neutral head position feels like.*

> Sit comfortably with your instrument nearby. (Don't pick it up yet.)
>
> Let your shoulders be relaxed. Release any tension in your shoulders so they fall away from your ears.
>
> Now imagine the back of your neck long. Think of making yourself tall, from your hips all the way to the cowlick in your hair.
>
> As you do this, chances are you'll lift your gaze and your chin will be more level. You may find that your head has drawn back to a position that's centered over the shoulders.

Come back to this neutral feeling periodically.

---

* Certain instruments must be played with the head and neck in a position that is decidedly not neutral. In that case it's all the more important to be *as neutral as possible in other ways* such as keeping the spine long, relaxing the shoulders. Plenty of expertise is available to help musicians minimize stress injury from playing instruments like these. If you feel you're at risk of injury, seek help from a knowledgeable teacher or bodywork professional.

As you play, remind yourself occasionally to check on your head and neck position. When you do, do you hear any change in your sound? Do you feel like playing is easier or more comfortable?

Today I'll pay attention to my head and neck and how I hold them as I play.

95   How to Jam

Jam sessions can be incredibly fun. They're a great way to meet other musicians, swap tips and ideas, and learn tunes. You don't have to worry about making mistakes: There are plenty of other players who will "carry" you.

As you get more comfortable in the jam setting you can try out new things and take advantage of the musical support of other players. They may provide rhythm backup, help you out with melody, sing along, or do whatever you ask. Fellow jammers can be extremely supportive.

Put It into Practice

Here are a few ways to make your jamming experience go more smoothly:*

- Attending your first jam session can be a bit daunting. Remind yourself that most jam sessions are full of extremely friendly people who want to encourage other musicians to join them.

- It's a good idea to show up a little early your first time, introduce yourself to the leader, and let them know it's your first time at a jam (or at this jam). This is a good time to ask things like, "Does anyone sing at this jam session?" "Where would you like me to sit?" or, "Is my hand drum welcome?"

- The first time at any jam session you're unlikely to know most of the tunes. This is true even for experienced players. There are a lot of tunes out there, and every jam session has

---

* There's a handy list of best practices for jamming in Appendix C.

its own set of favorites. It's OK to ask the names of tunes you liked. Write them down. Maybe choose one or two to learn for next time.

- Bring a recording device. (It's polite to ask before recording, especially if there are professional players at the session.)

- Most jam sessions don't use sheet music. This is a good incentive to learn to play without the "dots."

- Most jams are organized around a style of music or concept (Irish/Celtic, Scottish, old time, song swap, English pub tunes, etc.). Before you go, check through your repertoire. If you have a tune or two in that genre, brush up on it in case you're asked to start a tune.

- Every jam has its own traditions, even "rules." It's important to watch and listen to get a sense of these before fully participating. Do they play single tunes or medleys/sets? How many times do they generally play a tune? Does everyone play the same version or do you hear variation among the players? Does the group stick to tunes within the stated genre, or are they open to variety? Is there an acknowledged rhythm leader?

- Breaks between tunes are good times to ask questions of fellow musicians. Don't be too shy! All these jammers were beginners once, too!

If you followed good jamming etiquette and you didn't feel welcomed, it's probably not about you. The members may have had a bad experience. Don't let this ruin jam sessions for you.

Many jam sessions have a mailing list, website or social media page. Some circulate lists of tunes played or favorite tunes. All you have to do is ask to get access to helpful resources for next time.

Today I'll think about attending a jam session, especially if I've never done it before.

96   Ring Finger, Little Finger

The physiology of our hands is a given. No matter what instrument we play, we can't change the fact that the ring and pinkie fingers are weak and are difficult to move independently of the other fingers.

In classical music, musicians need to be able to use all the fingers even to play basic repertoire. Part of classical training includes exercises that increase finger independence and strength, especially in these "last" two fingers.

Many trad musicians who haven't had that type of training develop workarounds or stylistic ways to compensate for the weakness of the pinkie and ring fingers. Some players avoid using the pinkie finger entirely.

If you're in the above category, **why not use all your fingers?** Why not learn to strengthen your ring and pinkie fingers, so you can play more evenly, with better accuracy, and have more options for how you'll play tunes?

Put It into Practice

Try each step below for a few days before starting on the next.

Tapping on a Table

(You can do this any time, not just during "practice time.")

- *Rest all four fingers lightly on the tabletop* as if you were typing or playing piano. Make sure your wrist is level with the top of the hand and your shoulders are relaxed.

- *One at a time, lift each finger and tap it down firmly on the table.* You'll notice that the last two don't lift as high and don't come down as strongly. At first, you may not even be able to lift the ring finger without lifting the middle finger at the same time.

- *Play around with different tapping patterns*, lifting and tapping your fingers one at a time.

Tapping on Your Instrument

- Place your fingers on the keyboard, fretboard or keyholes. Slowly and deliberately, finger four notes, one for each finger. Don't bow or sound the instrument. As with the tabletop, play with different patterns. Do this for a minute, at most two, before you begin your regular practice.

Add Sound

- When you add sound, however that's accomplished, listen carefully for changes in tone, rhythm, or dynamics that may arise from the difference in finger strength and independence.

Finger independence exercises can be found for many instruments, from piano to banjo. Many are available for free online. If you don't find exactly what you need you can probably adapt an exercise from a related instrument.

Look for exercises that interest you. Don't keep it up if it's boring. Feel free to develop your own exercise, based on something you're working on.

Be careful not to overdo it. If the fingers feel sore or tired, stop. If you're still sore after you finish practicing, take a break from this exercise for a week or more. It's not worth straining your muscles or developing an injury.

Today I'll work on increasing strength and independence in my ring and pinkie fingers.

97 Mental Flexibility

When I began to practice the martial art of aikido, I quickly learned the importance of maintaining mental flexibility. We were taught that, even though we learned specific techniques in class, in a real-world situation anything could happen. A skill that we learned perfectly in these ideal circumstances could be undone by something as simple as uneven ground or bright sunlight.

When I started learning to play jazz, I realized that being flexible and open to the unexpected were also valuable skills for improvising. In the succeeding years I've found it's not just jazz musicians or improvisers who can benefit.

Whether you're just trying to add a variation to a tune or the singer forgets the lyrics and you have to vamp, being able to play flexibly, to make a musical "switch," with poise and equilibrium is of great benefit. And, as with self-defense, real-world musical situations don't always go down the way we practice them.

Put It into Practice

> Strengthen your ability to stay mentally responsive and equanimous as you practice by *drawing attention to how you respond to change as you play*.
>
> The change may be musical, as with transition from an A to a B section or when you try a phrase with or without an ornament. Or it may be something else: Perhaps you flubbed a note or a bellows switch. Do you physically tense? Does your inner voice warn, "Uh oh"?
>
> Simply noticing these subtle physical and mental reactions is an important first step. Then you can use the tools from your practice toolbox[*] to help you respond more smoothly.

Who knows? You may soon find yourself looking forward to the opportunity to respond to change.

Today I'll draw my attention to being mentally flexible.

98   Positioning Exercise

This technique can be very useful when you're trying to make big movements with accuracy. Big movements, or jumps, are more common on certain instruments than others: piano, piano accordion, hammered

---

[*] The Practice Pyramid, described in Appendix A, is an excellent all-around tool for practice.

dulcimer, and stringed instruments come to mind, but this exercise can be adjusted to work on any instrument where you have to reposition your hand from a "home" position.

Put It into Practice

- Play right up to the place where you will move your hand.
- Move to the new position, but stop before making any sound.
- Take a moment to experience what this new position feels like. Where are your arms in relation to your body? Where are your hands?
- Now play the note. Is it correct? Does it sound the way you want it to sound? If it isn't, don't get frustrated.
- Do this a few more times – for 3-5 minutes, each time making sure to pause before you make a sound, and really connect with the way your body feels.
- When you do have a successful result, give yourself a strong positive reinforcement. Think of your brain as a dog you're training with praise, and give yourself a mental treat.
- When you finish, make sure to stop after one of your better attempts, so you'll feel good about your progress.

Don't expect perfect results after one session. This is an exercise that can take a few days, a week, or even longer before you have consistent results, but *they will happen*.

Today I'll try a positioning exercise.

99 Watch and Listen

When I first started practicing aikido, there was a brown belt student who had just had knee replacement surgery. For six weeks she came to class, twice a week, and sat to one side watching. One day I asked her why she came since she couldn't practice. She told me *she learned at least as much from watching as from practicing.*

Don't overlook opportunities to watch and listen.

If I'm at a jam session and I don't know the tune, I try to resist the tendency to pull out my phone, zone out, or even to try to fake the tune. I remind myself to be present, listening to the other players and noticing everything I can.

There are amazing rewards to watching and listening to other players. I notice aspects of the music that are subtle, impossible to put into words. I never would have heard these subtleties without paying attention.

Today when someone else is playing, I'll treat it as a learning opportunity.

100   Sleeping with a Key

In this book I advocate that musicians devote effort to becoming more focused and mindful while practicing. Yet the direct opposite, what's called "diffuse thinking," is also vital to learning and to creativity.

Diffuse thinking happens when we're not focused on, or preoccupied by, a particular topic or train of thought. According to those who study neuroscience and learning, during this "free movement," the brain is able to make connections among new and abstract concepts. We can approach problems from different angles, using ideas from different disciplines. The resulting mental "models" are both stronger and more deeply rooted.

Stories abound of creators, from Keith Richards to Thomas Edison, who have made use of the type of diffuse thinking that occurs between sleep and wakefulness. Salvador Dalí called this state the one "most appropriate to the exercise of the art of painting."[12] He would induce it by napping while holding a key above a metal plate. When he fell asleep, the key hit the plate and woke him. He would then have access to the ideas generated in this liminal state.

You don't have to wait until bedtime to engage in diffuse thinking. Exercising, meditating, taking a shower, even grooming a dog can elicit this unfocused state. Here is how you can integrate diffuse thinking into your practice routine:

Put It into Practice

- Bring your attention to bear as you normally do, *until you're at the limit of your ability to concentrate*. This might be after a certain period of time, when you find your mind wandering, or when you're about to shift gears for some other reason.

- *Set a timer for five minutes.* During the break, let go of thoughts about the learning at hand. Let your mind wander. Some light or repetitive activity – stretching, pacing, washing your teacup – may be helpful. Avoid tasks that require focus and attention.

- Think of the short break as *part of your practice time*. Let your subconscious work, and don't worry about the results too much. When you come back it doesn't matter if you continue with the same activity or do something else. Your brain will have done the work on its own.

Today I'll recognize the role of diffuse thinking, and see if I can work it into my practice routine.

101 When to Move On

When I practice, I usually set out with some kind of a goal. The goal might be to play through an entire tune without a flub, to play an exercise through four keys using the metronome, to be consistent with my bellowing, or to play with more dynamics. It's in my nature to be fairly dogged about getting that thing right, whatever it may be.

This doggedness is helpful in many respects, but it can also be a burden: No matter how much I've worked, no matter how far I've come, a little voice is always telling me I could do more.

One of my teachers gave me excellent advice:

Recognize progress, even if it's not perfection, and move on.

Work for a period of time – it could be five minutes or 20 – until you make *some* progress, then move on. Make a note so you can come back to it tomorrow.

This method has multiple benefits:

- Your overall progress will be faster than if you hammered away at the same thing for just one day.

- Your practice time will be more interesting, as you'll work on more concepts, techniques and tunes.

- By explicitly recognizing that you *have* made progress, you'll be more satisfied with the results of your work, and be more enthusiastic about coming back to it again.

- Focusing on progress is a much healthier mental attitude than focusing on what's *not* right.

Today I'll recognize progress, even if it's not perfection, and move on.

102   Learning the Secret Language

The first time I attended an Irish seisiún (jam session), everyone seemed to have ESP. The musicians all switched to a different tune at the same time. If someone sang, the melody players knew when to take a musical break, who would take it and for how long. And each set of tunes ended with a flourish, as if it had been rehearsed.

Musicians don't read minds, of course, but there is communication going on between them. This language incorporates gestures, body language, vocalizations, and musical cues. Sometimes the exchange is subtle – a nod, a look – sometimes it's less so – a loud "Hup!" Learning to respond to, and provide, this communication makes playing in a group a lot more fun.

Communicating with others while you play can be a bit like rubbing your tummy and patting your head: It looks easy, but it's surprisingly awkward, especially at first. When I first tried calling "Hup!" before switching to a new tune, it was months before I could do it at the right *time*, not to mention doing it without my own playing falling apart. Even then, it sounded like a dog was getting its tail stepped on. Luckily my fellow players had all been there before.

It's much easier to become aware of signals from other musicians when you've made a practice of *not staying head-down in your instrument*. The best way to learn is by watching how other musicians communicate. As you try to do it yourself, it will eventually become easier and easier.

Today I'll watch how other musicians communicate, and work on getting better at it myself.

103   Make vs. Allow

A wise friend once told me, "You can't *make* yourself relax. You have to *allow* yourself to relax."

There are many things *we want so much to happen* when we play. We're used to doing things by trying harder. But in this one area, *relaxing*, trying harder actually has the opposite effect to the one we want.

The idea of *allowing* applies to more than just relaxing, however. It can be quite transformative for our playing if we wonder:

What other things could we allow to happen, instead of trying to make them happen?

- What if I *allowed* myself to create a particular type of sound instead of focusing on the technical aspects?
- What if I *allowed* myself to feel good about my playing?
- What if I were *allowed* to express *myself*: freely and fully, not trying to play like someone else, but to *play like me*?
- What if I *allowed* my fingers to fall exactly to the right places, where my mind/body *already knows* they belong?

As you practice, try asking yourself, "*What am I trying so very hard to do?*" What would happen if you believed that you already could do it, and that all you needed to do was *let go and allow it to happen*?

Today I will think about what I can allow *to happen in my playing. Is there something I can let go of that will open up more potential?*

104 Upper Body Stretch

Here's a great refresher to use when your brain is jumbled with notes, ideas and frustration.

Put your instrument down and stand up. Take a deep breath and exhale slowly through your mouth.

Reach Up

Hold your arms above your head. Stretch your spine upwards and long, keeping the heels on the ground. Work to straighten the arms. Imagine someone was holding your fingertips, and let your shoulders fall away from your ears. Breathe.

Palms Together

Hold your arms in front of you with the palms facing each other. Relax your shoulders and let your shoulder blades ease down over the back of your body.

Breathe deeply. Slowly open your arms as wide as you comfortably can and still stay relaxed. Bring your arms slowly back together again with the palms facing each other. Breathe.

Palms Up

Turn your palms so they're facing up and do the same stretch, opening your arms out to either side. Breathe deeply as you slowly bring your arms back together.

Palms Down

Turn your palms face down, and again open your arms wide, breathing deeply. Bring your arms back together keeping the shoulders relaxed.

Palms Facing Away

The last stretch is a bit of a challenge to do without "caving in" the front of the body.

Face your palms away from each other with the thumbs down. Let your shoulders relax. Open your chest, imagining that you're making space in the front of the body. Now open your arms wide, breathing deeply. This stretch may feel good in the front of the body. Bring your arms back together with the backs of the hands facing each other.

Sit back down and continue practicing.

Cautions:

Always exercise common sense with your own health. Stretching and movement should feel good, not painful or intense. If you have a back or neck injury or another health concern, or if you experience pain during one of these stretches, stop and seek professional advice.

Today I'll take a break and give my arms, shoulders, and back a chance to relax and reset.

105 Creating Lift

> When the dancers are in the air, you have them."
> — Martin Hayes[13]

The vast majority of traditional music is intended as dance music. We musicians may think of hornpipes, gigues, reels, waltzes and mazurkas as "tunes," but these are all names for dance forms. The tunes are written to match the dance. To communicate their essence, we need to make them *danceable*, even when there are no dancers. Musicians often call this giving a tune "lift."

The nuts and bolts of "creating lift" can be hard to pin down. The best way to begin thinking about lift is to remember:

The lift, or movement, in a tune, happens on the off-beat, because that's when you have to lift your foot to move it.

The first step (pun intended) to creating lift is to give *more emphasis to these weak, or off-beats.*[*]

Put It into Practice

Reels

- Choose a reel to play: a tune counted either **1**- 2 - **3** - 4 or **1** + 2 +. The dancers would take steps on the beats in bold face.
- Play your reel and walk (or skip or dance), stepping on the strong beats (e.g. beats 1 and 3). If you can't walk and play your instrument, sing instead.
- Keep playing (or singing) and walking, and add more emphasis to those strong beats.
- Keep playing (or singing) and walking. Switch your emphasis to the weak beats. Do you feel more like dancing?
- Play around with how much emphasis works best. How flexible can you make your playing? Can you shift, adding more or less "lift" or weak-beat emphasis?

Other Dance Forms

Jigs have six eighth notes per measure, played in groups of three. The strong beats, where the dancers step, are beats 1 and 4. To create lift in your jig playing, try putting more emphasis on the beats *just before* the strong ones: 3 and 6.

Most waltzes have three beats to a measure. Think about waltzing: You take a strong step on the first beat, that moves you around the dance floor. On beats two and three you rock back and forth. As with a jig, the place to create lift is where the dancer lifts their foot, just before putting it down on the strongest beat. This would usually be beat three. If there is a note between beat three or beat one, even better!

---

[*] Many musicians use the term *upbeat* instead of off-beat or weak beat. Music theory textbooks define the *downbeat* as the first beat in the bar and the *upbeat* as the last beat in the previous bar. I'm using these more "proper" terms here.

There are lots of tune types, dances and time signatures, but humans have two feet. Dances get divided rhythmically into groups of three or two. (In quite a few dances there's some of each.) Between reels, jigs, and 3-beat waltzes, you have the tools you need to get the feel of creating lift.

A Few More Thoughts

Most of us feel the "dance" underlying the tunes we play – That's part of their appeal. We may assume we're transmitting it in our playing. Is that truly the case? Could you do more? Could you do better? The most reliable way to find out is to *record yourself.*

Now that you've begun to listen for "lift," you can better hear the way other musicians emphasize it. There are no hard and fast rules. As you get to know the individual dances (and you should!) you'll begin to feel where the movement of a hip, a change in weight, or a turn can be emphasized to energize the dance. Using dynamics, cutting some notes a little short, letting others hang over the beat, leaving out notes entirely – all these can be part of giving "lift" to a tune.

Today I'll give attention to how I express lift. I'll start by learning to emphasize the off-beat.

106   Wild Takes

As a video producer, I often worked with voice-over artists. At the end of an ad or TV promo there's usually a final line called a tagline: something like "Tonight at 9, on WXYZ" or "Best Practice: Practice Smarter, Practice Happier."

When recording these taglines, we'd ask the announcer to do a few "wild takes": to read the tagline a few times in different ways. The best voice-over artists would give three completely distinct-sounding reads. Each would have a different rhythm, emphasize a different word, or have a particular emotional feeling.

This turns out to be a *great* practice technique for musicians. It can help give us more flexibility in the way we approach what we're playing.

Put It into Practice

- Choose a short phrase of music that you like – maybe the end of a tune, or any other zippy little bit that appeals. It should be just a few notes – a measure or two.
- Set the metronome on a nice, playable setting and play the phrase several times. *Play the exact same notes each time*, but try to vary the feeling each time, using emphasis, phrasing and dynamics. It may help to pause for several metronome beats between each "wild take."

If you're having trouble making your wild takes sound different, try one of these ideas:

- Think about *dynamics*: can you get louder and louder? Softer and softer? Rise and fall? It doesn't matter what's "right" – you're just playing with ideas.
- Are there places where you can open up *space between the notes* without changing the time? Shorten a note or two? What happens if you change which notes you do this with?
- What about *phrasing*: Can you make one long phrase? Two shorter phrases? Everything detached?
- What happens if you *sing the notes* instead? Can you sing them in different ways? If you added words, would you emphasize certain words?

Think of those great voice-over artists, and see how many ideas you can come up with for a single phrase.

Today I'll try some "wild takes."

107 A Direct Connection

As soon as you're able, go online and look for a video from 1933 of Louis Armstrong singing "Dinah."

Some players (and singers) are able to immerse themselves fully in the music they create, drawing upon their personality, emotions, memories and experience to create something that's entirely unique and entirely personal. This can reveal unexpected beauty in a tune we may have heard a hundred times. This ability is not bestowed from birth on certain sanctified artists. It's something we can all do by playing and practicing, all the time, *as if we really mean it.*

A friend of mine touched on this idea of immersion when he was explaining to his daughter how to speak better French. "Try speaking English with a *really overdone French accent,*" he said. When they did, as you might imagine, plenty of silliness ensued, including funny facial expressions and body language. "Now," he said, "Say something in French, but with that same accent." Suddenly, when she spoke French, she sounded...French.

This isn't a perfect metaphor, but it does point to the way we often hold back, whether we're playing, singing, or speaking a foreign language. It's not enough to "play the correct notes," or "use the correct grammar and pronunciation." We need to create a direct connection to what we're expressing. This involves engaging our entire *being* – emotions and thoughts, memories, experience, hopes, ideals – into what we play. Here are a few ideas that may help:

Put It into Practice

- Try imagining that words were not available to you, and that music was the only language you had to express yourself. Play the tune.

- Play as if this music were the most beautiful poetry you had ever heard. You owe it to the poet to express his or her ideas as well as you can.

- Try acting as if you were part of a fairy tale. The princess will be let out of the tower; you will not have to sign away your soul to the Devil; the room will be filled with gold, if your playing causes the antagonistic [king/troll/angel of Death] to experience just one true emotion.

These ideas may sound over the top, but sometimes we need something fantastic to jog us out of complacency. Why not give it a try?

Today I'll make a direct connection to the music I'm playing.

108   Learn a New Skill in 45 days

Is there something you've always wanted to be able to do?

- Sing while you play
- Play comfortably in F
- Nail a complex chord progression in every key
- Tap your feet while you play
- Get better at vibrato

Put It into Practice

> First, decide to stop thinking, "I really wish I could…" Instead, say to yourself, *"I'm learning how to…"*
>
> Next, set your goal. Make sure it's well-defined. This will help you know when you've reached it. For example, if you want to learn how to improvise, set yourself a goal like *being able to improvise, using the blues scale, in the key of F*. If you're trying to learn to sing while you play, set the goal of *learning to sing and play one song*.
>
> Decide what your practice technique is going to consist of. Then, every time you practice, you'll spend a few minutes working on your skill. Work deliberately for 5-10 minutes, then stop. Don't focus too much on whether you made progress. Just make sure you do a little of this work *every time you practice*.
>
> Every day, write down a few words about what you did in your practice notebook. Simply writing down that you did it is enough. The purpose is not so that you can read it back later, but to help "fix" the activity in your mind, to make it more memorable. A side benefit is that it will help later, when you want to look at the progress you made.
>
> Keep this up for 45 days.[*] When the time has passed, look back at how far you've come.

---

[*] Why 45 days? A widely-quoted study found that it takes an average of 21 days to break a habit, and 66 days to form a new one. There's quite a bit of variability, including what the

If you start today, in just a month and a half you'll be able to do something you've always wanted to do. You may make satisfying progress even sooner.

Today I'm going begin learning one thing I've always wanted to do.

109   Spaced Repetition

Spaced repetition is a well-respected method for memorization that's supported by a great deal of scientific data. The basic premise is that when we want to commit something to memory, we'll be most successful when we recall it *multiple times, over increasing intervals of time.*

Spaced repetition is commonly used in many fields, from language study to memorizing legal precedents. It also works for remembering tunes.

The neuroscience behind spaced repetition is based on the idea that *forgetting is essential to building memory.* You don't want to forget so much that you have to relearn the tune, just enough to increase the effort. That increased effort actually strengthens the memory.

I have a friend who developed a simple computer program to help him with tune recall. From the date he learns a tune, the program might pull it up after a week, then two weeks, a month, three months, a year. If he had trouble remembering the tune at any point, he can bump it up to a higher frequency.

Another friend has a simpler system: a "recall" list that he goes through once a week. If he can't start a tune, he marks it to try again. Both of these friends can recall a seemingly infinite number of tunes.

As a side note: Once we realize that *struggling* is an important part of memorizing and learning, it casts a new light on all our mistakes. We need mistakes, because the experience of working through them makes our learning more "sticky." **Mistakes, and even failure, are natural and even essential experiences on the path to mastering new material.**

---

habit is. Forty-five days falls roughly in the middle of 21 and 66, but it also fits with the experience of many people I've spoken with.

Today I'll start using spaced repetition to remember tunes.

110   Headwind

My brother likes to say that if you don't feel a headwind, you're not moving forward.

The fact that we're having difficulty with something *could* be seen as an indication that we're just innately terrible at it. Or it could simply mean we're working on something that's difficult to do.

String crossings. Crans. Learning by ear. Altered fifth chords. Double stops. Dynamics. Triplets. All of it. *Embrace the difficulty*. It means you're working and progressing.

Today I'll try to remember that feeling a headwind means I'm moving forward.

111   You've Got Five Minutes

It's great to have a substantial block of time set aside for practice, one that includes time to think about a goal for the day, warm up, and then get focused. But some days are just not like that.

Consider organizing your day's and week's goals[*] so that if you do encounter a little slice of time (waiting for the school bus, the egg timer, the phone to ring), you can slide on over to your instrument (instead of your computer or phone or some chore) and get productive.

To be successful using short blocks of time, you need a way to get to work quickly. Your instrument needs to be available, not in a case or needing 10 minutes to set up. You should have very clear ideas about what you're working, so you don't waste time fumfering around, remembering tune names, downloading audio files, or trying to remember what passage you had difficulty with.

---

[*] For more about setting daily and weekly goals, see 9 – Having a Plan.

If you keep a notebook, this yet another way it can be helpful. And if your notebook *wasn't* helpful, now you know how you can improve it.

Used well, even a five-minute practice period can be very rewarding. It forces you to keep the focus small and limited. It turns a little "dead" time into something productive, and hopefully leaves you with a great tune floating in your head.

Today, when I have five minutes, I'll bring out my instrument. If that turns out to be a problem, I'll make sure that next time it isn't.

112   Human Potential – A Story

Takeru Kobayashi is a world champion who redefined the sport of competitive eating. He holds several records, including eight Guinness World Records, for eating everything from hot dogs to tacos to pasta to ice cream. His story provides insight and inspiration in ideas of what we believe is possible.

In an interview,[14] Kobayashi talked about his approach to hot dog-eating contests. The first thing he did when approaching competitions was to **redefine the problem.** Previous competitors asked, "How can I eat just a little bit more?" Kobayashi asked, "How can I make one hot dog easier to eat?"

Since the goal was to eat a lot of hot dogs, and it was a requirement to eat the buns, contestants naturally ate the hot dog and bun together. Kobayashi realized that it took less time to eat the hot dog and bun separately. With some experimentation he found that if he dipped the buns in water and mashed them into a ball, he could eat them even faster. The first time he tried this technique, he *doubled* the previous competition record.

Kobayashi attributes his success to the fact that he *doesn't allow himself to be mentally limited by what is believed to be possible.* Previous eating competitors were limited themselves by thinking of the previous record as a kind of ceiling they had to push against. ***"The potential of human beings is great,"*** he said. ***"It's huge, compared to what they actually think of themselves."***

I am not advocating any type of magical thinking. I am not trying to pretend that absolutely anything is possible for anyone if we set our minds to it. What I am saying is that all of us have untapped potential that can be released by changing the way we think.

Today I won't limit my thinking to my belief in what is possible. Instead, I'll focus on how I can improve.

113   Dynamics

There is a simple way to make your playing more musical, to communicate more, and to draw the listener in to your playing. It is to focus on the use of dynamics. Dynamics help the listener organize and make sense of the music.

One way to think about dynamics is to think about how you might change the volume of short groups of notes, or phrases.[*] For example, you may want a phrase to get louder or softer toward the end. If a phrase is repeated, the second repetition might be at a different volume. As a passage goes higher, you may want to play louder, and then softer as the notes get lower. You might want to sound certain notes louder or softer to bring out a melodic idea.[†] Depending on your instrument, you may have the ability to change the dynamics in the middle of a note: letting it grow in power or fade away.

Another way to think about dynamics is to think of creating an arc for the entire tune. One tune, played a number of times, could be imagined as a story with a beginning, middle and end. What would the loudest part be within the tune? The softest? What would happen over the course of the repetitions? Do you want to build to a climax the last time through?

One way to get used to playing with dynamics is to exaggerate. Really lay on the schmaltz. Think lounge lizard, Rubenstein, Liberace, Italian love songs. Chances are what seems exaggerated to you may not sound as

---

[*] For more about phrases, see 20 – Play Better with Phrasing and 142 – Phrasing and Expression

[†] See 85 – All Notes are Not Created Equal

overdone as you think. If you want confirmation, record it both ways and listen.

A final thought: If you set out to *make every note either louder or softer than the one before it*, you're on your way to giving dynamics the importance in your playing that they deserve.

When you get used to playing this way, others will notice the change in your playing.

Today I'll use dynamics when I play.

114   The Tone Starter

I took a week-long workshop for beginning fiddlers with Andrea Larson at Ashokan Northern Week. One exercise, which we did for almost a half an hour every day, was called the *tonstarter*.[15] *Tonstarter* is Swedish for – you guessed it – tone starter.

Many of us launch into a tune without much attention to the beginning. If we're honest with ourselves, our first notes are often quite feeble. Yet the quality of even the very first note sets the listener up for *everything* they will hear. It's worth focusing some attention on how we start that first note.

In teaching aikido, I teach students about something we call "first contact." Generally, we want an attacker not to begin resisting until it's too late, until we have them in a position where their resistance is ineffective. If you start your response gently but purposefully, by the time they realize what's happening they're already compromised and off balance.

What possible relevance could this martial arts idea have for a musician? A lot, actually. We want the listener to be *drawn in* to the music from the very first. We don't want them to be distracted by feeble notes, odd sounds or scratchy strings. Once the listener is engaged and involved, once the tune has laid itself out in all its beauty, our fumbles are less disturbing.

Put It into Practice

Spend a few minutes each time you practice, for the next week or so, focusing on the very first sound you make.

- Sit calmly. Draw attention to your posture, your balance, your breathing. Set your fingers carefully and consistently.

- Play one note. Stop. What did it sound like?

- Try again. Can you be both relaxed and firm? If the note is part of a tune, does it evoke the music that's to come?

- Try four or five times until you have a fairly good result, then put it aside for tomorrow. Remember to take a quick note on what you did.

Today I'll work on making my first sound a beautiful one.

115   Time Off

There are days when all the diligent, attentive practice is too much. We all need to recharge our creative batteries occasionally, and let the fishpond of ideas and enthusiasm restock. If you need to put your instrument down for a few days or more, go ahead and do it.

It may be difficult to take time off without feeling guilt. We've all heard that, "Practice, practice, practice," is the way you get to Carnegie Hall. We may berate ourselves for lacking discipline.

If this sounds like you, keep in mind that, while discipline is important, it can be overrated. "Discipline" may not even be a helpful concept for an adult who is playing primarily for enjoyment. Why not go ahead and take time off, and use the time to remind yourself why you love playing?

When I take time off, I appreciate having more "spare time," but I also miss playing. I miss the creative expression, the physicality of playing, the ability to be immersed in the present, and the sense of accomplishment as I progress. If I were to let myself get caught up in thoughts of how I lacked discipline, it would be harder for these positive associations to surface.

If you need to take a break, give yourself full permission to do so. And, while you're at it, see if you can bring to mind the aspects of playing you miss the most. You may learn something.

Today, if I need to take time off, I'll give myself permission.

116 Smile

> Mona Lisa's smile is light, just a hint of a smile. Yet even a smile like that is enough to relax all the muscles in our face, to banish all worries and fatigue. A tiny bud of a smile on our lips nourishes awareness and calms us miraculously. It returns to us the peace we thought we had lost."
>
> — Thich Nhat Hanh[16]

While leading a pickup band for a contra dance I set up an experiment. I held up a sign with a frowny face, directing the band to frown the next time through the tune. The next time through I held up a happy face sign.

Later I asked the dancers, the band, and anyone listening whether they could hear the difference. The response was unanimous: **The band sounded better when everyone smiled.**

Happy feelings make us smile, but it works the other way, too: When we smile, we feel better. When we feel better, we play better.

Try giving your smile a little special attention today. Sit comfortably with good posture. Close your eyes. Imagine happiness filling you from the inside out. Feel the corners of your eyes lift a little, the furrow between your eyebrows releasing. Let the muscles of your jaw become soft, unclenched. Let the smile grow from your deepest being. Feel it spreading through your body, to be expressed, finally, in your face.

Spend a minute more enjoying this open-hearted lightness. When you open your eyes, see if you can bring that feeling to your practice.*

---

* A visualization exercise based on this idea is available at www.judyminot.com/bestpractice/

Today I will give my smile some special attention.

117   What Key Is It In?

This story may sound ludicrous to some players and completely familiar to others: I played trad music for several years before I had any sense of what key a tune was in, or associated the tune with the key it was played in.

I was trained as a classical pianist. As such, I learned to play comfortably in (almost) every key. Classical pieces often start in one key and wander through* several more before (usually) returning to the original key. For the most part I didn't think about it. I played the notes.

Only after learning the fiddle did I begin to understand the importance of associating the key with the tune, and being comfortable playing in that key. The patterns, finger placement, and even tuning of different keys are different enough on a fiddle to make the activity of playing in different keys quite noticeable.

Reasons to Know the Key

- You only have to focus on 7 (or maybe 8) of 12 possible notes. This helps reduce your cognitive load.

- Your fingers will be more accurate on common scale and chord patterns, especially if you practice that scale and arpeggio once in a while.

- You'll know what are the most likely chords or chord tones to play.

- If you want to provide harmony or improvise during a vocal break, just playing within the scale, or playing chord tones will get you most of the way there.

- It can help you to remember a tune, if, instead of thinking "Jerry's Beaver Hat," you can think "'Jerry's Beaver Hat'– in D, starts with a D arpeggio."

---

* Or "modulate to"

I'm sure you can think of more advantages of knowing what key you're in. Hopefully you won't wait as long as I did to make use of the information.

Today I'll begin to associate the key with the tune.

118 Stop While You Feel Good

Do you sometimes dread sitting down to practice? Maybe it's because you usually *practice until you feel bad*.

Most of us have some kind of goal or expectation for a particular day's practice. We often unintentionally set these goals a little too high. Thus, when we finish our practice session, we've seldom met our goals.[*]

Sometimes (since we're human) we're interrupted and can't practice for as long as we intended. Or maybe we think, "I'll just play until I'm tired."

One consequence of any of the above habits is that, no matter what happened *during* the practice session, we walk away with a negative overall impression. This is because the *last thing we did before we stopped was to feel bad*: tired, unfinished or dissatisfied. Instead, **stop practicing while you feel good.**

Put It into Practice

If you take steps to help end with a good feeling, you can change your entire attitude toward practicing. Here are a few ideas:

- Make your daily practice goals less ambitious.
- Shorten the length of time that you practice, so you're not physically and emotionally tired when you're done.
- Use a timer. Stop practicing when you said you would. Don't keep going until something frustrates or tires you.

---

[*] For more about setting achievable goals, see 9 – Having a Plan

- Pick up your instrument (or sit down at it) whenever you have a few minutes of free time, and play something just for fun.

- Build something really enjoyable into your practice time – like a tune you know and love. Play it at the end.

Today I'll come up with some ways to make sure I finish practice with a good feeling.

119   What's Next?

Both in practice and in my daily life, a lot of my attention is focused on trying to stay mentally *present*. It's easy to say this, but of course we constantly slip into preoccupation about the past and the future.

My Achilles heel is thinking about the future. When I'm doing something, I often realize I'm thinking about what I'll do next. I think all day about how I can't wait to be practicing. Then while I'm practicing, I think about all the other things I could be doing instead.

Put It into Practice

When you become aware that you're thinking about what you'll do *next*, instead of what you're doing *now*, these techniques can help you *become more present again:*[*]

- Pause. Take a deep breath.

- Draw your attention to your body and how it feels. Take another breath.

- Improve your posture. Sit up straight, lengthen your back and neck. Find your physical center of balance or *one point*.[†] Imagine it radiating energy. Take another breath.

---

[*] Of course, the same techniques will work if you tend to think about what you just did, too.

[†] More about finding your center in 47 – Keep One Point.

- Relax some part of your body that feels tense. Take another breath.

- Say to yourself, "I *am* practicing."

Today I'll take steps to stay more present as I play.

120   What's on the Technology Menu?

Everyone has a different level of comfort with computers, mobile devices, the Internet and technology in general. You may think of technology as fun, a time sink, a challenge, or a daunting, fearsome monster. Yet there's no denying that technology can be a powerful tool for musicians.

One issue we all have is that there are so many options. It can be difficult to know where to start or when to stop. I approach my use of technology for music the way a New Yorker friend taught me to look at a 15-page deli menu. "Instead of browsing the entire menu," he said, "shut your eyes and *decide what you want to eat*. Then open the menu and find the closest thing to that."

Starting with a decision about *what you want to do* and *what you need the most* can help you be more efficient in using the options available through technology. If you can think this way, you may end up spending fewer hours browsing the Internet. Or you may decide it's worth buying a new, fancy recording device or getting help with an app you've hesitated to try.

Today I'll consider how I can use technology more effectively, beginning with asking myself what I want and need it for.

121   Playing Fast and Slow

A very productive way to practice a tune or section of a tune is to alternate playing fast and slow.

I'm an advocate of playing slowly – more slowly than we usually do – to help deepen the mental connection between the sound we want to hear and the physicality of playing. Yet it's possible to get so used to playing slowly that it's a struggle to play faster. Or we may be used to playing fast-but-sloppy that we have difficulty even hearing or our mistakes.

Put It into Practice

Use your metronome for this exercise.

- Play a passage slowly enough that you get it more or less right and in time, without slowing down for mistakes. Make a note of the metronome speed.

- Increase the speed to one that's just barely possible for you. It should be fast enough that you make mistakes, but you don't crash and burn. Make a note of this metronome speed.

- Play the passage at the fast speed a few times. Hopefully you'll start to "get" a few more of the notes. See if you can try to relax your body a little and feel a little of the "groove" at this speed. At the same time, try to get a few more notes consistently correct. Don't expect to get it perfect, just aim for comfort and a little improvement.

- Now go back to the slow speed. Bring to bear all your ability to be musical, rhythmic and accurate. Note how much more relaxed you feel. Pay attention to all these aspects with as much focus as you can.

- Alternate between fast and slow. You can do this in any way that makes sense for you: One time through for each speed? A few minutes at each speed? It's up to you.

You don't have to do this exercise for longer than five or ten minutes. You can make it part of your regular practice, or just use it when you think it would help what you're working on.

There are many benefits to playing fast and slow. It can help you transfer the way you feel when playing slowly to playing fast, bringing more musicality to your faster playing. It can expose things you're doing at one or the other speed that you may want to change. Finally, it can help you become more comfortable playing a tune faster (or slower) than you're used to playing it.

Today I'll try alternating fast and slow.

122   What You Have

We all want to improve. That is why we're involved in this endeavor. Unfortunately, in the process of trying to improve we spend a lot of time thinking about what we don't do well. When other musicians have talents or skills that seem beyond our reach, it can leave us feeling even more bereft.

If you've realized that someone else's ability is making you feel diminished, take a moment to focus on the capabilities you do have. Are you good at sight-reading? Picking up tunes by ear? Finding the chords? Memorizing? Writing lyrics? Creating harmonies? Picking up new instruments? Keeping the beat? Do you learn slowly but retain what you learn? Are you good at articulating ideas to others? Do you have persistence? Organization? Maybe your tone is poor (so far) but you have great musicality.

When something comes easily to us, we tend to undervalue it. This is true of everyone, even (especially) very talented, experienced, accomplished musicians. To balance out that thinking requires a bit of effort and attention, to point out to ourselves that there are things we don't have to work so hard at.

Why go through this process? When we feel good about ourselves, we learn and remember better, we're more easily inspired to play and practice, and we may even sound better.

Today, if I find I'm comparing myself to others, I'll remind myself of a few things I'm good at.

123   Mute

An important element of mastery is what I call *knowing*.* The *knowing* I refer to is primarily non-verbal. It's not rote learning, like, "The key of A has three sharps," or, "A half-diminished chord is a diminished triad with a dominant seventh added." The *knowing* I refer to is the result of deeply

---

* See 78 – Playing and Knowing

exploring an idea, sound, tune or technique, combining your physical senses and your mental faculties.

One way to better *know* what you're playing is to practice playing without making sound. It can be a great technique to use when you're ironing out a trouble spot.

Put It into Practice

There are various ways to practice without sound. Some are more appropriate for certain instruments. With a little experimentation you can find a method that works for you.

- Work on one hand at a time. Where do your fingers need to be on the fingerboard/fretboard? Once you're sure of that, work on the other hand: Which strings or keys will sound and in what order?[*]

- Move your hands and fingers to the position for the next note or chord. Stop. Look. Is this the place you want them to be?

- Close your eyes. Hear the tune in your mind and visualize the hand shapes or finger positions. Where do you get tripped up?

- Violinists are fond of "air bowing": moving the bow, nowhere near the strings, in the rhythm of the bow strokes. You may be able to do "air fingering" or "air bellowing" on your instrument.

You'll quickly find that the aspects of the music that you *really know* become a foundation for better, richer playing and faster learning in future.

Today I'll try playing without making sound.

---

[*] More about playing one hand at a time at 43 – Left Hand – Right Hand

124   Making a List

I noticed a friend quietly consulting a piece of paper at an Irish music session and asked him about it. He had a list of tunes: four sheets, printed front and back, tightly spaced, sorted by style, with tune name, key, and the letter names of the first few notes.

When I first started attending Irish sessions, I brought a list of the tunes I knew, so that if I was asked to start a tune or a set I'd be able to remember the tunes. I had assumed that was a "beginner thing to do." Yet my friend is a consummate fiddler, steeped in the Irish tradition from childhood.[*]

This experience gave me "permission" to write a list of the tunes I know, to have on hand at home. That was eight years ago. I now have lists of tunes for various styles and instruments, as well as (the endless list of) tunes I want to learn.

It would be nice to think you could remember every tune you ever learned, but let's face it, since the invention of the printing press our memory skills have atrophied as a culture. Online search engines have only accelerated that process.

There are plenty of benefits to keeping a tune list:

1. It's necessary if you want to use spaced repetition to remember tunes.[†]

2. When you get together to play with someone, or you actually get some kind of gig, you can quickly go through your list(s) to compare what you both know, or pull up what you've been working on recently that you love.

3. It's *such* a good feeling to see *all those tunes* that you actually know (or at least, that you learned once).

Store your tune list as index cards, a spreadsheet or in a notebook. Write it by hand, with a computer, or in an app. Organize it, sort it, put in lots of detail or a little. Keep it up to date, leave it in a pile and forget about it

---

[*] It is important, if you bring a list of tunes you know to a jam session, to consult them in such a way as not to disrupt the pace of the session.

[†] See 109 – Spaced Repetition

– it doesn't matter. A tune list can help you whether you use it every day or not.

Today I'll make a list of the tunes I know.

125   Six Human Needs

Life coach Tony Robbins lists six human needs we all seek. Whether or not this is *the* definitive list, it's an elegant way to think about what drives and motivates us.

- *Certainty:* We all seek some assurance in how things will be, as well as assurance that we'll be able to get what we want and avoid what we don't want.
- *Variety:* Paradoxically, while we all want to know what to expect, we also need the stimulation of unexpected and new things and ideas.
- *Significance:* We want to feel like we're special, important, needed or noticed.
- *Connection:* We seek a feeling of closeness or union, usually with people, but perhaps with a cause or group.
- *Growth:* We're more fulfilled when we feel we're expanding in our knowledge, ability and understanding.
- *Contribution:* We all share a need to help, give, and to support others.

It can be interesting to consider this list in the light of your musical goals, and what motivates you to continue playing and practicing. If your practice isn't bringing you joy, if you're feeling kind of "flat," is there anything in this list that can inform you? Are you getting what you need in each of these areas?

You may feel a stronger connection with some areas than others. You may change your mind about what's important the next time you look at the list. Or you may want to substitute your own ideas.

Today I'll ask myself which basic human needs are satisfied by my practice.

126   Rhythmic Precision

Have you ever thought about being more precise with your rhythm? I mean *super, super precise*. It's a good thing to work on. Practicing rhythmic precision can help you develop fine motor control in your fingers, leading to more accuracy and control. This can be a big benefit, especially when you want to play fast. A habit of playing with rhythmic precision will also help you achieve a more "tight" sound when playing in a group.

Here some ideas to help you develop precision. Make a choice that works for your instrument, your playing level and your inclination.

Put It into Practice

> A metronome will keep you honest and give you a benchmark to return to tomorrow.
>
> Try to land your notes right in the center of the metronome's "click."
>
> - Isolate a short passage that has even notes. Play it at a slow speed. Stop, and play it again at a speed that pushes your ability to be precise. Switch back and forth. If you can't stay right on the beat at the faster speed, slow down the faster speed by 10%. Keep in mind that it can be as hard to be precise at a slow speed as a fast one, we just don't always notice it.
>
> - Play the passage as a dotted rhythm (long-short, long-short). Switch to short-long, short-long. Then play the passage evenly. Doing this just a few times can help even up your playing.
>
> - Put heavy emphasis on the first of every two eighth notes in the passage. Switch to putting emphasis on the second note. Try to play them all evenly. Switch back and forth.
>
> - Find a passage with triplets, or make one up. Play the triplets as evenly as possible while listening to the metronome. You will be playing three notes while the metronome clicks either once or twice (depending on the type of triplet). Add in some eighth notes before and after the triplet so that you're switching from straight eighths to triplets.

- Find a phrase that ends with a long note. Using the metronome, work on letting that long note have its full value.

- Choose an unusual or new (to you) rhythm from the music you're playing. Isolate that section and work for as much precision as you can.

Certain factors make it difficult to maintain precise rhythm, including increasing speed, difficult fingering, using the ring and pinkie fingers and string crossings. Stay alert for these. When you find them, isolate them and work on them with the metronome – slow and fast, dotted and even, varying the emphasis, or even as triplets.

If there's a technical issue complicating your ability to get a rhythm correct, try simplifying. Play the rhythm on open strings, slower, or more basic rhythm. Switch back and forth between the simplified and the "preferred" way of playing. This can help you get the rhythm into your ear, making it easier to execute it despite the challenge.

It can take an unusual degree of focus to listen for rhythmic precision. It can also be challenging to screen out unrelated issues: intonation, wrong notes, or anything else that may bother you about what you hear. Try to let those aspects slide, just for now.

Working on an exercise like this occasionally can really improve your accuracy and control. It doesn't take long at all to have an effect.

Today I'll try an exercise in rhythmic precision.

127   Embodying the Tune

What would happen if you played one tune for, say, 45 minutes? It's a challenging idea. Forty-five minutes is a ***lot*** of times through a tune that takes 45 seconds to a minute to play.

It is interesting to see what happens as you play far beyond your usual number of repetitions, "blowing through" things that might normally cause you to stop. After a time, you may not have to focus much attention on playing the notes. You might find yourself "zooming out," getting a drone's eye view of how it feels to play. You may notice that you're holding your instrument in a death grip, or recognize exactly when you tense your left shoulder. You may realize that crossing your legs isn't actually comfortable.

Finally, you may be able to give yourself fully and wholly to the tune. Just play it. This is a difficult process to describe, but when it happens, anyone listening will notice the difference. Hopefully it will feel different to you as well.

You may actually reach that point and pass through it, finding that the tune has lost its charm. Try to keep playing and see what happens.

Put It into Practice:

- Consider using a metronome to keep you at an even pace. It's natural to speed up after you start getting more comfortable and fluent.
- If you do decide to speed up, make it a decision, not an accident. And don't make that a goal of this exercise, as in, "I'll play this 100 times until I can play it faster."
- ***Don't play with pain.*** Notice stress before it becomes pain. If you can't relax or change your position so that it goes away, switch to a tune that's not painful, or do this on a different day.
- Be kind to your body. Take a break every 15 or 20 minutes.

This should be a fun practice that can help *all* your playing.

Today I'll try playing one tune for a long time.

128 Wu (Weight Underside)

I've long been familiar with a concept that in aikido we call *weight underside*. I stumbled almost accidentally on its benefits in playing music.

Talking to a violin teacher about my frustration with poor tone, she asked me to play a tune through twice. The second time through, I used *weight underside*. "I don't know what you did differently the second time," she said, "But if you're looking for better tone, *do that*."

Here's an exercise to help you get the feeling of *weight underside.*

Put It into Practice

- Sit comfortably.

- Pick up your instrument.*

- Choose a simple tune or phrase, and start to play. You want to be active enough that it takes some attention, but be able to reserve some focus for the exercise.

- Draw your attention to the front of your shoulders, your upper arms, and back. Where is the tension? Chances are you're tightening the front of the shoulders and the tops of your arms, curling your body forward and bearing down with your arms.

- Keep playing, but imagine someone had their hand in the middle of your back, near the base of your shoulder blades. Imagine them pushing gently forward and a tiny bit up. Settle into that imaginary hand. Do you feel your front shoulders and the tops of your arms relax?

- Now imagine a little more heaviness in the bottoms of your arms. Explore this feeling a little by trying some different visual ideas. Imagine you're taking a hot shower and it's pouring over your shoulders and back. Relax into that. Relax your arms, shoulders and upper back as much as you can and still hold your instrument. Now imagine you're holding something heavy in your arms, like an armful of wood or books. Gravity is pulling your arms down and you are just keeping the wood from falling. Do you feel different muscles come into play?

- You may stop playing without realizing it, as you try to get used to this novel feeling. Try to keep the feeling as you start to play again.

---

* If your instrument is particularly heavy (e.g. a 35 lb. accordion), make sure it's well-supported, or choose a lighter instrument for this exercise if you have one.

Exploring this idea can help you subtly relax muscles that are not needed to play. This can reduce fatigue, increase your comfort while playing, and make it easier to play accurately and even faster.

Today I'll try to get the feeling of weight underside.

129 Everyone Is My Teacher

One afternoon in a seminar, a high-ranking aikido instructor confounded me by saying, "I consider everyone to be my teacher. Not just the people who instructed me, but my own students. Even my beginning students."

What did a seventh-degree black belt, with 35 years of experience, have to learn from a beginner?

I wrestled with this idea. I realized that most of the time, whether I was being officially "taught" or getting informal advice from another student, I was *labeling* that instruction with either a thumbs-up or a thumbs-down. My decision on whether to listen or ignore what I heard was based various things, some rational, others not so rational:

- what I thought of that person's aikido practice
- whether I liked them personally
- whether they had more experience than I did
- who their teacher was, etc.

As a result, I essentially ignored input from anyone but a select few teachers and students.

After hearing this chance comment, I began *to seek actively to find something to learn from every single encounter.* My practice changed enormously as a result. Even if all I learned was, "I don't think that will work for me," I opened my mind to new ideas instead of trying to find ways to shut them out.

This is a mental habit I have brought to bear in my music practice. I try to learn from every interaction, *actively seeking out something to take back to my practice space.* Because of this attitude, I've learned extremely helpful concepts, sometimes from quite unexpected people. I've become a better listener, and I've found myself enjoying musical gatherings far more.

Whether or not we have a formal teacher, we all benefit from opening our ears, hearts, and minds to learning from everyone around us. It can take energy at first. At the same time, it helps us develop better insight and discernment and opens up a world of creative input and inspiration.

Today I'll start regarding everyone as my teacher.

130   The Dotted Quarter Swap

In a workshop with Kevin Burke we explored simple ways to vary a tune. Once you get the hang of this you can use the technique in other tunes.

Find a jig that has at least one pause in the rhythm, i.e. one note that lasts for three of the six beats in a measure: a dotted quarter note.

"The Rose in the Heather" is an Irish jig that offers a good example. Here's the sheet music of the beginning of the jig as it's often written and played:

The Rose in the Heather

Traditional (Ireland)

The very first note in the jig is a dotted quarter note – its rhythmic value is three eighth notes. The squiggly line above it means that this long note is often ornamented with a long roll.

But there's no rule that says you have to use that ornament at all.

In that three-beat space you can choose what to play from among many options. Here are a few:

- Just the dotted quarter note (no ornament)
- The same note three times

- The note, the note above, and the note again
- The note, the note below, and the note again
- The note, the note two notes above, and the note again
- The note, the note two notes below, and the note again
- The note repeated twice in a loping, dotted rhythm (quarter note and eighth note)
- The note three times, in a long-short-short rhythm (quarter note and two sixteenth notes)
- The note and a triplet: three notes taking the place of the second two beats

Here are all the above ideas written out for the first measure of the jig:

Except perhaps for the triplet, none of these variations requires any new technical ability to play. It can take practice, however, to get used to playing something you're not used to.

Play through these variations. You may not like the way they all sound *in this tune*. In another tune, who knows?

You can try the dotted quarter swap for any tune where you find one longer note. You can even try swapping out *any three notes* in a jig with one of these variations. Sometimes you'll like it, sometimes you won't.

Put It into Practice

- Choose a jig you're familiar with that has at least one longer note (dotted quarter note) – or use "The Rose in the Heather."
- Swap *one* of the variations above for the longer note.

- Practice a snippet of the tune with the variation. You may want to include a few measures before and/or a few measures after.

- Go back to playing it the way you're used to playing it.

- Now make a loop of your snippet and alternate between your "normal" way and the variation.

- Try a second variation. Play it a few times on its own. Make a loop and alternate the second variation with your "normal way."

- Add complexity if you wish, looping them however makes sense to you, for example:

  A – B – A – C
  A – B – C – A – B – C

- Making it challenging is OK, but don't make it so hard that it's impossible or frustrating.

After you're comfortable with adding these variations to jigs, you may be able to work out how to incorporate the same idea into tunes with other rhythms, like reels and waltzes.

Working on the dotted quarter swap will help improve your playing flexibility. It will also make it easier to incorporate variations into your playing.

Today I'll try the dotted quarter swap and see if I can work it into my playing.

131 Playing with Distractions

I once had a doctor, I'll call him Dr. Paul, who, early in his adult life, had been a concert pianist. I asked him why he changed careers.

According to Dr. Paul, he began his professional music career playing small recital halls, mostly in Europe. During one of these concerts an audience member arrived late. Hearing the door open, Paul looked up momentarily. When he returned his attention to the music he had completely lost his place. He barely rescued the performance but he was severely shaken. Within a few weeks he had decided to abandon his musical career and enroll in medical school.

I think about this story sometimes when I play Irish sessions in pubs. Playing in these conditions has really helped me get used to "imperfect" performance conditions. We're continually jostled as we play. Someone walks into the bar, bringing in a blast of Arctic air. The waitress asks me if I'll have my usual (not just while I'm playing – while I'm singing!), expecting an answer. An argument erupts near the toilets and I wonder how serious it's going to get.

Don't let distractions cannonball your playing.

Put It into Practice

> It's nice to have the confidence that your playing will stay rock solid, even if something unexpected happens. Here are some ideas to try at home, under more controlled circumstances.
>
> - Change your gaze. Look at the hand you don't usually look at. Look up. Focus out the window and then back at your hand. Move your head left and then right. Changing where you look can be very destabilizing to your mental focus.
>
> - When there's a space or long note, take your hand(s) off the strings, keys, frets. Way off – lift it/them in the air. How about scratching your nose with one hand and find the right hand position again?
>
> - Play a wrong note on purpose and then get back to the right one without breaking rhythm. Or just play the same note a few times, or play nothing for a measure, and then come back to the melody without a hitch.
>
> - Talk. Just start with a word or two. Even being able to say "Hi!" can be pretty hard at first. Sometimes I try to name the notes or chords out loud, or try to sing, "Up bow, down bow."

I'm not advocating that you do this in order to be able to play without being engaged in your playing. The idea is to be able to keep centered in your playing even while barraged with other sensory input. Is this a necessary skill? No. Maybe it's just a fun thing to try on a rainy day, or a party trick. Who knows? It may even come in handy some time.

Today I'll explore the idea of keeping my focus despite distractions.

132 Accepting Limitations

> "You must accept the fact that you are capable in some directions and limited in others, and you must develop your capabilities."
>
> – Bruce Lee[17]

All of us have a physical body and a mind which, essentially, limit us. We are all individuals. You may have longer or shorter arms, fat or skinny fingers. You may be 32 with rheumatoid arthritis or 67 with ADHD. Sometimes we attach a great deal of importance to the way these issues affect our playing. (Usually we focus on the negative aspects.)

There are some things about the physicality of playing that we can change and others that we can't. If we want to become better musicians, we're better off if we can be clear-eyed about our capabilities and our limitations, rather than spending time wishing they were otherwise.

If I could stretch my fingers to reach a tenth on the piano, many, *many* playing options would be open to me. I *could* wish it were otherwise. I *could* devote extra practice time trying to do something that, in reality, I will never be able to do. I serve myself better by accepting my limitation in this area, and by looking to the capabilities I do have and developing them.

We can all name influential musicians who have inspired us despite their having serious physical challenges. For every one of these musicians there are dozens, even hundreds more who face limitations that you or I are not aware of. These artists have found ways to accept those physical limitations and develop their capabilities.

Today I'll try to accept my limitations and work on developing my capabilities.

133 Practice "Upside Down"

Let's say you're working on a tune you learned a few days ago. Chances are, when you start practicing the tune, you start at the beginning.

*What if you **didn't** start at the beginning?* What if you started practicing on the B part, or the challenging part, or the bridge, or the last thing you worked on?

Many tunes start out simply, and build. In the process, there's often an element introduced that's unusual, tricky, or that only happens once.

If you always start practicing at the beginning, it's likely you'll get stuck there. You'll find something to work on and get involved in that. By the time you get to the later part of the tune you'll have expended focus and energy and may not have much left for the hardest or most unusual part of the tune.

If, instead, you start with the trickiest or most unusual element of the tune, you'll become more familiar and comfortable with it. You'll be setting yourself up to approach that section with equanimity *whenever* you play the tune.

Put It into Practice

> Stop practicing tunes from the beginning! Practice "upside down": Practice the B part first. If you know what the trickiest part is, go right to that part first.
>
> If your goal is to spend more time practicing the complex parts of the tune, you have to be able to identify those parts clearly and quickly. Keep notes. Use a highlighter on sheet music. If you don't use sheet music, find some way to get yourself right to the good stuff.

There's no rule that says we have to practice a tune in any particular order, so why not practice it in the order that's most efficient for learning? An advantage of practicing the tune "upside down" is that it can help us stay more engaged and focused.

Today I'll practice "upside down," and dig right in to the trickiest part of a tune.

134 Free Play

In the process of learning to improvise, I started doing something I call *free play*.

For 2-5 minutes, I play whatever comes to mind. I try to have absolutely no restrictions: no preconceived idea of format, rhythm, style or structure. I don't try to "write a tune." I don't try to stay in a particular key, be "compositional," or even "sound good." I leave behind any and all thoughts of judgment or criticism. I sometimes record what I'm doing, but only if I'm sure that won't inhibit me: This is not for posterity.

I set a timer. At first, even two minutes seemed like a long time. Now, a year or more later, the timer is usually a reminder for me to stop.

In practicing *free play*, **I reawaken a deeply-held belief in my own ability to create music.** Freed of the requirement to be "correct," I can be completely present. It doesn't matter what I just did since I'm not saving or preserving it. It doesn't matter what I'm about to do because it's not going to be wrong. I just listen. What music do I give life to today?

Another thing that happens when I engage in *free play* is that **I improve my ability to translate the sounds I imagine to my fingers and my instrument.** This is an essential part of developing mastery. We'll *always* play more evocatively if we play what we *hear*, rather than playing what we *see on a page*, or what we *think we're supposed to play*.

Many musicians are quite fearful when they think about playing something that is not written down. They may be afraid of playing the wrong notes, getting the rhythm wrong, forgetting a repeat, or clutching the whole tune. With *free play*, there's nothing to forget and nothing to remember. Just play.

If you're hesitant of your ability to play what's in your head, simplify. Start with just a few notes. Even if you only play two or three notes, you can use rhythms and patterns to create interesting music. Some drummers have only one drum that has two sounds, yet they manage to get a lot out of those two sounds!

You may have realized that *free play* is a form of improvisation. I don't want to scare anyone who thinks they can't improvise. Don't let your playing be constrained by any ideas of what you think improvisation is or isn't, or whether "improvisation" fits into your style of playing. This is not about style. It's about creativity and about making music.

Today I'll try free play.

135   Heuristics

In the language of psychology, a "heuristic" is a mental shortcut that we use to make decisions and take action. We might have a heuristic that leads us to be afraid of big dogs or to assume that people who look a certain way can be trusted. Once we've formed a heuristic, it functions, for the most part, without our conscious awareness. Most of our heuristics are extremely useful. In fact, heuristics allow us to function in daily life without subjecting every bit of cognitive input to a lengthy analysis.

Our brains are continually creating new heuristics in response to situations we encounter and adjusting or downgrading existing ones. One way of thinking about musical practice is as ***a process of constructing heuristics that are helpful, and dismantling or deconstructing those that are not helpful.***

When you encounter a sticky challenge, a mistaken "groove" you can't seem to get out of, it's natural to attempt to solve the problem through repetition. However, if you suspect there's a heuristic in play, repetition may reinforce the problem. You'll need to use some other tools.

Put It into Practice

> Addressing a mental shortcut we want to reroute requires giving the problem lots of cognitive attention. There's no "one-size-fits-all" solution. We need to approach the issue with focus, looking at it in multiple ways. It can help to take a section down to its component parts and put it together again step by step, or try practicing it in a novel way to shake up our notions about it.
>
> There are techniques described other sections of this book that you can bring to bear. These include playing very slowly, playing in

different rhythms, using all your senses, singing, playing without making a sound and visualization.*

Unpacking the brain's "stored notions" about a section of music or a habit can require lateral thinking, or thinking "outside the box." Consider this example from my own playing:

I had a problem with certain passages on the violin. My teacher noticed that when I switched to the E string (the highest string) I was tilting the bow much more than necessary. As a beginning fiddler I had trouble controlling my bow to keep it from sounding more than one string. Because the E string is the highest string, I could tilt the bow a lot, knowing I wouldn't hit another string. I realized I had a non-verbalized association of "E string" with "safe zone." Because I was less precise (in other words, sloppy) in my bow position, I had trouble building speed and efficiency.

Once I unpacked all this I was able to create a new heuristic, deliberately working on the physical feeling of a more efficient bow angle.

The next time you find yourself repeating a mistake and you can't seem to resolve it, try teasing apart the tangled mental map you've made about that passage or issue. If you can discover the heuristic that's not helping you, you can work to recode it.

Today I'll see if I can dismantle a heuristic that is not helping, and construct a new one that does.

136   Habit vs. Willpower

Sometimes the hardest part of practicing is just sitting down. There are days when you just don't feel like it, when you're not feeling the love. You come up with 100 reasons why you shouldn't practice today. Days like this are the reason it's important to make practice a habit.

Habit is the lack of need for willpower.

---

* Here are a few: 15 – Please Explain That More Slowly; 78 – Playing and Knowing; 87 – Engage Your Senses; 90 – Visualization; 121 – Playing Fast and Slow; 123 – Mute

Willpower requires effort. Willpower typically involves stopping something that is enjoyable, or something you're already in the habit of doing, to do something different.

When something is a habit, your need to make decisions is reduced to almost nothing. You don't need to decide whether or not to do it, or what exactly to do or how to start. If you have a routine, and stick to your routine, you'll conserve your mental energy for practicing, instead of using it up deciding whether and when to practice.

To achieve the goals we seek, it's vital to build the right habits. Willpower may be required at certain times, but habit is also a powerful asset for continued success.

Today, instead of berating myself for lack of willpower, I'll work to build a habit.

137   Fly Blind

What happens when you close your eyes as you practice?

From Turlough O'Carolan to Blind Lemon Jefferson, the image of the blind musician has an almost mythic quality in traditional music. There are probably good reasons for this. According to Oliver Sacks, systematic studies of children who were blind from birth have shown that they're more likely to have exceptional musical ability and are more likely to have perfect pitch.[18]

A third or more of the cerebral cortex is devoted to vision. Most of us use our eyes when we play: to check the alignment of the bow, to see where the chords will fall. Even when we play an instrument where we rely on touch, if our eyes are open, the visual cortex is engaged.

For some musicians, closing the eyes is very calming. Others are so flummoxed by not being able to see their hands, it becomes much harder to play. Still others find they're more liable to daydream and lose focus.

For me, the difference is striking. When I close my eyes as I play, I immediately have a more intense listening experience and am more aware of the subtleties in the sound I'm making.

Since this seems like an advantage, I often make a point of closing my eyes to play. When I run into a problem or have a random thought, my eyes often pop open. For a few months I tried using a sleep mask. Eventually, however, I found that even gazing into the distance was enough to remind me to listen more and look less.

Today I'll try flying blind.

138 Set Yourself Up for Success

If you're in a situation where you want to sound good, it's important to set yourself up for success. Here's an example:

> I go to a jam session I've never attended. When it's my turn to choose a tune, I pick one I've been working on. It's kind of hard (and a bit impressive, I hope!). I'm a little nervous, so I start it a smidge too fast. About five notes in, I realize I'm just not happy with my playing. In the end, I even if I don't totally crash and burn, I don't play as well as I know I can. I go home feeling kind of crappy. I'm not even sure I'll go back to that session.

What if I'd done this instead?

> Someone asks me to start a tune. After listening to what the group is playing, I pick a tune I'm pretty sure everyone knows. I start it at a pace that everyone can play. They all join in. There's a reason everyone knows it: It's a good tune. I play well, they play well. Everyone feels good about themselves and about me, including me. I go home and mark my calendar for the next session.

It's important to challenge yourself, of course. In this case the challenge is *playing in a new situation, for a group of people I don't know.* There's no need to pile on more difficulty than that.

Set yourself up for success. No matter whether you're playing in public or for your best friend: Choose a simpler tune, or a simpler version. Take a moment to remind yourself of the tune and any tricky spots. Put both feet on the floor. Start at a slower speed than your gut tells you. Make things as easy for yourself as you can.

Today I'll remember to set myself up for success.

139   Timed Modules

I want to learn so many things, yet there are only 24 hours in a day. I want to become a better singer, develop better violin tone, improve my *podorhythmie*, learn one new tune a week, practice for my band, and compose new tunes.

In theory, every day I could spend half an hour on each of these six things. I'd get everything done in three hours. OK. I'll do that every day. [Right!] But then I have a dentist appointment. I have to shovel the driveway. My spouse wants to go out for dinner.

Practice modules can help you move forward on multiple parallel goals, even though you have limited time to do it. If you already organize your practice time in 20-minute intervals,* integrating this idea will be easy.

Put It into Practice

- Make a list of the things you want to work on.
- Assign each a certain amount of practice time, and a priority.
- Every day, work on one, two or three or more of the modules, depending on how much time you have and how you've prioritized them.

At the end of your practice time instead of being left with a vague feeling that you didn't do enough, you'll know that you took one, two, or even more separate steps toward your goal.

These modules can be useful for those of us who can't allot the same amount of time to practice every day. Let's say you coach soccer on Wednesdays, but Friday is always completely open. You can do one module on Wednesday and four or five on Friday. Every time you sit down, you'll know exactly what to work on.

---

* See 21 – The 20-Minute Interval

You can make a list, or you could be more organized and plot your modules on a calendar. That's up to you. Of course, you can always ignore today's program and just sit down and play! But knowing what you're working toward and how you're going to get there will make practicing simpler and more rewarding.

Today I'll try setting up timed modules, so I can work on a few each day.

140   Your Inner Critic

When you hear that little voice, ("You're never going to…", "You should have…", "If only you had…",) first, remind yourself that the voice you hear is *not you.* Next, see if you already have a mental picture of the person who's giving this "advice." Finally, imagine that person as *someone you control, not someone who controls you.*

You can tell your inner critic, "Thank you for your input, I've got this one. Why don't you go for a walk and come back in about an hour?"

You can imagine your critic looking ridiculous. The sillier, the better. Put her in a funny costume. Imagine him naked in a business meeting. Shrink her into a mouse or a squawking blue jay.

Today when I hear my inner critic, I'll transform it into something that I control, not something that controls me.

141   Tensegrity

Tensegrity is a word coined by architect R. Buckminster Fuller to express the idea of "tensional integrity." In a tensegrity system there are two types of "building blocks":

- **Rigid elements** (like a piece of wood, iron bar)

    and

- **Non-rigid elements** (like a piece of string, a rubber band, cloth, a length of chain) that are under tension

The resulting structure is stable, but overall, it's able to move in response to stress and change.

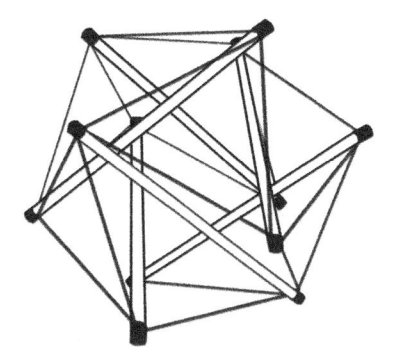

This sounds complex until you "get a visual." The image I often call to mind is called a *tensegrity icosahedron*. You may have seen one, it's a popular kids' toy. There are six dowels with slots in the ends, arranged in a spherical shape and connected by rubber bands. The dowels don't touch anywhere.

The tension between the dowels and the rubber bands creates a balanced structure. When you push down in one area, the rubber bands in other areas adjust. All the dowels move into a different alignment. The structure may look stable, but some of the rubber bands have more tension than others. When you let go, the figure springs back into balance.

The muscular-skeletal system is often described as a "biotensegrity" system. The rigid elements are the bones, and the non-rigid elements are the muscles and connective tissues. We usually think of our bodies as being bones stacked like blocks ("The thigh bone's connected to the hip bone…") but in a healthy system, our bones don't actually touch.

According to the principle of biotensegrity, the entire system of bones and connective tissue is interrelated. A problem in one area – tightness, chronic contraction, scar tissue – can pull the entire system out of alignment.

To play at our best, we should do what we can to optimize this biotensegrity system (the body), so it will provide support, flexibility and responsiveness.

Start by considering your posture. Instead of imagining yourself settling, with your bones like stacked bricks and your muscles slack, think of your muscles and connective tissue being in alignment, with the muscles engaged just enough to provide stability without rigidity.

Scan your body for particular areas of tension or for anything out of alignment: a cocked hip, habitually slumped shoulders, crossed legs. Remember the tensegrity icosahedron: Too much tension in one area can pull the whole system out of whack. What can you do to bring it back into balance?

Today I'll think about my body as a biotensegrity system. What can I do to bring that system into better balance so it will support my playing?

142 Phrasing and Expression

Even when we're able to hear the phrases in a tune, we usually don't do enough to *express them in our playing*.*

There are some things that take a while to get good at. There are others, like expressing the tune's phrasing, that we can accomplish quite quickly. The challenge for the second group is in doing it consistently and habitually.

Bringing out a tune's phrasing is a habit that you can develop. One thing that can help is to provide your brain with clear *examples of the difference between expressing phrasing and not doing so*. Think of your mind as a rather stubborn student who is refusing to give up their favorite way of doing something. You need to make this lesson very obvious in order to awaken in your "student" the desire to change.

Put It into Practice

- Sing the tune (or a section) out loud. As you do, clearly note to yourself where the phrases are, and particularly where you naturally took a breath. Singing is useful because we don't (usually) worry about the technicalities of making the music happen.

- Sing again, this time completely exaggerating the phrasing you chose. Take big pauses at the end of each phrase. Ham it up.

- Sing it again with the phrasing completely "wrong." *Try as hard as you can to mess it up*. Imagine someone reading a poem who put all the punctuation in the wrong place.

---

* For more on hearing phrases, see 20 – Play Better with Phrasing

- Sing the tune again, with absolutely no phrasing, as if a computer were playing back the notes.

- Go through the same exercise, this time playing the tune instead of singing. Play your "natural" phrasing, then exaggerate. Play it completely wrong and then play with no phrasing at all. See if you can stay focused on the expression of feeling, and not get caught up in technical issues.

- Come back to what you think of as your "natural" phrasing and emphasis. Little by little, start to incorporate more emphasis and expression into your playing of the tune. Think about your very exaggerated version and try to "dial that in" bit by bit. At what point is it too much? This is a personal choice, but many musicians find they can incorporate far more expression than they realized.

This type of experimenting is excellent training for your ear, and also helps you get better at making each tune "your own."

Today I'll play with phrasing and expression.

143 Sooner, Not Faster

One way to approach playing faster is to stop trying to play faster. Instead, focus on moving sooner.

To get your fingers where they need to be on time, they have to start moving sooner than you're probably used to.

Put It into Practice

An important element of "sooner, not faster" is *really knowing* the music.[*] If we know where we're going, the mind can chart the most efficient route on its own.

---

[*] See 78 – Playing and Knowing

The second element is *training ourselves to think ahead*.* Especially when we know something big is coming up (a hand position jump, a bellows change, a string crossing), we can't be ready to move there if we're not ready.

The final element is to move. Just be ready to move – not quickly, but without hesitation.

Once you know the music, work on building speed by moving your fingers – not faster, but sooner. You're likely to notice the difference immediately. You may feel less rushed and overburdened, or even less tense and fearful. Moving sooner, not faster, can also allow you to focus on the sound rather than the technicality of playing.

Today I'll think about playing sooner, not faster.

144   How Good *Am* I?

We spend more time than we'd like to admit wondering, "How good am I?" "Am I good enough?" "Am I better than ____? Better than I used to be?"

Consider that when a musician, or any artist, asks herself, "How good am I?" we often come up with an answer that's skewed by our own perceptions. I spend a lot of time focused on fine details of my playing. A listener, on the other hand, responds to the overall arc of the music. For that reason, I'm really not the best judge of whether I'm "good."

Here are some questions that may be more useful to consider:

- How good do you want to be?
- How good do you feel you need to be in order to enjoy playing?
- Do you enjoy playing now? Do you want to enjoy playing more than you do?

---

* See 62 – Thinking Ahead

- Do you feel you're improving? Does that/would that make you enjoy playing more?

- Are you playing to give others pleasure or to please yourself?

- Do you enjoy playing with others? Is that (or could it be) a goal in itself?

- Can you be more specific about who you want to be "as good as"? *What is it about their playing* that you admire, that you want to emulate?

- Are there specific *things* you'd like to be able to *do*? (play for a dance, attend a jam, play a certain tune or type of tune, accompany a singer)? Are there *techniques* or *styles* you'd like to be better at?

Articulating the answers, or even simply thinking about some of these questions, can be helpful. You may realize that some of your goals are very achievable and others are so unlikely that they may just be causing you frustration. You may be able to shift your ambitions to those that involve personal fulfillment.

Today I'll try to stop wondering how good I am, and think more specifically about what I want to be good at.

145   The Two-Tempo Rut

Most of us are comfortable playing at two tempos: a faster one and a slower one. We start "fast tunes" at the fast speed and "slow tunes" at the slow speed.

This "two-tempo rut" limits our flexibility. I don't know about you, but I really don't want my playing to be limited to two arbitrary tempos. I want to be able to play at the tempo that's right for the way I want the tune to sound.

When a player is limited to two tempos it can cause problems in group playing. If someone else in starts a tune, that player will often unintentionally push the tempo either faster or slower, heading toward their "comfort speed."

If you ever play (or hope to play) for dancers, you'll need the ability to play at whatever speed is right for them. You'll need the ability to slow down or speed up quite precisely, and then stay there reliably.

Getting out of the "two-tempo rut" is one of the best reasons I know for practicing with a metronome.

Put It into Practice

- Start the tune at the speed that your ear hears it.
- Find out what that speed is on your metronome. Write it down.
- Now set the metronome slower –10, 20 or even 30 beats per minute (bpm) slower. Play at that speed for a few minutes. Really get the sound of the tune at the slower tempo into your ear.
- Next, set the metronome 10-20 bpm faster than your "natural" speed and play the tune again. Don't worry about whether you make all the notes, just try your best to *hear and feel* the tune at the faster speed.
- Tomorrow try playing this tune again. What speed did you naturally choose? Use the metronome to check. Compare the speed you chose today to the one you chose yesterday. Is it different? If so, do you like it this way?[19]

Today I'll start trying to get out of the two-tempo rut.

146 Playing with Swing

Sometimes you may look at sheet music and see a note at the top that says "swing 8th notes," or, "swing feel." Or perhaps someone you play with might comment that such-and-such a tune is usually played "with swing."

What is "swing"? Very simply, it means that four eighth notes are played in a loping, long-short, long-short rhythm, instead of evenly.

Some musicians describe "swing" as a dotted rhythm. Others think of it as a triplet with the middle note missing, which is a bit of a softer feeling. To get a sense of the difference, try saying it out loud:*

    even eighth notes: **<u>one</u> and <u>two</u> and**

    dotted quarter notes: **<u>one</u>**-ey and **a <u>two</u>**-ey and **a**

    triplet: **<u>one</u>** and **a <u>two</u>** and **a**

"Swing" is often considered a feature of jazz music, yet many traditional tunes are played with swing. Whether the swing feels more dotted or "triplet-y" can depend on the tune, the tradition and the player. Trad musicians can be quite intentionally all over the map within the same tune. This is where you may find out that many trad players have an *extremely* refined sense of time.

Try swinging a tune you know. Then play it straight. Practice switching back and forth. Stay flexible. Have fun.

Today I'll play with swing.

147   Mukudoku

An aikido student who also practices the "way of tea" told me this story:

> "Each week in my tea ceremony class the instructor selects a scroll to hang from the wall of the alcove. These are often chosen for the occasion. Sometimes they are more general, yet still in the spirit of the 'way of tea.' One week, the scroll said, '*mukudoku.*'

> "When I asked about the word, my teacher told me of a famous dialog between Bodhidharma and Emperor Wu. Emperor Wu said 'I'm a faithful Buddhist. I built many temples and made various offerings to monks. What kind of reward can I expect?' To this, Bodhidharma answered, 'Mukudoku!' meaning, 'No reward whatsoever.'"

---

* I have added bold face where you'd play the notes and underlined the strong beats. You can think of the other sounds as "spacers."

When we play and practice, we often do so with the expectation of some kind of reward. We may hope that our musicianship will be recognized by others. Perhaps we'll be invited to join a group or play a gig. Or we hope to be welcomed by other musicians and audiences. At the very least, we hope to be rewarded by our own progress, by reaching some goal.

Mukudoku involves the idea of *letting go of the motivation of reward*. It means trying to live our lives with the understanding that every moment, whether beautiful or painful, is exquisite and perfect.

Would it be useful, even liberating, to practice just for the experience of it, not for some future expectation? To let go, even for a moment, of the idea of improvement, measurement or quid pro quo? Try it and see.[20]

Today I will try to practice without the expectation of reward.

148   Playing with the Masters

Most of us spend at least some of our practice time playing along with recordings of other musicians.

There are "slowdowner" apps that allow you to input audio files, slow them down, and make loops, so you can play along without interruption. When you can adjust the speed of the music, you can relax while playing, and also capture every note and nuance. Playing in a loop helps you stay engaged, without having to stop, rewind, and reset.

Purchasing an app such as this is *one of the best investments of money and effort you can make*. The best ones let you create loops from audio files on your computer, tablet or phone, slow them or speed them up, change keys, save your loops, and even organize your files in folders.

Even when you use a slowdowner app, capturing the essence of an artist's style can be elusive. Here's an exercise I learned from pianist David Leonhardt that is very helpful.

Put It into Practice

> Find a tune by an artist whose style you're looking to capture. It doesn't need to be the tune you're working on, but it should have the

same general feel. You don't *need* to be able to loop it, but being able to slow it down can help.

- Play the *tune you're working on* for a minute or two – look at the clock or set a timer. Choose a manageable section, at a speed you can play, rather than playing the whole tune.
- Listen *to the artist you're emulating* for a minute or two. Just listen without playing.
- Play your tune again. Try to imitate the feeling, without thinking about it too much. Don't get too focused on playing the right notes; act as if you already know how to play them.
- Go back and forth like this for 10-12 minutes.
- Now stop and reflect. What interested you? Did you gain anything from this?

The whole process looks like this:

Play → Listen → Play → Listen → Play

Reflect

Total: 10-12 minutes

As you play back the artist's version, try to listen without focusing on any thought in particular. See if you can use diffuse thinking[*] to help you absorb stylistic elements without articulating them.

Today I'll try a 10-minute practice exercise for listening to a musician whose indefinable "sound" I want to imitate.

149   Learn on the Fly

Some people can learn tunes quickly. In a jam or a session, after three repetitions of the tune you'll see them playing along. This isn't magic. Whether they're aware of it or not, players who learn tunes quickly are

---

[*] For more about diffuse thinking, see 100 – Sleeping with a Key

using the core skills of learning by ear, supplemented by a few more "tricks."

If you really want to build your skill at learning on the fly, you can. You'll have to work step-by-step, and it will take time, but it's an achievable goal.

Put It into Practice

To start, choose a tune to learn – one that's on the simple side.

- Find a recording that you like. If you can, find one with a solo player. If you have a "slowdowner" app, load in the tune and set up a loop to play the whole tune once through. If it's a recording of a band, the first time through the tune is often the simplest part of the arrangement, so choose that as your loop.

- As with learning any tune by ear, first establish the rhythm in your mind: Is it a jig, a reel, a waltz? Try to sense the general rhythm.

- Try to determine what key the tune is in, and if it's in a major or minor key. Quietly play the note you think is the "tonal center," i.e. the key the tune is in. If you're right, that note should sound good played over most of the tune.

- Listen for the structure of the tune. Is it AABB? AABA? Something else?[*]

- With a little practice you'll be able to establish all three of these elements: rhythm, key and structure, the first time through a simple tune.

- Next, listen for musical patterns *within* the tune. You may notice melody patterns first. Listen for rhythmic patterns as well.[†]

- Try to hum or lilt along with the tune. You may get some of it or most of it. There may be parts you're not sure of. Don't worry about those for now.

---

[*] See 37 – Tune Structure

[†] See 48 – Listening for Patterns and 65 – Give Me That Rhythm

Now that you've done your prep work, start trying to play along:

- Keep looping the tune and try to play just the first few notes. The first phrase is often a motif that shows up over and over – so just play it every time it comes up.

- Next, listen for easy wins: Is there another pattern that's like the first few notes but starts on a different note? You may hear a scale pattern or a set of notes you've played before on another tune. See if you can add one or two of those in.

- Practice just playing along, "letting go" of the notes you can't play or can't hear, and sticking with the notes you've worked out.

- You may be able to pick up a few more notes here and there. It depends on the tune. At some point you'll be aware that to learn the rest, you'll need to slow down the tune even more or pause the recording and work the notes out a few at a time. That's a good place to stop.

The idea behind this exercise is to pick up as much as you can *without pausing the tune*. Don't expect to be 100% successful. The first few times you may only be able to lilt or sing along with some of the tune. If you were able to play along with just the first few notes, as they repeat throughout the tune, consider that a win.

As you build this skill, you'll be able to learn more and more of any given tune on the fly. Your level of success will always be dependent on the complexity of the tune and how slowly you're looping or playing it. To challenge yourself you can always speed up the loop or work on a more complex tune.

The ability to learn tunes on the fly is not something you'll pick up in a day or a week. It will take either occasional practice over a long time or consistent practice for a month or more. If this is something you'd like to be able to do, why not start today?

Today I'll practice the skills of learning a tune on the fly.

150   Comfort Zone

Every musician has a comfort zone. Every. Single. One. Once we get outside our comfort zone, we usually don't sound so great. This may sound obvious, yet it can be helpful when we're listening to our musical idols, comparing their glory with our own paltry progress and abilities.

Even renowned musicians may falter when asked to play a tune they haven't rehearsed. Great classical musicians may not be able to improvise. There are excellent sight readers who can't play "Happy Birthday" without sheet music and world-class trad players who read sheet music very, very slowly, not to mention killer old-time players who can *not* get the feel of a Swedish tune.

In our day-to-day practice, for the most part, we spend time working on areas that are outside our comfort zone. That can be demoralizing, especially when we make the comparison to the players that we want to emulate. It's good to remind ourselves that there are plenty of things, musically, that would be a challenge for them as well. They might even be things *you* do well.

Today I'll remind myself that everyone has a comfort zone.

151   How Does It Really Go?

Variations in tunes are so common in traditional music that it's quite common to hear three players playing a tune three different ways at a jam session. Usually these versions don't musically "clash" (too much), but sometimes they're different enough to be disconcerting.

No matter what your level of accomplishment, it can be a frustrating experience, after painstakingly learning a tune, to show up to play it with others and find that they play a different version or variation.

Which is the "Right" Version?

The answer is, "It depends."

One of the appealing aspects of traditional music is that every tune has a history. The longer a tune has been around, the deeper and richer this history is likely to be, and the more variety there's likely to be in how it can be played. If you really like the tune, it's worth digging in to find out where and when it came from, who were the seminal players, or how it's played in different regions or settings.

Which Version Should I Choose to Learn?

Pick a version you like. Make that your go-to version.

Then What?

Any time you introduce a tune in a group setting like a jam, it's wise to be prepared for others to play it differently.

If you're leading the tune in a jam, most would agree that it's your option to play the tune the way you want and let others fit themselves to you. If the difference is just a few notes, it may not be noticeable to anyone but you.[*]

If you're not leading the tune, you may be able to noodle quietly and figure out someone else's variation. You might even figure out the differences on the fly, or at least get enough that you can go home and work on it. Alternatively, during a break in playing, ask someone to play you their version.

Many musicians embrace the opportunity to play a tune "flexibly" or "multidimensionally." Some common tunes have many variations. You could make a study of them and learn a few. A little project like this can reward you, pointing to the places where you can simplify or add notes, and also highlighting the areas that are seldom changed.

Today I'll reconsider the idea of the "correct" version of a tune. Maybe I'll learn a few ways to play some tunes.

---

[*] There *are* stories about jam sessions whose leaders insist that tunes be played a certain way. Though this may make the ensemble sound a bit more polished, many experienced and creative players don't enjoy having such a strict experience in a jam session.

152   Ikkyo, Nikkyo, Sankyo

The hands and wrists contain many small bones, ligaments and muscles. Here are three warmup exercises used in aikido practice. They can be beneficial for releasing tightness in the wrists, and stretching the hands and fingers.

Called *ikkyo*, *nikkyo* and *sankyo undo* (first, second and third exercises), each moves the wrist joint in a different way. In the process they stretch and move the hands and fingers.

Before You Start[*]

- Stand comfortably and naturally, with your weight balanced evenly on both feet. Make sure to stay relaxed and especially not to let your shoulders tighten as you move.

- Visualize your center of balance, or *one point*, just below your navel, in the middle of your body towards your spine. Imagine that center being very powerful and concentrated.

Your goal with these exercises is to feel *some* twisting and stretching in the wrist, but *don't stretch to the point of pain.* Try to make the movement smooth and not jerky. Make sure to stay relaxed and keep good posture. Keep your chest open and your shoulders relaxed.

Ikkyo Undo (First Exercise)

- Hold your left arm in front of your chest with your elbow bent and your wrist flopping down – a bit like a prairie dog. Relax your left shoulder. Grasp the back of your left hand with your right, with your right fingers around the pinkie edge of your left hand.

- Keeping the left elbow where it is, raise your left hand. The wrist will bend. At the same time, apply a little pressure with the right hand and twist the left wrist a little away from you.

- Do this movement five times on each side.

---

[*] It may help to view the video at www.judyminot.com/bestpractice/

As you move, keep your elbows heavy and your hands, arms and shoulders relaxed. Keep your breathing relaxed, your posture natural. Imagine that with each movement you're becoming stronger, more centered, more balanced, more relaxed.

Nikkyo Undo (Second Exercise)

- Hold your left hand in front of your chest with the palm facing the chest. Rotate your hand and wrist so your palm is facing toward your left.

- Grasp the thumb edge of your left hand with four fingers of the right hand and apply pressure against the back of the left hand with the right palm. Let the right thumb rest loosely against the back of the hand.

- Gently drop the left hand and wrist, maintaining the pressure with the right. As you do, the left wrist will twist clockwise and away from you.

- Do this five times on each side.

As you move the wrists up and down, keep your elbows heavy and your shoulders relaxed. To help you keep good posture, imagine making the distance between the fronts of your shoulders as wide as possible.

Sankyo Undo (Third Exercise)

- Hold the left arm in front of you, elbows bent, with the palm facing away from you and the fingers pointing to the right. Grasp the left hand with the right, with the right fingers around the pinkie side of your left hand, and the right thumb against the back of your left hand.

- Straighten the arms, and as you do, twist the left palm away and upward.

- Do this five times on each side.

Make sure that your shoulders don't creep up to your ears. Keep the front of the chest open, and the shoulder blades relaxed over the back of the ribcage. You may not be able to twist very far. That's OK.

Even though your arms are moving away from your center of balance, imagine your center becoming stronger and more powerful with each movement.

Shake

- When you've done all three exercises, stand comfortably with your hands at your sides.
- Shake your hands vigorously as if you were shaking off water.
- Let that shaking expand up your arms…and then to your whole body, until you're bouncing up and down on the balls of your feet.
- Stop.

Stand for a few seconds before continuing with your practice session.

Cautions:

Be careful, as you move, not to stretch to the point of pain. Try to make the movements smooth and not jerky. As always, exercise common sense with your own health. If you have a back or neck injury or another health concern, or if you experience pain during one of these stretches, stop and seek professional advice.

Today I'll try some wrist stretches: ikkyo, nikkyo and sankyo undo.

153   Checkerboard

Here's a practice method that can help you become more flexible *and* focused, and may help lift you out of a rut.

It involves switching back and forth between a "standard" way of playing a section of a tune, and a different approach or "concept." Your concept can be drawn from anything that inspires you. Here are a few ideas to start with:

- Put in as many ornaments as you can.

- Play as relaxed as you can.
- Play with exaggerated dynamics.
- Play only the notes of the chord names.
- Play every other note.
- Play staccato, legato, long bows or short bows.
- Play harmony notes.

Put It into Practice

Choose a section of a tune that you're already comfortable with. Select a concept to work on.

- Set the metronome 10-30 bpm slower than you normally play.
- Play the section through a few times to get the feeling of it. This will be your standard or "baseline" version.
- Pause for a few beats.
- Play the section again, incorporating your concept.
- Go back and forth between the two a few times, pausing between the loops. The pause is optional if you don't need it.
- It's important to keep going back to the baseline version, and working to distinguish the two in your mind.

If you want to keep going, you can:

- Switch to a different concept.
- Expand the area you're looping.
- Get rid of the pause.
- Switch to a different section of the tune.

Switching back and forth keeps you mentally alert and helps you become more flexible. Returning to your baseline version gives you a mental breather. As you focus on your variation, you'll probably find yourself becoming more and more solid and relaxed playing the baseline version. You'll probably come up with your own list of benefits of this useful practice technique.

Today I'll try checkerboarding a section of a tune.

154   Personal, Pervasive, Permanent

Here is a concept that sheds light on our reactions to the mistakes or problems we encounter. Psychologist Martin Seligman uses the terms *personal, pervasive* and *permanent* to describe the negative ways we explain our experiences.[21] Musicians are quite susceptible to these specific ways of characterizing the things that happen as we practice and play.

Personal

> When we make a mistake, it *is* personal, in that we can say, "I did that." Yet we often berate ourselves as if we did something intentionally. In reality, most of our musical mistakes happen either because we don't really understand what we're trying to do, or because we don't yet have the technique, strength or control. *It's not appropriate to blame ourselves for making a mistake when we didn't understand or weren't capable of doing otherwise.*

Pervasive

> We often connect the thought, "I did that," with, "I *always* do that." The mind runs away with itself, selecting memories and knitting them together into a straightjacket of incompetence. *We don't need to buy into that narrative.*

Permanent

> Perhaps the most debilitating story we tell ourselves is that it will always be so. We fall into believing that we will always be incapable, unable to learn and improve, and that we will stay "stuck" in this place forever. *Instead, we can think: "At this moment, this happened."*

Recognizing these three common reactions gives us more freedom to find the true source of the problem and to decide how to act to solve it.

Today I'll listen for the narrative I create when I make a mistake. Do I make all my mistakes personal, pervasive and permanent?

155   Wasted Motion

When I was a kid learning to play baseball, my brother taught me not to waste motion before I swung the bat. I would position the bat over my shoulder for the swing. Yet as soon as I saw the ball leave the pitcher's hand, I instinctively pulled the bat back another 30 degrees before swinging for the ball.

My brother explained that if the pitch were at normal speed, instead of a practice softball lob, I wouldn't have time to be moving the bat *away from the ball* before swinging *toward* it. "Hold the bat where it needs to be to deliver the hit," he told me. "You don't have time for wasted motion."

This concept can be used to make playing easier, more natural and less frantic. Pay attention to the way you move, with an eye to whether there is wasted motion. Are you moving your hands, the bow, the pick, in the most relaxed, efficient and direct way? Are you moving backward before you go forward?

This is a simple idea that you can call on at any time to help make your playing easier and more effortless.

Today I will pay special attention to wasted motion.

156   A New Environment

You may have a personalized, comfortable space where you practice, with all your "stuff" around you: your perfect chair, instrument and music stands, pens, notebooks, headphones, mirror, and more.[*]

Why not try playing somewhere else?

Play in your bedroom. In the park. In the kitchen. Not everyone (a pianist, for example) has all these options, or many options at all. If that's the case, can you move your chair to face the other wall? Raise the piano lid? Hang up some different artwork?

---

[*] See 17 – A Space of Your Own

Why do this? It's a fairly well-accepted scientific finding that novelty enhances learning. *Changing the environment can help make what you learn today more memorable.*

Changing your practice space can also help you *avoid relying on environmental cues to be comfortable in your playing.* This can help if you ever want to play anywhere besides in your comfy space.

Finally, as you move into different spaces you may *notice changes in acoustics.* Is there one that you like more? When your instrument sounds good, you're likely to feel more like playing. Maybe you can practice in that space more often.

In my house, the violin sounds best when I stand halfway up the staircase. It does not make my housemates happy when I play there. But when they're not home…

Today I'll try changing the environment I play in.

157 People Will Like My Playing

Our thoughts can sabotage our playing, undoing in an instant what took weeks, months and years of practice. Especially when we play for others, fear of criticism can be paralyzing. There are many fine musicians who seldom venture outside their practice room for fear of what others may think.

Contrary to what you're telling yourself, **most listeners actually will like your music.** I have had confirmation of this many, many times. Generous tips given after our "worst show ever," fellow musicians saying, "*You* were great but *I* made so many mistakes!" Even professional musicians rarely face a critic who's anxious to expose every flaw.

All of us can name a particular exception, perhaps even involving family or friends, but as a rule your audience wants to have a good time and they want you to succeed.

For years I kept a sticky note on my piano that said, "People will like my playing." Sometimes I take a moment to internalize this thought, letting it suffuse my mind and body with certainty. Staying with this idea for 30-60 seconds can send a powerful, calming message to your mind.

The next time you're going to play for others, remember that people want the best for you. See if you can connect with that positive feeling whenever you play.

Today I'll find a way to internalize the belief that people will like my playing.

158   Scales and Arpeggios

I used to have quite a powerful negative reaction when anyone suggested practicing scales or arpeggios.[*] This may be because as a teenager I spent hours practicing scales and arpeggios, in what eventually became drudgery.

Scales and arpeggios can actually be the opposite of drudgery, as long as the practice is *relevant to what we're learning* and *we understand the reason* we're practicing them.

Why Practice Scales and Arpeggios?

> Most music, not just trad, is organized into patterns of notes.[†] Many of these patterns are recognizable as either scale passages or chord tones. As we become more comfortable with playing these patterns, they act like power tools. Tunes become easier to learn, play and remember.

Put It into Practice

> *Play the scale.*
>
> – Before you start playing any tune, play the scale it's written in. You can play just one octave, the scale notes from the

---

[*] An arpeggio is just the notes of a chord, played one after another, either up or down.
[†] See 48 – Listening for Patterns

lowest on your instrument to the highest, or just the range of notes in the tune.

- Play these notes as deliberately, evenly and beautifully as you can.

- Listen intently and try to connect the *sound* to the way it *feels* to play. When it sounds best, what do your fingers feel like? How do your arms, back, neck, even your face feel? How are you sitting in your chair?

Play the arpeggio or chord tones for the key the tune is in.

- Now play the arpeggio for that key. If the tune is in D major, play the notes in a D major chord (or triad) one after another. This may take a little thinking if you're not sure what those chord tones are. As with the scale, choose how high and low you want to go, from an octave to the whole range of your instrument.

- Again, bring your attention to creating a beautiful sound and relaxing your body to make it feel easy.

- Resist the urge to be goal-oriented. You don't need to play at 120 beats per minute, play three octaves with one bellows push or play in every key.

Look for scale and chord patterns in the tune.

- Play through the tune and listen for "scale patterns" a few scale notes.

- Now do the same and listen for the chord tones. For now, stick with chord tones for the key the tune is in. If you find other notes that sound like chord tones or arpeggio patterns, you can file that for thinking about later, or, if it's interesting to you, try playing those arpeggios, too. It's up to you.

- If you want, you can use one or two of these scale and chord patterns to create a custom exercise for your tune. Try different rhythmic, bowing or bellows patterns, different phrasing, dynamics, etc.

- Keep in mind that this process should be interesting and fun. Try to stop *before* it becomes overwhelming or tedious.

You're likely to hear and feel a difference in your playing after just a few days of playing with scales and arpeggios.

We can all work on getting these patterns "under our fingers" in a way that makes the work relevant, holds our interest and produces results.

Today I'll try practicing scales and arpeggios in a way that's relevant to the music I want to play.

159   Do Say Do

Why is it that, even when we repeatedly remind ourselves *not* to do something, we do it anyway?

It has been said that our brains don't do well with negation. If you tell yourself, "***Don't forget*** to pick up cat food," you're likely to forget. Why would this be the case?

First, your brain has to form the concept, "***Forget*** to pick up cat food," in order "not" to do that. You're devoting cognitive attention to imagining the very activity you want to avoid. If you want a better result, you're better off re-wording your reminder: "***Be sure and*** pick up cat food!"

Put It into Practice

> Using this model can help you get more effective, lasting results out of the insights you have in practice. When you notice something you want to change, you may typically think in the negative:
>
>> "Don't let my mind drift."
>> "Stop grabbing the neck of the guitar with the thumb."
>
> Instead, deliberately re-word your instructions. Give yourself a positive instruction instead of something to avoid.
>
>> "Listen to the sound of the instrument."
>> "Relax the thumb against the guitar neck."

If you tell yourself what to do instead of what not to do, you'll find you're more likely to act on your own advice.

Today I'll remember to tell myself what to do, instead of what not to do.

160   Ending the Tune

One year I played in a fancy pick-up band for an annual contra dance. The band had six rehearsals for the dance. One thing we practiced *a lot* was finishing the tunes in a way that would signal to the dancers, "Hey, the end is coming!"

I'd been a contra dancer for years before I began playing the music. I'd noticed that the dancers usually knew instinctively when the end of the dance was coming and would often try to finish gracefully. Even though I was myself a musician, I had no idea that communicating this was a technique that bands actually practiced.

In that pick-up band, one of our favorite ways to indicate "the end is near," was to use the "anti-penultimate omission" or "APO." The name APO is a shibboleth of New Jersey/Philadelphia contra dance musicians, but the technique is quite common. It's done by leaving out a few notes, about a measure before the end of the tune.

There are plenty of other ways to end tunes including adding a flourish at the end, changing the last chord or the last few notes, and just slowing down.

As you listen to recordings, watch online video and play with friends, you can start to get a sense of the ways that other musicians signal the end of a tune, whether they're doing so for the benefit of dancers, musicians, or an audience.

Why not choose one and practice it on a tune you like to play?

Today I'll start thinking about how I end tunes.

161   Jumps

I learned a great practice technique in a workshop with guitarist Max Cohen. This method is very helpful when you're trying to move your hand a long way, or to a new position or a new chord shape. It can iron out frustrations in just a few minutes.

This technique is very useful for rhythm players (piano, guitar, accordion, mandolin, etc.) who often have to make new chord shapes with the entire hand. Melody players will also find it helpful any time they have trouble getting their fingers or hand quickly into a new position.

Put It into Practice

- Select a section of the tune to practice that has a jump you want to work on. You'll be playing in a repeating cycle, so include a little lead-in to the part you're having trouble with and enough at the end to make a comfortable loop.

- Set your metronome to go very slowly. You want to work slowly enough that you have time to move to the new position accurately and in a relaxed manner.

- Practice the loop, playing each chord or note as precisely "down the middle" of the metronome beat as you can. Don't forget to make the sound beautiful.

- As you begin to get comfortable, your first reflex will be to turn up the metronome. Instead, keep the metronome at the same tempo. Just move your hand more quickly to the new position and keep it there ready. Play the next chord or note precisely on the metronome beat.

- As the movement becomes easier, move your hand to the new position sooner and sooner. Again, don't speed up the metronome. Just focus on playing beautifully, staying relaxed, and making the rhythm precise.

- Eventually, you'll start to be able to move quickly and confidently. For me the test is that I'm not experiencing any mental "turmoil": There's no sense that I don't know what to do next or that I'm afraid I may not make it in time. *At that point*, you can change one of two variables: Increase either metronome speed or the length of your "loop."

- Go easy. Make small changes and pay attention to what happens to your playing. If you do speed up or lengthen the cycle and you can't maintain your progress, take a step or two back: Slow down or shorten your loop. By proceeding slowly you'll make faster progress.

Today I'll work on getting better at jumps.

162 Rich Musical Soil

It's hard to feel like you've made progress – that you've absolutely nailed something – and then have to go "backwards." When I dust off a tune I know well, it's not easy to admit, for example, that I actually can't play the high notes in the B part anymore, and that perhaps I may *never* have played them as well as I thought.

It can feel a bit crushing, remembering the effort you put into learning a tune, to hear that you're not playing certain notes evenly, or you're hesitating just before the difficult section (again). Even harder is to do what needs to be done: Put on the metronome. Slow down. Dissect the passage into its component parts until you really *know* it.

The work we do follows a spiral path rather than a circular one. We may revisit some issues, but, whether or not we realize it, we do so from a new, higher level.

In addition, as we become more accomplished, we become more efficient at doing the work. The resistance to what we need to do gradually eases. The ground that was once hard clay, difficult to break with a shovel, becomes loamy soil, and each time we plant a new seed, it becomes more fertile and productive.

Today I'll remember that it's OK to go over ground I've worked before. I'm creating rich musical soil to make it more fertile and productive.

163 Look Up!

We practice alone. As we do so we develop habits. When we play with others, not all those habits are useful. One example is keeping our eyes on our instrument. While practicing, why would you have reason to look away from your instrument, your fingers, or the floor?

Yet when you're playing with others, having the freedom to look around can be extremely useful. You can see the visual signal that someone is switching or finishing a tune. You can watch the singer's breathing or another violinist's fingers and work to stay in perfect sync. You can make sure you're playing at the right speed for the dancers. You may simply want to enjoy seeing the happy faces of listeners or watch a child dancing to the music.

When we look up from our instruments, interesting things happen. I often listen better. As a result, I relax more. Of course, I also lose my place in the music, my fingers hit the wrong piano keys, and my bow slides over the bridge.

That's why we need to *practice* looking up while playing. Create some kind of reminder for yourself. Set up a mirror and glance at yourself. Put something nice in your practice space that you want to look at. It will become easier to lift your head, and it will make you a better musician.

Today I'll practice looking up while I play.

164   Child's Pose

There are a few yoga poses that are quite therapeutic and relaxing for musicians. One is Child's Pose.* Child's Pose is a resting pose that offers an opportunity to recharge during a quick practice break. It can help you release tension in the shoulders, upper arms and hands. Because you're supported by the floor during the pose, using gravity to help with any stretching, the pose can be very relaxing. Child's Pose also gently stretches the hips, lower back and thighs, which can get tight and stiff from sitting.

Today I'll use Child's Pose as a way to recharge during a break from practice.

---

* If you're not familiar with Child's Pose, you can view the video on www.judyminot.com/bestpractice/

165   Simplify Your Approach

The principle of Occam's razor is that the simplest solution is usually correct.

When I'm having difficulty with a knotty problem, I look for ways to simplify my approach. I slow down. I play a smaller portion of the music. I play using one hand at a time.

When I'm looking for a way to present a tune, to arrange it, to bring out what's best in it, I try simplifying, bringing it back to its bare bones, to see if I can find the core of it.

While this might seem obvious in hindsight, often it's not what we actually do.

As soon as you realize you don't understand something or you're not getting something, stop. Look for something to simplify. If you sense internal resistance – "Just one more time and I'll get it for sure!" – take a deep breath and tell your ego to take a walk around the block.

Today I'll simplify my approach.

166   Pleasure, Praise, Fame, Gain

In almost everything we do, we're motivated by one of these:

         Pleasure   Praise   Fame   Gain

If we aren't seeking one of these four, we may be trying to avoid their opposites:

         Pain   Blame   Disgrace/Obscurity   Loss

Buddhists call these motivations the *eight worldly winds.*

When you have strong emotions about something that's going on in your playing, it's worth asking yourself: "What am I seeking?" or, "What am I seeking to avoid?"

Is there something from the list above that rings a bell? Is your identity tied to some level of achievement, how others see you, or whether you get external validation? Is it no fun unless it's easy? What mental calculations are you making about whether it's "worth it"?

If we can be more aware of the underlying impulses that give rise to strong thoughts and emotions, we can be less blown about by these "winds." Like a boat with ballast, we can stay on course more easily, and perhaps even be content in our playing, just as it is.

Today I'll consider whether I'm motivated by any of the "eight worldly winds."

167   Make It Stick with a Memory Trick

Over the years I've had many teachers, musical and non-musical. The best ones knew how to make their points memorable.

Musically, there are many things we may want to recall: a feeling, a tonality, a phrase, the name of a tune, an idea. If there's something you want to remember, use the power of your attention and try one of the techniques used by great teachers.

Put It into Practice

> ***Sound:*** Playing with sound, such as adding words to a musical phrase, using alliteration or rhyme, or exaggerating a sound, can help make an idea more accessible to memory recall.
>
> ***Humor:*** Jokes, unusual juxtapositions, and things that surprise us are memorable. A joke draws the focus of the mind to an entire sequence of events, and can help us remember what happened just before the joke was told.
>
> ***Physicality/Kinesthetics:*** Many of us learn better when the learning is associated with a physical sensation in the body. Zen masters used to rap their acolytes with a bamboo stick during meditation to help them stay attentive to the present. I don't recommend you hit yourself, but you can certainly bring your awareness to pleasant physical sensations as you play.

Visuals. We depend heavily on our sense of sight and often ignore our senses of touch and hearing. Yet there are times when paying attention to what we see can help lock in an idea.

Today, if there's something I want to remember, I'll focus my attention and use a memory technique.

168   Plays Well with Others

Playing well with others is a skill worth cultivating. When other musicians sense they're being supported musically, they relax and play with more confidence. The result is that everyone sounds better. It is an amazing feeling when the group sound "clicks" and you know you had a part in making it happen.

Playing well with others is a bit like being good at conversation. The most enjoyable discussions are often with those who leave space for others to voice their ideas and opinions, who try to find points of agreement, and who, when they're not speaking, really listen.

Like *looking up*,* the skills of playing well with others are challenging to work on at home. When I'm practicing, I'm always the leader. There's no one else to react to in real time. I'm focused on making the tune sound the way *I* want it to sound. I don't have to adjust my speed to someone else's, help them recover the beat, or help others in the room hear the melody.

Playing and jamming with others offers a great opportunity to improve your skill at being a more supportive group player.

Put It into Practice

> ***Practice being a follower.*** If there is a leader at a music gathering, listen carefully to their speed, their sense of rhythm and their phrasing. Try to match your playing to theirs as much as you can.

---

* See 163 – Look Up!

Dump your ego. We all want to be recognized and appreciated for our ability. If that motivates you, imagine there's a secret, stealth award for the ability to "mind meld" with another player. In my experience, musicians that can do this *are* recognized and appreciated, especially by other musicians.

Practice being flexible in your playing. Violinist Hilary Hahn has said that when she practices, she actively works on being able to play the music in different ways. For Hilary that flexibility may involve changes in dynamics, tempo or phrasing. Traditional musicians can also change the notes![22]

When you get the chance, step back! Intentionally put yourself in a supporting role. Work to do everything you can to make the leader (the singer, or whoever you choose) sound as great as possible. Can you help bring out their melody notes? Strengthen a weak rhythm? Help other players recognize the tune?

Today I'll think about the qualities that go into playing well with others. How can I cultivate these in my own playing?

169   Continuous Growth

I am convinced that what separates most great musicians from "the rest of us" is not that they have some innate ability, but that they specifically aim for continuous growth and lifelong improvement. How can we aim for continuous growth in our own playing?

When we learn a skill, there are typically three stages:

Cognitive – We devote lots of energy to thinking about it and discovering ways to do better. We make big leaps in skill level.

Associative – As we improve, we make fewer errors. At the same time, progressive gains in skill become more subtle.

Autonomous – As skills become automatic, it takes less attention to carry them out. Progressive gains are hard to see on a day-to-day basis. At this stage we often stop devoting attention to improvement.

When we get to the stage when things become easier, it feels great to kick back and relax after all those years of struggle and self-doubt. But so much more is possible!

How can we jog ourselves out of the autonomous stage, and lift ourselves off a practice plateau?

Experts in various fields offer several methods to help rise from a learning plateau, to engage in continuous growth.

Stay Engaged, Stay Challenged

Once we've learned a skill (say, riding a bicycle), our brains shunt the performance of that skill to the background. This makes our cognition available for other stuff we might need to pay attention to (Sabretooth tiger! Speeding bus!). I've written in other chapters about techniques to stay attentive and keep our brains from going into "screensaver" mode.* Working on new skills is another way to keep our minds engaged. Anything that doesn't come easily, or that uses existing abilities in a new way, can serve this purpose.

Study the Greats

You probably know which artists you want to emulate. Thanks to technology you have the resources to study them. Don't just watch and listen. Really go deep. Slow the music down. Focus on the artist's face, posture, hand position. Listen for every nuance you can. As you do, ask yourself: "Why did this person decide to do exactly that at this time?"

Treat Your Practice Like a Science

If you're in the habit of planning and taking notes,† that habit will pay off here. Research which practice techniques work for you and which don't. What's your most productive time of day? What's the best length of time for your practice sessions? Develop a theory and

---

* See 4 – Being Present; 28 – Interrupt the Loop; 79 – Interleaving
† See 9 – Having a Plan; 18 – Taking Notes; 54 – Tracking Small Wins

test it. Study the things that challenge you and find the most successful approaches to remedying them.

Get Immediate and Constant Feedback

In most areas of medicine, doctors' skills improve over time. One area this is not true is in mammography. It's been suggested that this is because the radiologists who study mammograms may not know if their diagnosis is correct for months, years, or, possibly, ever.[23] Getting feedback right away helps us learn. The more often we get feedback, the better.

A great teacher is invaluable, but the best and most immediate feedback is *listening to yourself*. Listen to your own playing as if it were someone else. Record yourself and listen back with discernment rather than criticism.[*]

Keep challenging yourself. Learn a new skill. Find ways to push past your comfort zone and rise above your practice "plateau" to stay on the path of continuous growth.

Today I'll work on continuous growth.

170   The Last Thing You Hear

I became a video editor in the early days of MTV. An editing style that was made popular by music videos was to make lots of quick cuts. This is a difficult technique to do well. If the editor is not skilled the visuals can become a blur of shapes that make no sense.

One trick I learned was that when a scene changes abruptly (i.e. when there's a video "cut"), the eye focuses on the very last thing seen before the edit. That image sticks in your brain like a little "freeze frame." If someone starts to stick out their tongue, a bird displays its tail, a dancer crooks her hip, that's what you remember. I made use of that knowledge over and over to get sequences that were smoother, more coherent and more interesting.

---

[*] See 74 – Discernment vs. Criticism

Since the brain processes what we hear as well as what we see, it's not surprising that, good or bad, we *remember the last thing we heard* before a pause or change. The "earworm" tune that won't leave your head, the mistake you kept making before you got up to take a break, the phrasing or harmony choices you made: All of these tend to reverberate.

It's easy to imagine ways that this tendency of the brain can frustrate our practice efforts. If I play a wrong note or play at an uneven tempo, or if I play well but not at my best, that sound will echo in my ear. I'll find myself mentally "practicing" the music *the way I don't want to hear it*.

We can turn use this tendency of the brain, to remember the last thing we hear, to create a useful tool. It's been said that the best way to get rid of an unwanted "earworm" is to *replace it with one you chose*. You can do the same with your memory of your own playing.

Put It into Practice

> If you're practicing a tune, before you switch tunes make a point to play once through as beautifully as you can before you stop.
>
> If, during practice, you play something unexpectedly well, pause to let that sound reverberate in your ear.
>
> You can even apply this idea to *thoughts* about practice. When you do something you're happy with, pause. Be explicit in commending yourself. "Wow, I did it!" "That's how I want it to sound." Help this good thought resonate. Give it a few seconds to sink in. Write it down.

We can't avoid the fact that we're not always happy with our playing. But we can do more to make sure the best sounds – and thoughts – resonate long after we've stopped playing.

Today I'll remember that my brain holds onto the last sound, and make that work for me.

171 Neurogenesis

Our ability to learn depends on the ability of our brains to generate both new neurons and new neural connections. It's reasonable, then, to ask: How much physical change can we realistically expect in our brains after we reach adulthood?

The vast majority of the neurons in the human brain develop before age 25. Yet there is fascinating and, for adult learners, encouraging research on the subject of neuron generation, or neurogenesis.

It turns out that in a part of the brain called the hippocampus, new neurons are made constantly: even after adulthood. The hippocampus regulates brain activity related to memory capacity, spatial recognition, and differentiation of similar memories. These are subjects that musicians deal with every day.

According to Dr. Sandrine Thuret,[24] there are many activities that have been shown to affect neurogenesis in adults. Some of them may be surprising.*

Activities that Affect Neurogenesis in Adults	
Increases Neurogenesis	*Decreases Neurogenesis*
Learning, mental exercise	Stress
Sex	Sleep deprivation
Exercise (running, dancing)	
Yoga and meditation	Aging
Calorie restricted diet (20-30%)	Diet high in saturated fat
Intermittent fasting	Diet high in sugar
Caffeine	Drinking alcohol
Foods high in flavonoids	Vitamin A, B or E deficiency
Zinc, folic acid, omega-3 fatty acids, resveratrol	Taking certain cancer drugs
Eating foods that are crunchy	Eating foods that are soft

Another benefit of performing activities that increase neurogenesis in the hippocampus is the effect on mood. If we generate more neurons, studies show we experience better mood. If we generate fewer, we feel more

---

* Since there is a great deal of current research interest in this area, it's likely that the above list will grow.

depressed. Conversely, if we do things that make us feel good, we generate more new neurons, and vice versa.

By this logic, if playing music makes us happy, then playing music will also help us generate new neurons, so we can learn more easily. This is a clear win-win!

Today I'll do something that benefits neurogenesis.

172   Wake Up Your Warm-Ups

Many of us spend a period at the beginning of practice "warming up." This is typically done to get the fingers and hands (and perhaps lips and vocal cords) physically warm and coordinated, to facilitate the flow of synovial fluid around joints and tendons, and to remind ourselves of common playing patterns.

Unfortunately, the music we choose to play when warming up is often not very…musical. For example, many musicians are taught to begin practice by playing scales, arpeggios and technical exercises.

There is no rule that you *must* do warm-ups in a certain way or even that you must warm up at all. The question for the musician is: *How will you approach the precious, memorable moment when you first sit down to play?*

Why not use the time at the beginning of practice to rekindle your relationship with your instrument: to reacquaint your ear with the beautiful sound you can make and the music you love most?

Warm up by playing a beautiful tune slowly. Wind your way through random notes that find themselves under your fingers, your favorite passage, one favorite scale, or a melody you can't get out of your head. There's plenty of time for repetitive exercises in a few minutes, or much later, played in the context of what you're working on.

Today I'll warm up with music that I want to hear.

173   The Gift of Listening

It's been said by wise people that if you want something, offer it to others. One thing I think all musicians crave is someone who listens to our music with a receptive, open heart.

I found out what it's like to play for such a listener when I went to visit my friend Kate. Her mom, known to everyone as "Tilliemum," had moved in with Kate following a stroke.

Kate and I played some chamber music (she on flute and I on fiddle). Tillie was an enthusiastic listener. Over the course of the weekend she asked me several times, "Won't you play your violin for me?" When I did play her a few tunes, comfortable for me but new to her, Tillie gave me her whole attention. Whenever I looked up her eyes were fixed on mine. I know her ears were wide open.

Having an attentive and appreciative audience is an incredible gift. It's not something most of us experience often. It made me a better player for those few minutes. I let go of my little mistakes and opened my ears to my own music, because Tillie was there to receive it. Thanks to Tillie, I try to offer this gift to other musicians whenever I can.

Today I'll offer the gift of listening with my full attention and an open heart.

174   Relaxed Hands

In an aikido seminar I was called on to demonstrate a technique. My teacher commented, "Your hands are like a bird's claws, hanging onto its perch!"

He went on to demonstrate that when the hands are tense, the arms, shoulders and entire body are tense. When I relaxed my hands, the rest of my body relaxed in turn. When I practiced the same technique with my hands relaxed, it was much easier to throw my opponent.

Learning to relax the hands can make a profound difference in our playing. It can be difficult to imagine how can we relax our fingers and hands when we are using them to play. The answer is simply to relax them *more*, rather than relaxing them *completely*.

Imagine you could fine-tune your body to the point that not a single muscle fiber was engaged in playing unless it was needed. This is our goal. As we progress toward that goal, playing becomes easier and more comfortable.

Put It into Practice

- First, minimize your area of focus. Start by working on playing just one note, one chord or even with just one hand.

- Begin with your hand away from the instrument. Allow it to completely relax. Let it fall to the correct position on the instrument, staying as relaxed as possible. Slowly, consciously, engage just enough muscle to press the key, string, cover the hole, or whatever the appropriate action is. Direct the focus of your attention to the way it feels in your hand, arm and shoulder.

- Do this movement again, but this time – if you didn't before – sound your instrument. Try to keep the relaxed feeling as much as possible. If you're not happy with the sound, carefully make any changes you need to, staying as relaxed as you can while expending the minimum effort needed to play. Make a strong mental connection between the sound that you enjoy and the feeling in your body.

- Gradually expand this practice to more notes or chords, or both hands, whatever feels right for you.

- Periodically "check in" with your body as you practice. See if you can re-engage with that relaxed feeling. If it helps, pause and go through the exercise again.

You obviously won't go through all these steps every time you need to make a sound on your instrument. Yet focusing on it for a week or so for just a few minutes a day, and then checking in during your practice time, can help you create a habit of relaxing your hands.

Take note of your progress. Return to the idea over the next few months. Gradually you'll find that having relaxed hands feels more and more easy and natural.

Today I'll spend some time learning to relax my hands as I play.

175   Harness the Power of Metaphor

> Your deep valleys are
> Only as vast as the space
> You need to rise up
> – Amanda Reilly Sayer[25]

Playing music involves the coordination of complex movements. Unlike, say, whittling, painting or sports, we're not creating an item we can hold, or even seeking a quantifiable outcome. We perform these complex physical movements *in order to produce sound*. Unless we're singing, we're producing the sound *through the medium of some other object*. When you look at it that way, the ability to play music is pretty marvelous.

This combination of complexity with an intangible result is one reason why the right metaphor can be so helpful to our learning.

A metaphor creates a vivid, memorable picture that concisely expresses a great deal of abstract and intangible information.

We're so habituated to using metaphors in everyday life that we're unaware of how they can define our reality. We "wrestle" with new concepts, we can't "stomach" unpleasant news, we "nurture" ideas so they can "take root and grow." Metaphors offer a great deal of potential to the musician.

A metaphor can help us make significant changes in our playing simply by helping us think differently.

It's worth considering whether the metaphors you use in your playing and practice help or hinder you.

- "My pipes are a finicky octopus that I have to coax sound from."
- "This tune is like a delicate flower that's quickly blown away in the wind."

– "To make a string crossing, I make a movement like flicking ash off a cigarette."

Nurture an awareness of the metaphors you use to make sense of your practice. Become active in deciding which ones to keep and which to let go of.

Today I'll become more aware of the metaphors I use in my practice, and make sure they work for me.

176 Both Hands Together

We play an instrument with two hands. For us to play well, both hands must be perfectly coordinated: bow and fingers, fretted notes and pick, melody and bass, and so on.

We produce better sound when both hands work perfectly together. If they don't, especially as we play faster, our playing can sound messy or worse.

Put It into Practice

Developing an exercise to improve the synchronization of both hands is in similar to other exercises you create for yourself. The important elements are:

- Breaking the movements, or the music, into more simple, well-defined elements
- Focusing your attention and listening
- Working slowly at first
- Increasing complexity gradually
- Using a metronome
- Working on the same idea for a short time, say 5-10 minutes, for at least a week
- Tracking your progress, recording yourself

Depending on your instrument it may be helpful to begin with just one hand, for example picking one repeated note on the guitar, or single bows on one string, and then adding the left hand.

Today I'll work on playing with both hands in perfect sync.

177 Between the Shoulder Blades

There's an area of the upper back, roughly between the shoulder blades, that, for most of us, is habitually tense. It's often the first area to tighten when we're under stress, even before the face or shoulders. This is the same area that dogs and cats tense in reaction to threat, causing their fur to rise so they look bigger. That response is not useful for modern, hairless humans.

Unfortunately many of us are so habituated to this stress reaction that the muscles in this area *seldom fully relax*, even when we're asleep. Even though we may be unaware of it, this constant tension puts an extra "load" on our bodies, limiting movement in other muscles, contributing to overall fatigue, and, of course, affecting our ability to play with ease.

If you make a practice of drawing your attention to the area between the shoulder blades and allowing it to release, you can begin to form a habit that can take on its own, healing momentum.

Put It into Practice

We're used to exercises that consist of doing something until it becomes a habit. This one is a little different. You might think of it as repeatedly *un-doing* something until it becomes a habit.

- Sit in a chair without your instrument. Draw your mind's eye to the area between your shoulder blades. Breathe in deeply, and as you exhale, relax the upper back. Notice any other areas that change. You may even feel the skin in that area relax.

- Take a few deep breaths. Try to stay focused on the feeling in this area. With each breath try to let go just a little more.

- Carefully pick up and hold your instrument. Try to maintain the relaxed, open feeling in your upper back.

- Play a few simple notes.

- As you practice, periodically pause and draw your attention to the feeling between your shoulder blades. Stop if you need to, and take a few breaths to bring back that feeling of open relaxation.

- Gradually, over a period of days, or weeks, you'll be more and more able to relax your upper back, even as you play.

It can be a challenge even to *feel* the muscles between your shoulder blades, let alone release them. If this is true for you, try minimizing distractions by lying on your back instead of sitting a chair.

Today I'll draw my attention to the tension in the muscles between my shoulder blades.

178   The Next Note after the Hard One

I've noticed that often, after I've "made it" through a challenging passage of music, I make a mistake just *after* the passage? These unexpected flubs can be very frustrating.

Years ago I read that when people lie, they often pause in their speech just *after* the lie. The working theory for why this happens, as I remember, was that the brain expends effort to construct the lie and to tell it believably. After all that effort, the brain needs a little cognitive rest. Hence the pause.[26]

If we imagine that the brain is seeking a little cognitive "vacation" after we play something difficult, it can help us avoid these unexpected mistakes.

Put It into Practice

After you've smoothed out a challenging area, practice *until you can comfortably play through the next few measures as well.*

Once you're aware of it, it won't be long before your brain doesn't need a break on the next note after the hard one.

Today I'll pay attention to what happens just after a challenging passage.

179 Develop Counterarguments

When I was in graduate school I took a course called Persuasion. We studied how people are persuaded, and also how to help them resist being persuaded. We looked at research on everything from smoking cigarettes, to voting, to eating choices.

It turns out that one of the best ways to keep from succumbing to an unhealthy or unwanted suggestion is to have "counterarguments" ready-to-mind. When the commercial for sugary breakfast cereal splashes onto the screen, if you can easily remember how lethargic and depressed it makes you feel to eat Frosted Sugar Bombs, you'll may not reach for the cereal box.

Try developing some counterarguments that will help you sit down to practice when your mind is offering up some other more exciting, but unwanted, behavior.

Put It into Practice

First, see if you can become aware of the thoughts that typically come to mind when you don't feel like practicing. Here are four that commonly come up for me:

- I don't have time.
- I'm too tired.
- I'll never be very good anyway.
- I didn't practice yesterday or the day before, so there's not much point in practicing today.

Develop explicit counterarguments for each of these "reasons." Here are some that resonate with me:

- All I have to do is pick up the instrument. I don't have to play for an hour.
- Practicing makes me energized, especially if I do something I enjoy.
- Look at where I was a year ago! Practicing really works!
- It doesn't matter what I did or didn't do yesterday. What matters is what I do from now forward.

With your counterarguments at the ready you'll be less likely to succumb to the inertia of not practicing.

Today I'll prepare myself with counterarguments, so I will *sit down to practice.*

180   Relaxing while Playing Fast

It's one thing to try to relax when we're simply sitting or standing. It's harder to stay relaxed when we're moving, and especially difficult when we're doing something as complex as playing a musical instrument. When we're trying to play fast, the difficulty of staying relaxed skyrockets.

I've often found myself hammering away at a musical or technical issue that only crops up at faster speeds, only to realize that if I could just stay relaxed, I'd quickly solve the problem.

You can learn to stay relaxed while playing fast. It just requires attention and practice.

Put It into Practice

The Practice Pyramid is an excellent tool to help you stay relaxed as you play faster.[*]

Remember that the ***base of the pyramid*** is:

---

[*] See the Practice Pyramid in Appendix A, and 5 – Working with the Practice Pyramid

- Always play *relaxed* and *in time*

You then **pick two** of the remaining three elements (***Play Fast***, ***Play Perfectly***, and ***Play the Whole Thing***) to focus on. Since you've already chosen to play fast, you can:

- Play the entire tune or section (***Play the Whole Thing***) and blow through your "mistakes" (don't ***Play Perfectly***)

- Choose a short snippet (don't ***Play the Whole Thing***) that you can play without mistakes (***Play Perfectly***).

When you use this tool, a goal of the practice is to allow your body and mind to absorb the way it feels to combine speed with relaxation. This may be a new feeling. When you return to a more typical, slower practice speed, staying relaxed is likely to be easier, too. Gradually the speed at which you can stay relaxed and accurate will inch its way up.

Today I'll practice relaxing while playing fast.

181 Transitions

Transitions plague us all. When we move from one tune to another in a medley, or from the A to the B section in one tune, we often falter. It can happen even when the notes or chords themselves are not particularly difficult.

The reason we stumble may be because we're interrupting a musical pattern. It may be that we play those transition notes less often than we play the rest of the tune. Whatever the reason, *we need to give special attention to transitions.*

Put It into Practice

- Practice transitions more than you practice the main body of the tune.

- Go over them mentally before starting the tune.

- Sing them.

- Visualize them.

- Color them with a mental highlight marker.
- *Know* the notes, *know* where they are going, why they are there.
- Use other tools in your practice toolbox, and apply them directly to the transitions in the tune.

Being able to flow smoothly through transitions can help your playing become more effortless, and let you stay focused on *making music*. Give your transition notes a little special care and attention and they'll reward you for it.

Today I'll give special attention to transitions.

182 Embracing Uncertainty

All of us are anxious when faced with uncertain outcomes. The world we live in is increasingly complex and interconnected. It can feel that we need tools to help us maintain equanimity in the face of uncertainty, simply to survive and stay sane. In a very real way, music practice can be one of those tools.

The work of practicing involves consistent, methodical, attentive and goal-oriented effort. This might seem to be the intuitive opposite of learning to be comfortable with uncertainty. At the same time, playing music is rooted in self-expression and responsiveness. Striving for some imaginary ideal of perfection and trying to erase every possible variable or unknown can lead to constant frustration.

We seek proficiency, control, comprehension, a broad repertoire. But we also need to be open and responsive, and have balance and composure in the face of the unexpected. Strengthening these qualities in our playing can benefit our response to stresses in daily life as well.

Improvising musicians train explicitly to respond to uncertainty: to take a curve ball such as a phrase played by another musician, an unexpected chord or note, or a mistake, and mold it into something great. The best trad musicians also put ideas into practice that allow them to take uncertainty in stride.

Violin bowing offers an example. Kevin Burke and Martin Hayes are two master Irish fiddlers who stress the importance of a fluid approach to bowing. They teach students to play Irish tunes without becoming attached to a particular bowing pattern. This is quite different from the way bowing is taught in a classical, especially orchestral, context.

Once a player is comfortable making the same sound with an up or a down bow, or easily switching from long, legato bow strokes to short, detached ones, it's easier to adjust phrasing, emphasis, rhythm or even notes, in response to a creative impulse.

Not all trad musicians play Irish music on violin. But all musicians can be alert for opportunities to accept, and even embrace, uncertainty and turn it into an opportunity for creativity.

Today I'll work on accepting uncertainty.

183 Consonants

If you were trying to sing and sound like a brass instrument, chances are you'd use a range of sounds from "brrrrrap!" to "pah pah pah" or "mwah." We often change the consonant at the beginning of the sound, pa, ba, da, zha, etc. Yet we often forget that it's not just horns that can make use of many of these sounds.

Consider how sound is produced on your instrument. Every note you make has a beginning, middle and end. Even after you stop playing the sound may resonate, both in the instrument and in the room. These four elements are called *attack, sustain, release and decay*.[*]

The first three elements, attack, sustain and release, are accomplished differently on every instrument, through plucking, blowing, bowing, etc. A given instrument may have more or less control over a note as it is sustained.

---

[*] Sound engineers would describe this somewhat differently, but this description should suffice for musicians who are not modifying the sounds after they're recorded.

If you think just about the possible "attack" sounds you can make, how many options do you have? The chances are there are more sounds are available than you're currently using.

Put It into Practice

- Playing one note, try to make as many different initial sounds as you can think of.

- You may not be able to make a "Brrrrrap!" sound on your instrument. What does it sound like if you play *as if you could*?

- Are there other, consonant-like sounds that are unique to your instrument?

- If you run out of ideas try lilting or "turlutting." What nonsense syllables best express your understanding of the music? Can you reproduce them on the instrument?

- Give special attention to the beginnings of phrases and repeated notes.

Consonants offer a new sound playground to explore in your playing.

Today I'll think about the "consonant" sound that I make at the beginning of each note.

184 Give Yourself a Gold Star

When I was seven, my piano teacher stuck gold stars on my music at the end of every lesson. Where are my gold stars now?

As we become more accomplished, we tend to focus on increasingly subtle details. It can be hard to stay motivated because it's more difficult to perceive our progress. At the same time, these results are real. It's important to find ways to give ourselves positive reinforcement. We need those mental "gold stars" to keep feeling good about our progress.

Put It into Practice

- In your practice notebook, **write down something you did well today**. Be specific, not just about what challenged you, but about how you succeeded. "Memorized B part!" "Good rhythmic accuracy." "Intonation in G minor!"

- When you're feeling frustrated, go back through your notes. You'll see the things you've got under your belt that were difficult even a week ago.

- **Make a benchmark recording**. You don't even need to record the whole tune. Just record what you're working on: an ornament, a snippet, intonation, an exercise. Listen later: At the end of your practice session. Tomorrow. Next week. In five months.

- **Listen to your playing** at the beginning of your practice session. Listen with great attention to detail. Then listen the same way at the end. Imagine you are a compassionate teacher. What would your teacher say?

- **Start and/or end your practice time with something positive**. Play something that has nothing to do with what you're working on: a song from childhood, a show tune, or something you love to play. Give yourself a treat– a cup of tea, a piece of chocolate – either while you play or afterward.

- **Give yourself an actual, verbal, "attaboy/girl."** You *did* practice for 5, or 20, or 60 minutes. You *did* work on that tune. Do a little dance. "Yeah! I did that!"

- Go ahead and **get a packet of gold star stickers**. Yes, they still sell them.

Today I'll give myself a gold star.

185 Six Direction Spine Stretch

Many of us stretch our backs when we feel tired or achy, but we seldom make an effort to move the spine in all six of the directions in which it has mobility.

Stretching our backs in all six directions can help bring the muscles of the back and spine back into balance, and can help us feel better overall. The bones of the back form the core structure supporting the entire body. Within the spinal column, the nerves in the spinal cord connect all the parts of the body to the brain.

As with any stretch, move to a point of comfort, not of pain. If you do feel discomfort, back off the stretch and see if you can re-approach the stretch in a way that offers a more comfortable, opening sensation.

Forward Bend

From a standing position, inhale deeply. Imagine yourself growing taller. As you exhale, bend forward from the waist, curling the back in a "C" shape. Bend your knees to make this feel comfortable. Unless you can easily reach the floor, rest your hands on something like a chair or a tabletop. This can help with stability and take the strain off your back, allowing you to relax more.

Breathe deeply and evenly. See if you can feel a little more release in the lower back and legs with each exhalation. Stay here for a few breaths or whatever feels good to you.

When you're ready to come up, do so as you inhale. Use the chair or table and your abdominal muscles to help you.

Backward Bend

From a standing position, put your hands on your lower back with the fingers pointed down, as if you were putting them into your back pockets.

Don't bend backwards yet! First, inhale deeply, imagining your spine becoming long. Let your shoulders relax away from your ears. Draw your belly strongly toward the spine. Keeping the abdominal muscles engaged, lift up the rib cage and let just your upper torso fall gently back. Rather than thinking about "bending backward," focus on becoming taller and opening the chest.

Some people are comfortable with a backward bend in their lower spine. That's fine, though it's not necessary *at all* in order to get benefit from this stretch. You can simply focus on lengthening the spine and opening the chest and upper back.

Side Bend (Both Sides)

Stand with your feet hip distance apart (best for stability), or closer together. Breathe in deeply and extend your spine long, from the hips to the top of the head. Imagine yourself growing tall.

Now begin the bend: Raise your left arm above your head with the palm facing toward the head. Keep the right arm relaxed at your side. As you exhale, lift your rib cage up and then stretch your torso gently to the right. Keep breathing. With each exhalation, see if you can find, and then release, a little more tightness and tension.

Try not to prop your right hand on your hip. If you feel you need more support or stability, release the bend a little or rest your arm on a table or countertop.

Switch to the other side.

Standing Twist (Both Sides)

Begin in a standing position, as with the side bend. Breathe in deeply as you let the shoulders relax away from the ears.

As you exhale, twist your upper torso to the right. Your arms and hands can be out to either side, gently wrapped around your body, with the palms on the back of your head, or relaxed at the sides.

Draw your attention to the feeling in your spine, abdominal area, and the muscles of the torso and chest as you breathe evenly and deeply.

Try to keep the hips facing forward. Resist the urge to "crank" your shoulders and head around. Let the head float freely. Relax the shoulders, lift the spine longer, and then, as you exhale, see if you can use the muscles in the waist, rather than your head and neck, to twist.

Switch to the other side.

Cautions:

> Exercise common sense with your own health. If you have a back or neck injury or another health concern, or if you experience pain during one of these stretches, stop and seek professional advice. If you have balance issues, hold onto something and go very slowly. If you have high or low blood pressure, take caution, especially with forward bends. A qualified instructor or movement therapist may be able to help you adjust any pose so that it is beneficial. If you are pregnant, be particularly gentle when practicing twists.

Today I'll try stretching my spine in six directions.

186 Writing It Down

> "La transcription est une trahison."
> "Transcription is treason."
> – Robert Bouthillier[27]

Whether or not you typically read sheet music, there are times when it's useful to be able to save and share music in written form. There's benefit also in the *activity* of writing music. It's well-established that writing down what you're learning helps you to understand and remember it.

You can probably think of many ***objections*** to the idea of writing music.

- ***It can be quite a struggle.*** Most of us are not used to writing musical notation. Even if we're used to reading it, writing it is quite a different story.

- ***It may seem impractical.*** Most of the tunes we play have already been written by somebody, somewhere. Why not just use those?

- ***It can take a lot of time.*** That might be time that you'd like to spend practicing.

Here are a few of the *benefits* of writing down music:

- It can help your note-taking to more details about specific notes, measures or passages you're working on.

- Writing something down, even just a measure or two, helps us process it cognitively and helps us remember it better.

- Your version of the tune may not be the same as versions you might find online or in books. You may want to add harmonies, different chords, a melodic variation, or something else.

- If you do something that you want to remember – or maybe if you write a tune! – writing it down may take longer than recording it. Later, though, it may be easier to access a written version than a recording.

- Seeing the music laid out visually can be illuminating. Whether it's the rhythm, the chords, note lengths, visual patterns or something else, seeing the notation can sometimes answer questions or solve problems.

- Being able to share tunes and versions of tunes with others is a great asset.

The *method* you choose to write music depends on both your purpose and your level of comfort with technology. If you're just keeping track of chord backup or writing arrangements, as one teacher told me, "As long as *you* can read it, it's OK." If it's only for you, your manuscript doesn't have to look anything like traditional music notation. Develop your own system, why not?

You can be as detailed as you want. It's your choice whether you write every bowing, accordion switch and chord tone, or just outline the basic tune.

In addition to writing music out by hand there are many computer-assisted options for writing music. Most of these offer the ability to play back what you've written through a MIDI interface and to transpose, print, share files electronically, and more. Each method has its advocates.*

There's also notation and tablature written for specific instruments and styles. If you're frustrated with the options available through standard notation, one of these may work for you.

Writing music can require patience, especially at first, but once you get past the initial struggles the ability to write music can be a great practice aid.

Today I'll try writing music down.

187   Shine

I often feel some conflict when it comes to my ego.

On the one hand I understand that *humility is good*. Nobody wants to hang around with someone who thinks they're the most important person in the room. In studying Buddhism I've read about the idea of "no-self." This idea proposes that our concept of a permanent, unchanging "self" or "ego" is illusory, so there's no point in trying to hang onto it. That makes at least *some* sense to me.

On the other hand, *self-confidence is good*. There are aspects of being a musician that can be ego-crushing. In the face of my insecurities, my awareness of how much I have to learn, the giants on whose shoulders I stand, and the talented young people coming after me, I do feel an urge to guard and protect my ego, to remind myself of my own value, progress and ability as a musician.

Playing in front of an audience, or even playing with a group, can cause some conflict between these two ideas. As a performer I want to draw people's attention, be engaging, interesting and worth paying attention

---

* I'm a personal fan of ABC notation. It can be used to quickly record a tune or snippet using pen and paper or keyboard without drawing horizontal staff lines. There's a lot of information available on the Internet. Many trad musicians are familiar with ABC notation and are happy to explain the principles.

to. Doesn't that sound a bit egotistical? Where does humility belong in all this?

Struggling with this idea, I asked one of my aikido teachers for his opinion. He said, "When you stand up in front of others, just shine."

Today I'll just shine.

188   Piano

I remember making a trip to Italy and hearing a mother caution her son in a restaurant, "Piano, Luca, piano!" The word *piano* is Italian for quiet. In sheet music, *p, pp,* and *ppp* mean piano, more piano, and as piano as you possibly can.*

Playing *ppp* is one of the most challenging things to do on any instrument. Most of us never play very quietly. We play either *moderately loud* or *very loud*.

The thought of playing quietly seldom even occurs to most of us. So, naturally, we're not good at it. When we try to play quietly our tone suffers. We have trouble creating a reliable sound. We end up in a vicious cycle, never playing quietly because we don't sound good, never sounding good at playing quietly because we don't practice it.

There are excellent reasons to be able to play quietly. The ability to play at low volume gives you a greater range of expressive options. Playing quietly can lead a listener to "lean in" and pay more attention to your playing. Having the control to play quietly allows you to accompany another instrument or a singer without overwhelming them. The ability to play *piano* may make you a more in-demand player with ensembles that include quieter instruments – particularly if your instrument is naturally loud.

It's true that *ppp* isn't an option for all instruments. Yet, whatever the dynamic range of your instrument, being aware and in control of the

---

* You probably know that the musical instrument we call a piano was originally called a pianoforte. This referred to the fact that, unlike a harpsichord, it allows for variation in volume.

quietest sounds you can make is an important aspect of your musicianship.

Today I'll work on having more control of my sound, even at ppp.

189   Aimaisa

An aikido student wrote to me from Japan where he was on an extended visit. He told me about an experience in a calligraphy class. When he asked the teacher, "How should I do this particular brush stroke?" she answered, "Boldly!"

The teacher was using the technique of *aimaisa*. *Aimaisa* translates from Japanese as something like "vagueness" or "ambiguity." If the teacher had given him the technical answer he was expecting, such as, "With a downward stroke" or, "Thin at the top, fat at the bottom," my student might have focused on trying to make his work *look correct.* By trying helping him connect with the *feeling* of drawing the character, she was offering a deeper level of understanding *based on direct experience.*

To create art, including music, we need to transcend the concept of playing "correctly" and find a way to *play from our own direct experience.*

It's fairly straightforward to learn things like good hand and arm position, to learn the notes of a tune, to get the "feel" of a style or idiom, or even to reproduce the nuances of an acknowledged master of the style.

How, though, do we connect with our playing on a deeper, more personal level?

Boldly![28]

Today I'll try to connect with my musicianship through direct experience.

190   I Can't Hear Myself

The first time I was actually paid to play piano was for a friend's CD release concert. Since I did not play on the recording, I had to learn all the piano parts. I practiced, we rehearsed, I practiced, we rehearsed, we sound checked. I was ready.

When we played the show on stage, I was completely taken aback: *I couldn't hear myself.* I now know that by normal standards I could hear myself fine. I just wasn't used to playing in a large hall with the other instruments amplified and the sound coming from speakers instead of from the instruments themselves. Without my usual auditory references, I was quite rattled.

There are many situations where you may not be able to hear your instrument: in a workshop full of other [*your instrument here*] players, in a noisy jam session, sitting next to a bagpiper, in a room with a bad acoustic. Experienced touring musicians will attest that even when you have an excellent sound engineer, things happen and you just have to carry on.

Playing without audio feedback is a challenge, but it's an extremely useful skill and, as in the example above, it could be a critical one. It can also be a challenge to find a way to practice that skill.

One way is to work on *knowing* what you're doing without the need for auditory confirmation.[*] Another way is to make use of situations like jams and workshops where you can't hear yourself, and to *use them as part of your practice.* You could even put yourself in those situations intentionally – after all, the seat next to the accordion player is often available!

Meanwhile, a broad-brimmed hat can be more than a fashion asset. It helps reflect your instrument's sound back to your ears.

Today I'll consider developing my capacity to play without being able to hear myself.

191   It's All Your Voice

I had a conversation with singer Laurel Massée about learning a new instrument. I mentioned that learning the accordion had made me aware

---

[*] See 123 - Mute

of the way the instrument uses air. I said it reminded me of the way a singer breathes, and that thinking about this had improved my musicality on the accordion. I burbled on about how that idea could be translated to a lot of instruments, not just wind instruments, for example that people talk about violin bowing in terms of inhaling (upbow) and exhaling (downbow)…

"It's *all* your voice," Laurel said, "every instrument."

I thought of my piano, a 7-foot black, wooden beast with a cast iron frame and strings that hold 30 tons of tension. That's *my voice*?

But Laurel expressed it perfectly. A musical instrument is a tool we use to express the sound of the original instrument, the human voice. When I think about it this way, I approach making music in a totally different manner.

Today I'll use my instrument as my voice.

192   Making a Recording

I decided to record an eight-song CD as a holiday gift for family and friends. It was a home-made affair, very simple, but I took it seriously. I tried to play well and make good quality recordings. The result was a gift not just for others but for myself, too.

When you listen back to a recording of yourself you hear your own playing stripped of the veil of what you *intended* or *hoped* to sound like. It is difficult at first. (Isn't that why we avoid doing it?) After a period of adjustment, however, the honesty can be refreshing and also instructive.

What I Heard:

> ***Rhythmic Precision.*** Despite playing with a metronome every day, I'm not nearly as rhythmically accurate as I want to be. I recorded with a "click track." Though the overall tempo was steady, I could hear variation within the tune, especially as I tried to play melody to my own backup track. When I imported my tracks to music editing software, these issues were visible on the timeline. Some notes were on the beat, some a little before and some a little after.

Musicality. Listening to a recording, it was much easier to hear the elements of "musicality" in my playing. Because I wasn't engaged in the process of producing the sounds, I could give listening my full attention. I listened for the effect the music had on me: whether it conveyed emotion and whether it held my attention. I experienced the effects of dynamics, the way notes started and ended, and changes in tone or emphasis.

Control. As I listened back I sometimes thought, "I'd like to do that slightly differently." But when I recorded another take, I often found I couldn't make the desired change *and* maintain speed, accuracy and calmness. I realized that this was another level of mastery I could set my sights on.

All the issues I described above are very addressable, when you're able to hear them. It's important to be a compassionate self-teacher and to be discerning rather than critical,[*] but if you're willing to do those things, recording yourself can be a very powerful tool.

There was a time when only professional musicians had access to high-quality recording equipment and to all the learning and insight that was gained as a result. Now that we can make a decent-to-excellent recording with a smartphone, a tablet, or a moderately-priced, hand-held recorder, *why don't we use this learning tool more often?*

Today I will use recording as a learning tool.

193 Fast Practice

When we play at fast speeds, we use different attacks, hand movements, phrasing, bow strokes, ornamentation and fingering. A tune's rhythm can change too. Dotted or "swung" rhythms can start to sound more even.[†] We may naturally add "groove" to rhythms that were more even and march-y.

---

[*] See 74 – Discernment vs. Criticism

[†] For more about "swing," see 146 – Playing with Swing

On the other hand, at faster speeds we can lose the control and rhythmic accuracy that are possible at a slower speed. This is one reason why many professional musicians say they spend much of their practice time working at faster speeds.

For most non-professional musicians, though, spending a lot of time playing fast is not necessarily a benefit. If we're practicing for control, rhythmic accuracy and musicality, and we don't have those elements at slower speeds we're not going to attain them by practicing faster.

When you're able to play at a measured pace, *and* stay relaxed, able to listen and think ahead, then it's worth working on increasing speed.

One benefit of fast(er) practice is that *it exposes anything you don't know deeply*. When you give these elements your full attention during practice, your ability will grow.

Here are three practice methods for building speed. Choose one that looks fun. If you want to work on this idea, make a plan to do it for at least a week. If possible, stick to it for six weeks or so. Record your progress. Use a metronome. Stay relaxed.

Put It into Practice

Fast and Slow

- Alternate playing a few times at the speed where you feel comfortable, musical and relaxed, and one where you can get somewhere between ½ and ¾ of the notes. Pause for several seconds to gather your thoughts before switching tempos.*

Bursts

- Set the metronome at your goal tempo. You're going to try just playing a few notes at that tempo. Listen to the metronome and imagine the tune at that speed. It may seem ridiculously fast for your fingers. If so, just repeat one note in the rhythm of the tune to get your body accustomed to the speed.

---

* See 121 – Playing Fast and Slow

- Keeping the Practice Pyramid* in mind, try playing a short section. It doesn't matter how short, even if it's just a few notes, as long as you can stay in time and relaxed.

- Pause. Gather your thoughts. Try another burst.

- After a minute or so, dial the metronome back to the slower speed. How does that feel?

- As an option, while you pause keep repeating one note until you're ready to try the burst again.

Listen and Repeat

- Set yourself up so you can play along with another musician's recording of the tune. This works best if you can use a "slowdowner" app or an online tool that lets you create loops of a recording. Set up loop of a few measures. At first, try this without slowing down the recording.

- Alternate between listening for four bars and playing along for four bars. Make sure to stay relaxed, and devote your attention to listening when you're not playing.

- If this speed is impossible, slow down the recording until you are able to play along with the segment. You may not be happy with your efforts – that's OK. As long as your fingers are moving, your body is relaxed and you're not literally dropping your instrument or your mallets, you're getting the feeling of playing fast into your body.

There are elements of fast playing – often unique to each instrument – that require their own approach. You may develop them yourself through trial and error or with the help of a teacher or musical mentor. Don't expect to become a speed demon in one practice session. It may turn out that this isn't the time for you to work on this particular skill. Whatever happens, it's sure to be interesting and may even be fun. Look for benefits in the practice itself rather than seeing it as a means to an end.

Today I'll try practicing for speed.

---

* There's more about the Practice Pyramid in Appendix A.

194   The Presentation Rule

> "Tell them what you're going to tell them. Tell them. Then tell them what you told them."
>
> – Advice given to business presenters

When you start an important presentation, it's common practice to begin with an outline, present the main body of your ideas, and finish with a summary.

The outline at the start allows the audience to create a mental framework so that later, when you're deep in the weeds of your presentation, your listener can fit each idea into that framework.

The summary at the end helps relate all the details they heard to the original message points. It makes it more likely that, as they walk away, the audience will retain the ideas you want them to.

I often use this presentation technique when I practice, with my own brain as the audience. I run through a list of what I'm going to work on before I begin. I might think,

> "Today, I'm going to refresh my memory on what I did yesterday. I'll work on that technical issue for five or ten minutes. Next, I'll warm up in three scales. I'll work on the two tunes for my group lesson, then maybe one or two more, let's see how far I get. For the last 10 minutes I'll just have fun, maybe play along with a favorite recording."

Then I do the work. If I have to take a break, it's fine. Because I gave myself an outline at the get-go, I know exactly where to pick up again.

At the end, I spend a minute or two writing down what I did. As I do, I'm very explicit in giving myself my "walk away" ideas: positive thoughts, progress, what I liked and didn't like.

At the end of a practice session, I feel I've organized my time well. I have ideas on improvements I've made, and about what I might work on tomorrow. And I've explicitly given myself positive thoughts that will stay with me until my next practice session.

Today I'll try the Presentation Rule, with my brain as the audience.

195 Overlearning

"Overlearning" refers to an approach in which you keep to a repetitive practice method far beyond the level where improvement is taking place. Rather than practicing until you get it right, you practice *until you can't get it wrong*.

Musicians, public speakers, basketball players and actors are among those who use this technique so they can perform at the same level even when under pressure or stress.

Overlearning is a useful tool, but only when you can play a tune the way you want to play it, in time, without obvious flubs. If you keep repeating wrong notes, or keep pausing or slowing down, you'll end up ingraining that sound into your ear and your fingers.

I've been a strong advocate in these pages of mindful and attentive practice. It might seem like a contradiction to advocate what sounds like mindless repetition. Overlearning is distinct from mindless repetition. When we learn a tune well enough that the *mechanics* of playing are no longer occupying conscious thought, we can devote attention to listening. Active listening is far from a mindless activity. Listening can occupy our entire consciousness.

While overlearning by itself doesn't make you a more musical player, it *can* free you up to play more musically. Having the confidence that you won't mess up – that you *can't* mess up – may help you relax, allowing you to listen more closely than you ever have before.

Today I'll try "overlearning."

196 Goal Setting

Goal setting can be a powerful practice. Articulating what you're hoping to learn or accomplish can help you decide how you should spend your practice time overall. It can also help you make choices about what you want to include in your musical life.

When you have a clear idea of your goals it's easier to work toward achieving them.

Many of us reject the idea of setting goals, perhaps because we've been disappointed by not reaching them in the past. Goals don't need to be a list of things you want to do. They can include things that are important to you in order to be happy and creatively fulfilled. Seen that way, the goal setting process can generate a lot of insight.

Put It into Practice

Think about the coming 12 months.* In the spirit of brainstorming, be ready to listen to anything your brain offers up no matter how unexpected or oddball. Don't ignore or belittle thoughts that occur to you. Make a mental note, or a written one.

- What, *musically*, would you like to attract into your life or do more of? What problems or issues would you like to solve? What would you like to see happen, both within you and around you?

- Think specifically about *your life* a year from now. What will it mean to have realized your goals? How will you be spending your time? Who will you be spending it with? What activities will you have done that you're proud of? What will you be preparing for?

- Next, look at the *activities* you spend time on now. You can use broad categories: Work, Take Care of Mom, Finish House Renovation, Practice, Leisure. You can make it a music-specific list: Practice for Lesson, Learn New Tunes, Practice for Band A, Mandolin Orchestra Admin, Practice for Gig B.

- Now look at the way the activities you listed *align with your vision*. It's unlikely that there will be a perfect match. There may not even be good one – that's simply life for many of us. Yet you may recognize activities that you don't need to continue. You may do these out of habit, a sense of obligation, or because you're used to having a certain role or status. Seen in the light of your goals, these activities may have less importance.

---

* You can also add goals for two years, five years or more if you'd like.

- Once you've defined your path, don't worry about it much. There's no need to hang anything on the fridge or track it with an app. Let your brain do the work.
- You may want to write down your thoughts so that, in a year or so, you can revisit your goals and see what happened.

Having clarity about our objectives can inform many small, daily decisions that can slowly add up to something meaningful. The power of attention is in some ways like a laser beam: It seems insubstantial, yet it can cut not only with force but precision.

Today I'll take some time to articulate my goals.

197   Simple Idea! Why So Difficult?

One night after an aikido seminar a group of students convened at a local restaurant with Sensei.* As everyone chatted about aikido topics, Sensei met my eye. In his thick Japanese accent he said, "Judy, Sensei is so skinny and small! How do *you* think Sensei beats so many strong students? And *so easy!*" He rolled up his sleeve to show how small his biceps are. "The secret is, Judy: *I never use muscle*! Such a simple idea! Why so difficult?"

I've seen Sensei roll up his sleeves and show his "unimpressive" biceps at least 100 times, and I've heard him say not to use muscle another 500 times. This principle, that we should relax and not force our way through technique, is one that Kokikai students are taught in every class.[29]

Because he is committed to practicing without muscle, Sensei is able to do things that, from a martial arts perspective, seem incredible. He easily throws people who are younger, physically much larger, who train with weights, who train in other martial arts. He has reached the age of 60, even 70, and this ability is still growing. In contrast, most aikido students revert to using muscle as soon as they face resistance or challenge. Sensei's idea, "Don't use muscle," is simple. But it's difficult to do in practice.

---

* The founder of Kokikai Aikido is Shuji Maruyama Sensei. We usually call him just "Sensei."

When we hear an idea that sounds interesting or helpful, we often think, "Yes, that makes sense, I understand." Our brains equate "understanding" with the ability to do something. In reality, incorporating even a single new habit into our playing takes repeated effort and attention. Changing an existing routine, whether it's a pattern of action or of thought, can feel awkward and uncomfortable. Consciously or unconsciously, we avoid change.

I hope I've encouraged, motivated or even goaded just a few musicians into doing more than just reading and saying, "Yes, that makes sense, I understand." These *are* simple ideas. They *can* be effective – if you make a commitment to practicing them with attention.

Today I'll make a commitment to my practice, even if I just work on one simple idea.

Appendix A – The Practice Pyramid

The Practice Pyramid[30] is a very useful tool for efficient and effective practice. It lets you focus on key elements in your playing without becoming overwhelmed by the need to do everything at once.

The Pyramid

Imagine a pyramid with a triangular base and three sides.

The base of the pyramid represents the foundation of your playing, the key elements that should always be present. The three sides represent variables that you can change, depending on what you want to work on.

The five key elements of the Practice Pyramid are:

- Fast
- Perfectly   } **Variables** – keep two, let the third go
- The Whole Thing
- Relaxed   } **Constant** – foundation
- In Time

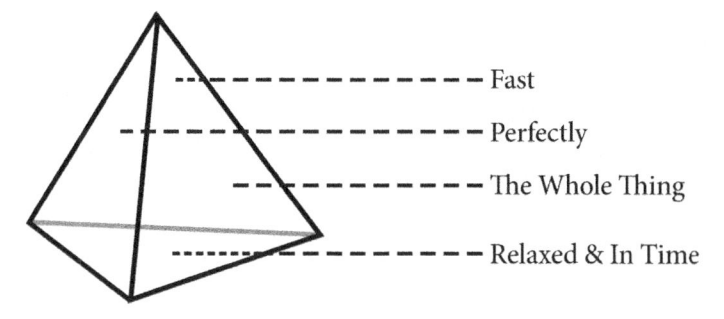

- - - - - - - - - - - Fast
- - - - - - - - - - - Perfectly
- - - - - - - - - - - The Whole Thing
- - - - - - - - - - - Relaxed & In Time

When you play and practice, your goal should be always to play in time, and play relaxed. That's the base of the pyramid.

Then you can choose how to practice, depending on which of the three remaining elements you want to focus on. *You'll keep two, and let the third go.*

Definitions

Play in Time

If you don't already, make it a habit always to practice "in time" or "in rhythm." No matter whether you're playing fast or slow, keep the beat evenly, without slowing down, speeding up or hesitating – even when you make a mistake. Use a metronome.

There are times when you need to practice "out of time." Think of these as special cases or exceptions. To put it differently, when you're not playing in time make sure it is a decision, not an accident.

Play Relaxed

Whenever you practice, perform or play with others, make it your goal *always* to remain as relaxed as possible. When your body is relaxed, you're more able to pay attention, listen, move accurately and efficiently, and even think ahead. I sometimes call this *playing with relaxed attentiveness,* but "play relaxed" will do.

Play Fast

What you consider "fast" depends on your ability and your goals. If there's a particular speed you're aiming for, like a dance tempo, you might work to play at that tempo. On another day, "fast" might mean "faster than you usually play," somewhere outside your current range.

Play Perfectly

Go easy on yourself as to what constitutes "perfectly." Make a decision as to what is a reasonable challenge in terms of notes, dynamics, musicality or whatever is on your wish list. What you consider to be playing "perfectly" will change as you become more accomplished. That's OK.

Play the Whole Thing

Playing "the whole thing" means not just playing a few measures or notes. You may decide that "the whole thing" is the entire tune, the A section, an entire medley of three tunes, or something similar.

Using the Practice Pyramid

Here are your three practice scenarios:

Let Go of Playing Fast

Work on the whole thing, *as slowly as it takes* to play perfectly while staying in time and staying relaxed.

Let Go of Playing Perfectly

Play the whole thing fast. *Accept all your mess-ups*, stay in time and stay relaxed.

Let Go of Playing the Whole Thing

Play as short a section as you need to while playing perfectly and fast, staying in time and relaxed. You may only be able to play a few notes.

A Note on Playing Relaxed

We know intuitively that we play better when we're relaxed. It's my experience that people also learn more quickly when they are relaxed. The Practice Pyramid is an approach we can use to **practice relaxing**, even as we work to hone our musical ability. Eventually, being relaxed while playing will become second nature, and feeling tense while playing will feel so strange that you'll immediately notice and correct it.

Appendix B – Jamming Best Practices

Jam sessions happen all over the world: in pubs, coffee houses, church rec rooms, living rooms and anywhere a few people can cram around a table. Attending a jam session is a great way to meet people, no matter where you live.

The etiquette of jam sessions is based on common courtesy and thoughtfulness. An understanding of the expected behavior in jams will smooth the way, not just for your own introduction in the jam, but for those jammers who may come after you.

Jamming Etiquette

- *Be a good listener first, a good player second.*
- A jam session is different from an open mic or a performance. The tunes that are often most welcomed are those *that allow for more participation*. Complicated tunes, esoteric tunes, or tunes that show off your own ability are not typically good choices especially at first.
- A jam session is usually based on a type of music or concept (Irish/Celtic, Song Swap, Old Time, Swedish, Balkan, etc.). If you don't know any tunes in that genre, *don't start tunes in a different genre* unless you're specifically asked to do so.
- *Be guided by what's going on around you, particularly the behavior of players you see as "leaders."* Depending on the jam and the genre, the players may be expected to stick to the melody. In others, harmony and riffing are encouraged. Some jams choose tunes by going around the circle, in others people just jump in with tunes. Still others are more formal, with a leader choosing most of the tunes and asking people to start tunes. Some jams encourage singing. In others, only a few or no songs will be sung.
- At most jam sessions there's time between the tunes for a little socializing. *Relax. You don't need to play every minute.*

- *Sheet music*: If the players in the jam don't use it (and most don't), leave yours at home. If you need a cheat sheet to start a tune, try writing notes on a small piece of paper or refer to a screenshot on your phone.

- *Be aware of your volume,* especially if you have a loud instrument. Give the quieter instruments (especially singers) a chance to be heard.

- *Resist the temptation to "noodle"* or play between songs. If you need to work out chord changes or go over the melody, do it silently or as close to silently as you can.

- *Make sure your instrument is in tune.*

- *Stick with the tempo of whoever started the tune.* If you can't keep up, pause until you can. If you like to play faster, this is your chance to practice sticking to a slower tempo.

- *Not all jam sessions are open to all comers or to all instruments.* If you're not sure, contact the venue or show up early and ask the session leader. If it turns out not to be appropriate for you to play, be ready to be a gracious listener instead.

Above All

Go out and jam. Don't be daunted. Even if you don't play much the first time or three, carry on!

Appendix C – Harmony Basics

Music theory is a vast subject that's been covered in countless books, videos and workshops. For the trad musician, however, it takes surprisingly little knowledge to get a grip on the harmonic structure underpinning most of the music we play.

Below is an overview of three major concepts. With an understanding of key signatures, scales, and simple chords, you will have the tools you need to play in any trad style.

Key Signature

Most[*] music is written in a particular key or "key signature." If you know the key signature, you know a few things:

- *The scale:* The key signature tells you the scale, or the notes used in the tune. For example, a tune in D major uses the 7 notes of the D major scale. Tunes in G minor use the 7 notes of the G minor scale.

- *The tonality or "sound" of the tune.* The note of the key is a tonal center that the rest of the tune revolves around. This is hard to describe in words. Try picking a tune whose key you know. Play back a recording while you play that key note on your instrument. Do you hear it as a tonal center? If you're not sure, try a different note that's not the key. It is unlikely to have the same "fit."

- *The chords:* Once you know the key signature, you can expect to hear certain chords more than others. More about that below.

Some tunes start in one key and then shift or "modulate." For example, the Québécois tune "Reel de Sherbrooke" (aka "Reel de Montréal") has an A part in G major and a B part in D major. In

---

[*] In music you can never say "all," because if there's a rule, then someone, somewhere has broken it.

French musettes, the third section, or "trio," is almost always in a different key.

Many trad instruments play far more easily in certain keys than others. An uilleann piper needs a separate instrument to play in the key of F, as do many accordion, concertina and flute players. Perhaps for this reason, *in every tradition, there are certain keys that are more commonly played than others.*

Scale

Each key signature has a scale associated with it. A scale is simply a subset of the 12 notes available.* There are many scales, but traditional music largely makes use of major and minor scales. These scales each have seven notes. If a trad tune is written using a particular scale, it seldom uses notes that aren't in that scale.

Here are all 12 notes (i.e. the black and white notes of a piano, or every fret on a guitar), with the notes of a C major scale circled.

Ⓒ C# Ⓓ D# ⒺⒻ F# Ⓖ G# Ⓐ A# ⒷⒸ

There's something about uneven spacing of the notes in a scale that makes the sound appealing to our ears. If you choose a rhythm and play it randomly on just the white notes of the piano (the C major scale or the A minor scale, depending on where you start), it will sound much more interesting than if you did the same thing using all 12 available notes. Try it and see.

Chords

A "chord" is simply a group of notes. There are many possible ways to group notes. Some of these chords sound better to our ears. Luckily, in trad music for the most part we make use of common chords that are also easy to describe: three-note groups (called triads) that use the notes of the scale we're playing in.

---

* In Western harmony there are 12 notes available between one note and the note an octave above it. There are, of course, more possible notes in between, but many of our instruments can't play them and Western music notation doesn't easily accommodate them.

Here are all the triads based on the scale notes of C major:

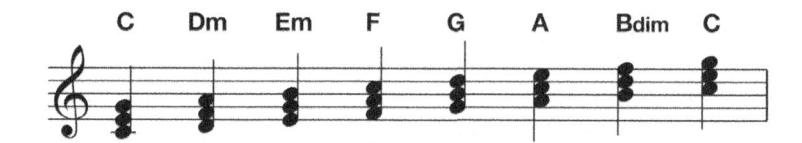

[Musical notation showing triads: C, Dm, Em, F, G, A, Bdim, C]

Even if you don't read sheet music you can see that these chords are formed by following a pretty mathematical format. If you want to try it on your instrument,* play notes 1, 3, and 5 of the scale. Then play notes 2, 4 and 6, and so on up the scale.

You'll probably hear the difference between the chords built on C, F, and G, and the chords built on D, E, and A. The first three are major chords, the second three are minor chords.†

Since this pattern is the same in every key, we often refer to the chords by Roman numeral, using upper case letters for major chords, and lower case for minor (and diminished) chords:

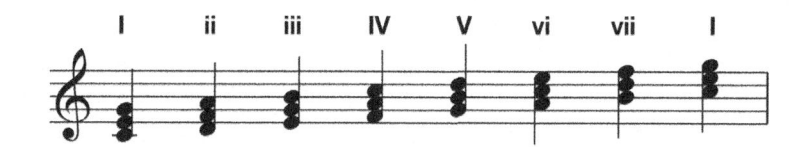

[Musical notation showing triads labeled: I, ii, iii, IV, V, vi, vii, I]

While it's interesting to see all seven options, we use certain chords much more often than others. The vast majority of the time, trad accompanists make use of just three chords, with a fourth thrown in as "spice."

The most commonly-used chord is I, and the second most common is V. You'll almost always start and end a tune with the I chord (reinforcing the *tonality*). The V chord is often played just before the I chord at the end. This combination of chords (V – I) reinforces the tonality even more.

---

* Playing the notes all at once or one at a time, depending on your instrument

† And if you ever wondered what a diminished chord is, one way to describe it is: It's the triad based on the seventh note of a major scale.

In major keys, the other two chords used often are (in decreasing order of likelihood) IV and vi. If you see or hear other chords than these, they're either optional, a personal choice of whoever wrote the chords or an idiosyncrasy of the tune.*

You may see chords labeled G7, G6, Gmaj7 or GΔ, Gsus4, or something else. These are usually triads with another note added. Since a chord is just a group of notes, there is almost an unlimited number of possible chords. There's no need to learn them all, or any of them. Major and minor triads suffice for most of the needs of traditional music.

An understanding of these three concepts will give you a practical foundation in music theory, and a basis on which you can learn more if it interests you.

---

* If you can play a minor scale, it's interesting to try building triads on each of those scale tones. You'll find the major and minor triads in different places. When we play in minor keys, the I and V chords are common, but other chords may be used, and with different frequency. If you're a chord player, this may be an area worth exploration.

Appendix D – Four Basic Principles

I learned these four ideas in the practice of Kokikai Aikido, where they are used as a mnemonic to help coordinate mind and body:

Keep One Point
Relax Progressively
Positive Mind
Correct Posture

The playing of music involves a combination of mental activity and complex physical movements. Working to coordinate mind and body can help make us practice more effectively.

Each of these principles coordinates mind and body in one of two ways: either by *bringing the attention of the mind to the body* or by establishing *an idea or concept, which then changes how we move our bodies*.

Here's a brief description of each of the four principles:

Keep One Point

One point is closely related to your center of balance. It's an imaginary point about two inches below your navel, within your abdomen, close to your spine. If you focus on this spot it can help you feel more calm, and make it easier to relax the rest of your body.

Relax Progressively

We all have habitual patterns of tension. Simply telling yourself to relax is not usually very effective. Instead, try relaxing a specific area of your body for a specific amount of time. Think about relaxing a little more today than yesterday. That's the idea behind "relax progressively."

Positive Mind

When we feel confident, capable and optimistic, those feelings can actually change our bodies and our minds. You can probably think of examples when your playing was strongly affected by your mood or mental outlook.

Correct Posture

Our posture affects our playing. Good posture makes it easier to move the body easily, in a relaxed manner. It reduces the likelihood of injury and makes playing itself more enjoyable.

I am a believer in subjective research. Try these ideas for yourself. If they work for you, then by all means, keep them in your toolbox.

Appendix E – Breathing Exercise

Most of us rarely, if ever, take a full, deep breath. We tend to breathe shallowly without using most of our lung capacity. Our ability to inhale deeply is diminished by things like poor posture, anxiety, tension, and lack of muscle tone.

A regular breathing practice can have immediate, powerful, and long-lasting results, improving mood, the quality of sleep, and even general health by allowing more oxygen to be available to the cells in the body. Regular deep breathing is the simplest way I know to improve health. It costs nothing except a little time. It can be done anywhere. Breathing has no unwanted side effects.

The exercise below is designed to help improve breathing capacity. At the same time it helps improve posture, strength and flexibility in the chest. I have tried many breathing exercises that are taught in the practice of yoga, meditation and elsewhere. This is the one I prefer. It's a modified version of the one taught in Kokikai Aikido.

I recommend a regular, daily (if possible) practice of 10 minutes, though this can be effective when done for as little as 5 minutes a day.

How to Breathe Deeply

- Find a time and place where you can relax without being disturbed. Sit in a comfortable position that you can maintain for 10 minutes. Try not to slouch or lean against a chair back – that may be too tiring at first, but as your back muscles get stronger try to make it a goal.
- Set the timer and start it.
- Close your eyes gently.
- Take two or three comfortable, deep breaths.
- Now breathe in deeply and fully, through the nose if possible. Then exhale through the mouth as slowly as you

can. *Continue breathing in this manner.* There's no need to make the inhalation slow. Just breathe in all the way.

- While you are exhaling, open your mouth slightly. Make a sound as you exhale, as if you are whispering "heee." Making a sound helps keep your mind focused on the breathing. It also gives you feedback on whether your exhalation is regular and relaxed. Try to make the sound as smooth as possible as you exhale.

- When the timer goes off, finish the breath you're on. Take one more easy breath and you're done!

Pointers

It may help to count, silently and slowly, as you exhale.

Try to be conscious of keeping the back long and tall and relaxing the shoulders, back, chest, throat and face.

Don't worry if the length of your inhalations and exhalations changes over the course of your practice session. Don't even worry too much about day-to-day changes in the lengths of your breaths. Just try to relax without any particular goal and stay comfortable.

If at some point you can't maintain the slow breathing, it's OK. Let your breath return to whatever is comfortable for you. *Remember that you are in control. There's no one requiring that you hold or extend your breath. It's just you.* Relax, let go of any goals or requirements you might have set for yourself. If you choose at some point you can continue at whatever pace works for you.

Cautions:

If you know your lungs are compromised, for example you have emphysema, COPD or asthma, seek a doctor's advice before trying any new practice.

If at any time during your breathing practice you feel dizzy or anxious, stop and allow your breathing to return to its natural rhythm. Remember that you are in control, and you can decide when or if you want to try again.

Notes

1 The Practice Pyramid is adapted from Kenny Werner's Learning Diamond, which was developed for jazz musicians. The Learning Diamond, as well as excellent advice on the "mind game" of practice can be found in *Effortless Mastery*, Jamey Aebersold (1996).

2 Ira Glass (2009) Excerpt from an Interview by Current TV (via Public Radio International), "Ira Glass on Storytelling Part 3." Available at https://youtu.be/X74yYfTZSWU

3 Gil Fronsdal is the senior guiding co-teacher at the Insight Meditation Center in Redwood City, California and the Insight Retreat Center in Santa Cruz, California. His talks to students of Buddhism (dharma talks), including guided meditations and introductions to meditation, are available at www.audiodharma.org/teacher/1/

4 The "10,000-Hour Rule" was a core concept of Gladwell's book, *Outliers: The Story of Success*, Little, Brown and Company (2008). Ericsson calls the 10,000-Hour Rule a "provocative generalization to a magical number."

Ericsson, K.A. (2014) "The danger of delegating education to journalists: Why the APS Observer needs peer review when summarizing new scientific developments." (blog post) retrieved January 23, 2021 from: radicalscholarship.wordpress.com/2014/11/03/guest-post-the-danger-of-delegating-education-to-journalists-k-anders-ericsson/. Sadly, Anders Ericsson died during the writing of this book.

5 Halberstadt, R. (2001) *Metaphors for the Musician*, Sher Music.

6 Krumm, J. (2017) *Rounds, Canons and Partner Songs*, available through www.johnkrumm.com.

7 These findings are fairly well-established in scientific literature. The results hold true, in general, for people who are awake in the daytime, eat lunch at mid-day and sleep at night.

8 Béla Fleck, in July 2020, answering a student question in an online workshop, as part of a subscription to the Chick Corea Academy www.chickcoreaacademy.com. Sadly, Chick died during the writing of this book.

9 A good layperson's overview of the status of interleaving is here: Pan, Steven C. (2015) "The Interleaving Effect: Mixing it up Boost Learning" *Scientific American* August 4, 2015. Available at https://www.scientificamerican.com/article/the-interleaving-effect-mixing-it-up-boosts-learning/ (accessed March 2, 2021).

10 Quoted multiple times on the Fred Rogers Center's Facebook page, including on November 27, 2018. Visit www.fredrogerscenter.org/about-fred/Fred-Quotes for more inspiring thoughts from "Mister Rogers."

11 Simon Fischer details the process of visualization with reference to playing violin in an article available on his website: www.simonfischeronline.com/uploads/5/7/7/9/57796211/mental_rehearsal.pdf. (accessed January 23, 2021).

In the CD accompanying his book *Effortless Mastery*, Kenny Werner provides several excellent guided visualizations for musicians.

12 Dalí, S. (1992) *50 Secrets of Magic Craftsmanship*, Dover Publications.

13 From a workshop attended by the author.

14 Freakonomics, Episode 173, available at freakonomics.com/podcast/a-better-way-to-eat-a-new-freakonomics-radio-podcast/ (accessed January 23, 2021).

15 This is a concept taught at the Eric Sahlström Institute, which hosts year-long programs focused on traditional Swedish music and dance.

16 Thich Nhat Hanh (1990) *Peace is Every Step: The Path of Mindfulness in Everyday Life*, Bantam Books.

17 Quoted in Hyams, J. (1979) *Zen in the Martial Arts*, Bantam Books.

18 Sacks, O. (2008) *Musicophilia: Tales of Music and the Brain*, Vintage Books.

19 Thanks to pianist David Leonhardt for this idea.

20 Thanks to Steven Syrek for this story.

21 Martin E.P. Seligman is known as the father of the science of positive psychology. His seminal book is *Learned Optimism: How to Change Your Mind and Your Life*. (1990, Alfred A. Knopf).

22 Listen to this great discussion over Chinese food with TwoSet Violin www.youtube.com/watch?v=oIJPIgfKvaI.

23 K. Anders Ericsson made this observation, referring to a study on mammographers: Beam, C.A., et al. (2003) "Association of Volume and Volume-Independent Factors with Accuracy in Screening Mammogram Interpretation," *Journal of the National Cancer Institute* 95, 282-90.

Ericsson, a cognitive psychologist, is considered by many to be the "expert on expertise," whose lifetime scholarly aim could be described as an attempt to answer the question "How do we get good at things?" Ericsson's work not only inspired the writing of Malcolm Gladwell (*Blink*), but also Angela Duckworth (*Grit*), Joshua Foer (*Moonwalking with Einstein),* and Stephen J. Dubner and Steven D. Levitt (*Freakonomics: A Rogue Economist Explores the Hidden Side of Everything).*

Chapter 8 of Foer's book, *Moonwalking with Einstein,* offers many insights into maintaining continuous growth, which he calls getting off the "OK plateau."

24 Sandrine Thuret, "You can grow new brain cells: Here's how" TED Talk, June 2015, available at: www.ted.com/talks/sandrine_thuret_you_can_grow_new_brain_cells_here_s_how (accessed January 23, 2021). Thuret is (at the time of writing) head of the Adult Neurogenesis and Mental Health Laboratory at King's College London.

25 Haiku #23, ©2019 by Amanda Reilly Sayer, used by kind permission. More of Amanda's poetry and art can be seen at amandaart.poetry.blog/

26 Those who make it their business to know, like detectives and forensic psychologists, are in general agreement that there is no infallible method of knowing when someone is lying. Even so, this is an interesting concept that holds true subjectively.

27 Quoted by Lisa Ornstein.

28 Thanks, again, to Stephen Syrek for this story.

29 The martial art of aikido is based on the principle that you can use the attacker's momentum and energy to take their balance, thus disabling or throwing them using minimal physical force or effort. As one of the first Japanese aikido practitioners to teach in the U.S., Shuji Maruyama Sensei taught students who had been trained in karate and judo. They were not interested in politely deferring to their instructor the way Japanese students did. If they could punch, kick or resist him, his American students did so. A further challenge was that Sensei was small, even by Japanese standards.

Rather than giving up, Sensei "doubled down" on the idea of throwing without using any more force than necessary. As he grew in ability, he invited his experienced students to learn other martial arts, to lift weights, and to challenge him more, even as he practiced responding with less and less effort.

30 The Practice Pyramid is adapted from Kenny Werner's Learning Diamond (*Effortless Mastery*).

Index

"10,000 Hour Rule," 49–50
20-minute intervals, 28–29, 155–56

ABC notation, 210
ability, 37–38, 49–50
accuracy, 56–57, 133–34
acoustics, 176
acting "as if," 103–4
adult musicians, 1, 14–15, 33–34
aikido
    see Kokikai Aikido.
aimaisa, 212
"air bowing," 136
Alexander Technique, 54
ambition, freedom from, 25–26
anti-penultimate omission (APO), 180
apps (computer/device applications), 20, 23, 164–65, 166, 217
arms, stretches for, 92–93, 116–17
Armstrong, Louis, 120
arpeggios, 130, 177–79, 192
associative learning stage, 187
"at speed," 35, 56–57
attack, 52, 203–4
attention
    and memory, 185–86
    and physical movement, 70
    attentive listening, 51–52, 219
    continuous growth, 187–89
    diffuse thinking, 112–13, 165
    efficient practice, 39
    listening as a gift, 193
    mistakes, 46–47
    one thing at a time, 91
    power of, 29
    relaxed attentiveness, 224, 225
    relaxing the hands, 193–95
    to pain, 79–80, 184–85
    very slow practice, 90
    see also awareness; being present; mindfulness.
audio feedback, playing without, 212–13
aural tradition of traditional music, 7
    see also playing by ear.
autonomous learning stage, 187
avoidance, 73–74
awareness
    and avoidance, 73–74
    body awareness, 76, 79–80, 95, 100–102, 157–58
    of all senses, 98–99
    of metaphors, 195–96
    of normative beliefs, 86–87
    of trouble spots, 61–62
    physical movement, 70
    playing and knowing, 87–88
    subtle thoughts, 40–41
    three things to focus on, 100
    while playing what you know, 99–100
    see also attention; being present; mindfulness.

backward bend (stretch), 206–7
balance, 54–55, 66–67, 156–58, 170, 232
beginning tunes, 102–3, 127–28, 149
beginning, adult learners, 14–15, 18–19, 31–33
being present, 9–10, 29, 75–76, 132–33

see also attention; awareness; mindfulness.
biotensegrity, 157–58
blindfolded playing, 153–54
blocked practice method, 88
Bodhidharma, 163
body awareness, 76, 79–80, 95, 100–102, 157–58
body clock, 65–66
Bouthillier, Robert, 208
bowing patterns, 203
breathing
   and phrasing, 26–28
   and playing music, 78
   being present, 132
   exercises, 234–35
   integrating into practice, 85
   opening up space, 82–83
   relaxation of muscles between your shoulder blades, 197–98
   upper body stretches, 116–17
   using the instruments as your voice, 213–14
"Britches Full of Stitches, The" (tune), 55–56
Buddhism, 184–85, 210–11
Burke, Kevin, 144, 203
Burrows, Veronica, 64
bursts, 216–17

center of balance
   see one point.
certainty (as a human need), 138
change, resistance to, 221–22
checkerboarding, 172–74
Child's Pose (yoga pose), 69, 183
chords, 130, 177–79, 228, 229–31
circadian rhythm, 65–66
classical music, 7, 70–71, 106–7, 130
cognitive learning stage, 187
cognitive load/cognitive attention, 72, 89, 130, 151, 179, 187, 198–99
   see also neural connections.

Cohen, Max, 180
comfort zones, 168
commitment, 2, 104, 222
communication, music as, 82–83, 114–15, 120–21
community, musical, 7, 34, 52–54, 58–59
   see also jam sessions.
connection (as a human need), 138
connection (through musical community)
   see jam sessions.
connection (through musical community), 7, 34, 52–54, 58–59
consonants, 203–4
continuous growth, 187–89
contribution (as a human need), 138
Correct Posture, 233
counterarguments, 199–200
couples dances, 74
COVID-19 pandemic, musical community, 59
creativity
   see individual expression.
criticism
   see self-assessment.

Dalí, Salvador, 112
dancing and traditional music, 6, 74–75, 117–19, 161–62, 180, 183
   see also jigs; reels; rhythm; waltzes.
decay, 203–4
diffuse thinking, 112–13, 165
"Dinah" (song), 120
direct experience, playing from, 212
discernment *vs.* criticism, 83–84, 189, 215
distractions, 51–52, 146–48
   see also listening, attentive; visualization.
"dotted quarter swap," 144–46
dotted rhythm, 139, 162–63

dynamics, 52, 99–100, 117–19, 120, 126–27, 211–12

ear, playing by
   see playing by ear.
earworms, 190
Edison, Thomas, 112
"Egan's Polka" (tune), 60
eight worldly winds (Buddhist teaching), 184–85
"embodying" a tune, 140–41
emotional response, evoking, 99–100, 184–85, 191–92
ending tunes, 180
"enlargening," 61–62
Ericsson, Anders, 50
expressiveness, 120–21, 158–59

face
   relaxation of, 94–95
   smiling, 129–30
fast practice, 133–34, 159–60, 200–201, 215–17, 224
finger strengthening, 108–9
Fleck, Béla, 85
flexibility, physical, 157–58
   see also mental flexibility.
foot tapping, 41–42, 75
forward bend (stretch), 206
Four Basic Principles of Kokikai Aikido, 232–33
"free play," 150–51
French, speaking, 121
Fronsdal, Gil, 40
Fuller, R. Buckminster, 156
fun
   and practice, 131–32
   enjoyment, 81–82, 93–94, 192
   jam sessions, 106–7
   playing as play, 93–94
   vs. perfection, 70–71

Gandhi, Mahatma, 40
Gladwell, Malcolm, 49–50, 50
Glass, Ira, 37

goals
   acting as if, 103–4
   and feeling good, 131–32
   and human needs, 138
   and moving on, 113–14
   and self-assessment, 160–61
   creation of a plan, 15–16
   eight worldly winds (Buddhist teaching), 184–85
   freedom from, 25–26
   learning methods, 122–23
   setting, 63–64, 219–21
   short blocks of time, 124–25
   short-term, 32, 63–64
   timed modules, 155–56
growth (as a human need), 138

habits, developing, 122, 151–52, 152–53
Hahn, Hilary, 187
Halberstadt, Randy, 56
hands
   both hands together, 196–97
   relaxation of, 193–95
   right or left, 50–51, 136
   stretches for, 50–51, 92–93
   see also finger strengthening.
harmonies, 52, 101, 228–31
Hayes, Martin, 117, 203
head position, 105–6
headwind, 124
hearing yourself, 189–90, 212–13
   see also listening; playing by ear.
heuristics, 151–52, 152–53
hook, musical, 60–61
human needs, 138
human potential, 125–26
humor and memory, 185

ikkyo undo (first exercise), 170–71
immersive experiences, 75, 120–21
improvisation, 58, 110, 130, 150–51, 202–3
inclusivity, of traditional music, 6
incremental progress, 2, 182

individual expression, 7, 65–66, 102, 150–51, 156, 168–69, 212
inflexibility, and mental resistance, 64–65
inner critic, 156
   see also self-assessment.
instruments, nature of, 79
intention, definition, 3
   see also goals.
interleaving, 88–90

jam sessions
   and "secret language" of, 114–15
   as a musical community, 53, 59
   audio feedback, 212–13
   different versions of tunes, 168–69
   etiquette in, 106–7, 226–27
   learning on the fly in, 165–66
   learning to play better with others, 186–87
   setting yourself up for success, 154–55
   watching and listening, 111–12
jazz, 110
Jefferson, Blind Lemon, 153
"Jerry's Beaver Hat" (tune), 130
jigs, 74, 118, 144–46
jumps, 180–82
   see also positioning.

Keep One Point, 232
keeping *one point*, 54–55, 66–67
key signatures, 130–31, 166, 177–79, 228–29
kindness, of great teachers, 45
kinesthetics, and memory, 185
Kobayashi, Takeru, 125–26
Kokikai Aikido
   about, 221
   and "yeah, buts," 64–65
   breathing exercises, 234–35
   everyone is my teacher, 143
   Four Basic Principles of, 232–33
   Keep One Point, 232
   keeping *one point*, 54–55, 66–67
   Maruyama, Shuji, 45, 78, 221
   mental flexibility, 109
   minimum effort for maximum effect, 8
   performance anxiety, 81
   recovering quickly, 66
   slow practice, 17–18
   weight underside, 141–43
   wrist, stretches for, 170–72
Krumm, John, 58

Larson, Andrea, 127
last thing you hear, 189–90
learning by ear
   see playing by ear.
Lee, Bruce, 148
Leonhardt, David, 58, 164
letting go, 163–64, 167
lifelong improvement, 187–89
lift, creating, 117–19
limitations, acceptance of, 148
listening
   and closing the eyes, 153–54
   and everyone is my teacher, 143
   and fast practice, 217
   and mindfulness, 76
   and tone, 76–78
   as a gift, 193
   attentive, 51–52, 219
   for patterns, 55–56
   learning from others, 111–12, 188
   not reading music, 73
   playing with others, 186
   practicing with recordings, 23, 164–65, 166–67, 205, 214–15, 217
   singing and playing, 86
lists, 137–38
living tradition (of traditional music), 7
local music community, 53
looking up, 182–83

martial arts, 13–14, 17–18, 18–19
   see also Kokikai Aikido.
Maruyama, Shuji, 45, 78, 221–22
massages, 92
Massée, Laurel, 213
McLane, Jeremiah, 61
melody
   and knowing what is correct, 168–69
   and rhythmic patterns, 23, 74–75, 95–96, 166
   bringing out, 96
   enhancing by opening up space, 82–83
   interpretation of, 79
   learning on the fly, 165–67
   memorization, 60–61
   note patterns, 55–56, 97
   playing both hands together, 196–97
   playing by ear, 23, 76–78, 159
   playing well with others, 186–87
   simplifying, 47–49, 95
   singing, 86
memorization, 35–36, 59–61, 88–90, 123–24, 185–86
   see also practice loops.
mental flexibility
   about, 109–10
   and "two-tempo rut," 161–62
   checkerboarding, 172–74
   differing versions of tunes, 168–69
   distractions, 146–48
   improvisation, 202–3
   intentional, 187
   using positive language, 179–80
   "yeah, buts," 64–65
Metaphors for the Musician (Halberstadt), 56
metaphors, effective use of, 195–96
metronomes
   alternating speeds, 133–34, 215–17
   and bursts, 216–17
   and checkerboarding, 172–74
   and "embodying" a tune, 140–41
   and "enlargening," 61–62
   and fast practice, 216–17
   and jumps, 181–82
   and playing both hands together, 196–97
   and playing in time, 224
   and recording, 57, 214
   and rhythmic precision, 139–40
   and thinking ahead, 72
   and two-tempo rut, 161–62
   and very slow practice, 90
   and "wild takes," 119–20
      see also Practice Pyramid, The.
   as practice tool, 11, 19–20
   in practice space, 24
mind-body coordination, 13–14, 87–88, 110–11, 115–16, 196–97
mindfulness
   "10,000 Hour Rule," 49–50
   20-minute intervals, 28–29
   and distractions, 146–48
   and efficient practice, 43–44
   and "embodying" a tune, 140–41
   and "free play," 150–51
   and music practice, 75–76
   and positive thinking, 176–77
   and recovering quickly, 66–67
   and technology, 133
   and "yeah, buts," 64–65
   before you start, 102–3
      see also attention; awareness; self-assessment.
   challenging assumptions, 125–26
   checkerboarding, 172–74
   connection to music, 120–21
   keeping *one point*, 54–55, 66–67, 232
   letting go, 163–64
   limitations, acceptance of, 148
   mind-body coordination, 13–14
   mistakes, 46–47
   musical priorities, 56–57

one thing at a time, 91
pain and stress, 79–80
power of, 29
practice loops, 35–36
slow practice, 21–22
staying present, 132–33
subtle thoughts, 40–41
thinking ahead, 71–72
watching and listening, 76, 111–12, 188
"when the bell rings, get up," 104
minimum effort for maximum effect, 8–9
mirrors, use of, 24, 36–37, 94, 105, 182–83
mistakes, 46–47, 198–99
mnemonics, 60, 185–86
motivation
   and adulthood, 33–34
   counterarguments, 199–200
   eight worldly winds (Buddhist teaching), 184–85
   expectation of reward, 163–64
   gap between taste and ability, 37–38
   mental gold stars, 204–5
   showing up, 38
   your inner critic, 156
   see also goals.
movement, 30–31, 159–60, 175
mukudoku, 163–64
multitasking, 91
music camps, 53, 59
music theory, 46, 228–31
musical community, 7, 34, 52–54, 58–59
   see also jam sessions.
musical notation, 208–10, 227
musical words, patterns as, 96–98
musicality
   alternating fast and slow playing, 134, 215
   and visualization, 101–2
   beautiful sounds, 76–78
   instruments as your voice, 213–14
   listening to yourself, 215
   of scales and arpeggios, 177–79
   optimal speed, 35
   playing slowly, 90, 99, 215
   priorities, 56–57
mute (playing without sound), 135–36

neck, stretches for, 92–93, 105–6
negative thinking, 12–13, 174
   see also positive thinking; self-assessment.
neural connections
   and interleaving, 88–90
   building, 60, 191–92
   diffuse thinking and, 112–13
   heuristics, 151–52
   spaced repetition, 123–24
   using positive language, 179–80
   see also cognitive load/cognitive attention.
Nhat Hanh, Thich, 129
nikkyo undo (second exercise), 171
non-practice days, 43–44, 100–102, 128–29
non-verbal communication, 114–15
normative beliefs, 86–87
notes and notation (musical), 227
   and dynamics, 126–27
   importance of, 208–10
   not using, 72
   ornamentation of, 144–46
   playing fewer notes, 82–83, 120
   scales and arpeggios, 177–79
   use of, 67–68, 95–96, 208–10
   use with challenging passages, 198–99
note-taking
   after practice, 218
   and continuous growth, 188–89
   and motivation, 205
   and musical notation, 208–10

and small wins, 64
and thinking ahead, 72
and tracking progress, 114, 122
and tune memory, 60
goal setting, 100
importance of, 25
tune lists, 137–38
use with challenging passages, 149
novelty, 51

O'Carolan, Turlough, 153
one point, 54–55, 66–67, 132, 170, 232
one thing at a time, 91
one-handed playing, 50–51, 136
online lessons, 53
opening up space, 82–83
"optimal" speed, 35
ornamentation, 95, 144–45
overlearning, 219

pain (physical), 79–80
pain, blame, disgrace/obscurity, loss *(eight worldly winds)*, 184–85
patterns, 55–56, 96–98, 166, 178
perfection
    and The Practice Pyramid, 10–12, 200–201, 224
    being good enough, 70–71, 113–14, 202–3
    discernment *vs.* criticism, 83–84
performance anxiety, 81, 102–3, 103–4
"personal, pervasive, permanent" reactions, 174
phrasing, 26–28, 82–83, 99–100, 120, 126–27, 158–59
    see also musicality.
physical self-care
    ikkyo, nikkyo and *sankyo undo*, 170–72
    keeping *one point*, 54–55, 66–67, 232
    mind-body coordination, 13–14, 20–21, 87–88, 110–11, 115–16, 196–97
    motion, 20–21, 30–31, 159–60, 175
    smiling, 129–30
    tensegrity, 156–58
    weight underside, 141–43
    yoga, 12, 25–26, 183
    see also posture; stretches.
physical sensations and memory, 185
piano (quietly), 211–12
planning
    creation of a plan, 15–16
    goal setting, 63–64, 219–21
    on non-practice days, 43–44
    organization of time, 28–29, 32–33, 124–25, 155–56
    tracking progress, 63–64
play "at speed," 35, 56–57
"play in time" (The Practice Pyramid), 11, 224
"play perfectly" (The Practice Pyramid), 10–12, 200–201, 224
"play relaxed" (The Practice Pyramid), 200–201, 224, 225
    see also relaxation.
"play the whole thing" (The Practice Pyramid), 200–201, 225
playing as play, 93–94
playing by ear
    about, 23–24
    and singing, 23, 86
    and tone, 76–78
    musical patterns, 55–56
    not reading sheet music, 73
    phrasing and expression, 159
    rhythms, 166
playing fast, 133–34, 139, 159–60, 200–201, 224
playing in time, 11, 224
playing with others, 34, 186–87
    see also jam sessions.

pleasure, praise, fame, gain *(eight worldly winds)*, 184–85
positioning exercises, 110–11
Positive Mind, 233
positive thinking
    and intention, 12–13, 176–77
    and realistic goals, 131–32
    focusing on one thing at a time, 91
    mental "gold stars," 204–5
    Positive Mind, 233
    setting up for success, 154–55
    using positive language, 179–80
    vs. negative thinking, 174
    what you have, 135
        see also negative thinking; self-assessment.
posture
    about, 42–43
    and being present, 132
    and mindfulness, 76
    and recovering quickly, 66–67
    and using mirrors, 36–37
    and weight underside, 141–43
    biotensegrity, 157–58
    Correct Posture, 233
    head and neck position, 105–6
    importance of motion, 30–31
    repetitive stress injuries, 79–80
practice loops
    and dotted quarter swap, 145–46
    and jumps, 181–82
    and learning on the fly, 167
    memorization, 35–36
    practicing with recordings, 164–65, 166–67
    trouble spots, 61–62
practice notebook
    see note-taking.
Practice Pyramid, The
    about, 223–25
    fast practice, 200–201, 216–17
    play at speed, 35, 56–57
    play in time, 11, 224
    play perfectly, 10–12, 200–201, 224
    play relaxed, 200–201, 224, 225
    play the whole thing, 200–201, 225
    thinking ahead, 71–72
practice space, 24, 175–76
practice techniques
    blocked practice method, 88
    changing the environment, 175–76
    checkerboarding, 172–74
    diffuse thinking, 112–13, 165
    "dotted quarter swap," 144–46
    interleaving, 88–90
    learning musical patterns, 55–56, 96–98, 166, 178
    learning on the fly, 165–67
    overlearning, 219
    playing as play, 93–94
    practicing with recordings, 23, 57, 164–65, 166–67, 196, 205, 214–15, 217
    practicing without sound, 135–36
    practicing without visual clues, 153–54
    simplification, 47–49, 72, 154–55, 184, 221–22
    slow practice, 17–18, 21–22, 90, 133–34
    spaced repetition, 61, 123–24
    three things to focus on, 100
    timed modules, 155–56
    see also metronomes.
practicing, as a practice, 5–6
Presentation Rule, The, 218
priorities, musical, 56–57
    see also goals.
problem areas, identifying, 39
progress
    and avoidance, 73–74
    continuous growth, 187–89
    headwind, 124
    incremental, 2, 182

tracking small wins, 63–64

quiet playing, 211–12

recharging, 43–44, 51
recording yourself, 57, 196, 205, 214–15
recordings, practicing with, 23, 164–65, 166–67, 217
recovering, 66–67
reels, 74, 118, 146
Relax Progressively, 232
relaxation
    and breathing, 85
    and fast practice, 217
    and "play relaxed," 200–201, 224, 225
    and playing, 78
    and stretches for wrists, 170–72
    and weight underside, 141–43
    Child's Pose, 183
    make *vs.* allow, 115–16
    minimum effort for maximum effect, 8–9
    mirrors, 36–37
    of face, 94–95
    of hands, 193–95
    of muscles between your shoulder blades, 197–98
    one point, 54–55, 66–67, 232
    playing with relaxed attentiveness, 224, 225
    posture, 42–43
    Relax Progressively, 232
    repetitive stress injuries, 79–80
    while playing fast, 200–201
release, 203–4
repetition
    and interleaving, 89
    blocked practice method, 88
    "embodying" the tune, 140–41
    identification of problem, 39
    novelty, 51
    of musical words, 96–98
    overlearning, 219
    patterns, 55–56
    practice loops, 35–36, 61–62, 145–46, 164–65, 167, 166–67, 181–82
    spaced, 123–24
    technical exercises, 38–40
repetitive stress injuries, 79–80
rests (musical notes and notation), 82–83
rewards, 163–64, 204–5
rhythm
    about, 74–75
    and creating lift, 117–19
    and learning on the fly, 166
    and playing by ear, 23, 166
    and technical exercises, 43–44
    dotted, 139, 162–63
    "dotted quarter swap," 144–46
    foot tapping, 41–42
    listening to yourself, 214
    play in time, 224
    playing slowly, 90
    rhythmic precision, 139–40
    swing, 162–63
    varying importance of notes, 95–96
    see also metronomes; playing in time.
Richards, Keith, 112
Robbins, Tony, 138
Rogers, Fred (Mr. Rogers), 93
"Rose in the Heather, The" (tune), 144–45

Sacks, Oliver, 153
sankyo undo (third exercise), 171
Sayer, Amanda Reilly, 195
scales, 130, 177–79, 192, 229
scheduling, 32–33, 43–44, 100–102, 124–25, 128–29, 131–32
self-assessment
    and ego, 210–11
    and "free play," 150–51
    and the Practice Pyramid, 10–12
    comfort zones, 168

discernment *vs.* criticism, 83–84, 189, 215
eight worldly winds (Buddhist teaching), 184–85
how to judge, 160–61
inner critic, 156
listening to yourself, 189, 215
"people will like my playing," 176–77
"personal, pervasive, permanent" reactions, 174
recognizing progress, 113–14
see also positive thinking.
self-confidence, 210–11
self-criticism
see self-assessment.
self-motivation, 33–34
see also goals.
Seligman, Martin, 174
senses, 98–99
see also hearing yourself; listening; sight.
shake, 172
shoulder blades, muscles between, 197–98
shoulder rotation, 68–70
showing up for practice, 38
side bend (stretch), 207
sight, 98, 153–54, 186
significance (as a human need), 138
simplifying, 47–49, 72, 154–55, 184, 221–22
singing
and phrasing, 26–28, 120, 158–59
and playing by ear, 21–22, 86
importance of, 58
practicing transitions, 201
trouble spots, 61–62
six direction spine stretch, 205–8
skillfulness, of great teachers, 45
slow practice, 17–18, 21–22, 90, 133–34
"slowdowner" apps, 23, 164–65, 166, 217

smiling, 67, 129–30
social aspects of playing music, 7, 34, 52–54, 58–59
see also jam sessions.
social media, musical community, 58–59
sooner, not faster, 159–60
sound, quality of, 76–78, 139–40, 164–65, 185, 203–4
see also musicality; tone.
spaced repetition, 61, 123–24
speed
alternating between fast and slow, 133–34
and "embodying" the tune, 140–41
and musical priorities, 56–57
and playing what you know, 99–100
and rhythmic precision, 139
and technical exercises, 43–44
arbitrary nature of, 35
fast practice, 200–201, 215–17
foot tapping, 41–42
slow practice, 17–18, 21–22
sooner, not faster, 159–60
two-tempo rut, 161–62
very slow practice, 90
see also metronomes; Practice Pyramid.
spines, stretches for, 205–8
standing twists, 207
stretches
arms, 92–93, 116–17
Child's Pose, 183
hands, 50–51, 92–93
"motion is lotion," 30–31
neck, 92–93, 105–6
shoulder rotation, 68–70
six direction spine stretch, 205–8
standing twists, 207
upper body, 116–17
wrist, 92–93, 170–72
sustain, 203–4
swing, 162–63

"sword nature," 78
synchronization of hands, 196–97

talent, 14–15, 49–50
teachers, 34, 45–46, 52–54, 143–44
technical exercises, 38–40, 192
    see also practice techniques.
technology, 133
tempo
    see fast practice; metronomes; slow practice; speed.
tensegrity, 156–58
thinking ahead, 71–72, 159–60
three things, 100
Thuret, Sandrine, 191
Tillie (Kate's mom), 193
time, organization of, 28–29, 32–33, 124–25, 128–29, 155–56
timed modules, 155–56
timers, 24, 70, 113, 131, 234
timing, 11, 41–42, 43–44, 224
    see also opening up space; playing in time; rhythm; speed.
tonality, 228, 231
tone, 52, 78, 130
tone starter, 128
touch, 99
traditional music, 1, 7, 44, 49, 56, 59, 71, 75, 119, 131, 163, 169, 203, 231
training, *vs.* talent, 17, 50
transitions, 202
triads, 229–31
triplets, 139
tune structure, 44, 55–56, 67–68, 74–75, 82–83, 166
tunes
    beginning to play, 102–3, 127–28
    choosing what to play, 99–100
    dance music, 117–19
    differing versions of, 168–69
    "embodying" of, 140–41
    ending signals, 180
    key, 130–31
    lists, 137–38
    memorization of, 59–61, 185–86
    play in its entirety, 200–201, 225
    see "Britches Full of Stitches, The" (tune); "Egan's Polka" (tune); "Jerry's Beaver Hat" (tune); "Rose in the Heather, The" (tune).
two-tempo rut, 161–62

uncertainty, embracing, 202–3
upside down practice, 149

variety, 28–29, 38–40, 138
versions, checkerboarding, 172–74
very slow practice, 90
visual clues, playing without, 153–54
visualization, 100–102, 136, 201
voice, your instruments as, 213–14
volume, 211–12, 227

waltzes, 74, 118, 146
warm ups, 124, 149, 192, 218
wasted motion, 175
watching and learning, 111–12, 114–15
weight underside, 141–43
Werner, Kenny, 31
when the bell rings, get up, 104
wild takes, 119–20
willpower vs habit, 152–53
workshops, 53, 59, 77
wrists, stretches for, 92–93, 170–72

"yeah, buts," 64–65
yoga, 12, 25–26, 183

About the Author

Judy Minot has played piano since she could reach the keys. She trained in classical music until age 16. In the "empty nest" years she began playing jazz, and at the same time discovered the vibrant community of traditional music. She now plays piano, accordion and violin, and has led workshops all over the Eastern U.S.

Judy began her working life in broadcast video, editing music videos, entertainment specials and documentaries for a long list of well-known musical artists. She went on to produce, direct and write for broadcast, cable and recording industry clients, eventually transitioning to work in digital marketing.

Judy holds a 4th degree black belt in the martial art of Kokikai Aikido, which she taught at Rutgers University for 12 years. She is also a certified yoga teacher.

Made in the USA
Middletown, DE
10 April 2023